A PRELIMINARY SKETCH.

of

PROPOSED GARDEN AND TERRACING

FOR THE ESTATE OF

W. H. COWLES ESQ

MONTECITO SANTA BARBARA, CALIFORNIA.

JAMES OSBORNE CRAIG ARCHITECT.

Spanish Colonial Style

Santa Barbara and the Architecture of
James Osborne Craig and Mary McLaughlin Craig

Spanish Colonial Style

SANTA BARBARA AND THE ARCHITECTURE OF
JAMES OSBORNE CRAIG AND MARY McLAUGHLIN CRAIG

PAMELA SKEWES-COX AND ROBERT SWEENEY

INTRODUCTION BY C. FORD PEATROSS

PHOTOGRAPHY BY MATT WALLA

RIZZOLI
NEW YORK

New York · Paris · London · Milan

IN ASSOCIATION WITH THE SANTA BARBARA HISTORICAL MUSEUM

First published in the United States of America in 2023 by
RIZZOLI INTERNATIONAL PUBLICATIONS, INC.
300 Park Avenue South, New York, NY 10010
www.rizzoliusa.com

In association with the Santa Barbara Historical Museum

This is a revised and updated Second Edition of a work of the same title, first published in 2015 by Rizzoli International Publications in association with the Santa Barbara Historical Museum.

ISBN-13: 978-0-8478-4612-2 (Trade Edition)
ISBN-13: 978-0-8478-7307-4 (SBHM Edition)
Library of Congress Control Number: 2015935597

Publisher: Charles Miers
Editor: Douglas Curran
Production Manager: Kayleigh Jankowski
Managing Editor: Lynn Scrabis

Illustrations and archival photography are credited on a case by case basis throughout the book or on the photography and illustration credits page (p. 272)

Page 1: El Paseo, Santa Barbara
Pages 2–3: 402 Plaza Rubio, Santa Barbara
Pages 4–5: Spaulding House, Montecito
Page 7: Drawing of Mary McLaughlin Craig and daughter Mary by Clarence Mattei, 1927

Designed by Abigail Sturges

Printed and bound in China

2023 2024 2025 2026 2027 / 10 9 8 7 6 5 4 3 2 1

Visit us online:
Facebook.com/RizzoliNewYork
Twitter: @Rizzoli_Books
Instagram.com/RizzoliBooks
Pinterest.com/RizzoliBooks
Youtube.com/user/RizzoliNY
Issuu.com/Rizzoli

This new edition of Spanish Colonial Style *has been made possible by the generosity of*

Lincoln F. Anderson
Mary Brooke Anderson
Sarah McLaughlin Thompson
Eleanor Van Cott
John Woodward

To Mary Osborne Craig Skewes-Cox

*I am transported by what I saw to be
old world prototypes . . . the simple
grandeur of the expression of
Spain's influence was satisfying. . . .*

J. Osborne Craig.

*Is not respect and emulation
of work well done a great thing?*

Mary McLaughlin Craig.

Contents

Introduction

C. Ford Peatross

PREVIOUS PAGES
Urmston House,
Pebble Beach

Today in America, the materials and architectural forms and details of the Spanish Colonial Revival are ubiquitous, an unquestioned aspect of everyday life. The irregular plans and picturesque massing, the planar stucco walls with arched openings and low-pitched tile roofs, the terraces and patios open to the sky, and the wooden beams and wrought-iron ornaments can still be observed and continue to be produced with varying degrees of authenticity, from Honolulu to Key West, from public buildings and vast residential developments to posh resorts and the local *taqueria*.

This highly influential and distinctive vocabulary was arrived at in the space of a few years in the late 1910s and early 1920s, eclectically and extravagantly in Florida, with a Mediterranean accent, by Addison Mizner, and more calmly and purely, inspired by Andalusian Spain and Mexico, in Santa Barbara, California, by two architects, George Washington Smith and James Osborne Craig. Smith's contributions have been recognized for some time, while those of Craig and his wife Mary have not received the attention they merit, in part due to Craig's untimely death in 1922, at the age of 33. *Spanish Colonial Style: Santa Barbara and the Architecture of James Osborne Craig and Mary McLaughlin Craig*, does much to rectify this deficiency by providing new information and insight into their seminal roles, and that of their patrons, and the *genius loci* that made Santa Barbara the birthplace of one of this nation's most durable and popular architectural styles.

The authors, Robert Sweeney and Pamela Skewes-Cox, examine the factors that coalesced to make the Craigs' work in Southern California so permeable, and his masterpieces, the Bernhard Hoffmann house and the commercial and residential development known as El Paseo, models for the entire nation.

Their achievements merit our attention and remain relevant because what happened in Santa Barbara did not stay in Santa Barbara.

From the time of the memorial exhibition and publication of Craig's works and architectural drawings in the August 1922 issue of *Architect & Engineer*, the architectural and shelter publications of the time regularly featured specimens of buildings inspired in part by their example, further spurring their proliferation. In the early 1920s Santa Barbara's Civic Arts Association began to support adherence to the materials and forms of the Spanish Colonial Revival much as George Washington Smith and James Osborne Craig had interpreted them. Following the 1925 earthquake and aided by the work of an Architectural Advisory Committee, and a Community Drafting Room that provided assistance and plans, the design of over 2,000 new projects was approved by Santa Barbara's Board of Architectural Review, one of the first of its kind. By 1926 the architecture of Santa Barbara had undergone an Hispanic transformation, and by the end of the 1920s almost every town in America had one or more examples of Spanish Colonial style buildings, including houses, stores, restaurants, theaters and even gas stations.

Santa Barbara was admirably situated to serve as a crucible for these developments. Its climate, scenic location, and legacy of colonial Hispanic architecture combined with the wealth, leisure time, and diversity of its residents to provide a near-perfect matrix in which both Craigs could flourish. He was a talented, imaginative young Scottish architect who had traveled in Spain and could draw beautifully, and she was an attractive, socially well-connected wife with unerring taste, who quite remarkably stepped into his professional shoes following his death. Respectively, they fit like kid gloves into Santa Barbara's

*James Osborne Craig,
Flagstaff, Arizona, ca. 1915*

business and cultural milieus. They were ready and able to provide something that was both old and romantic and new and exciting to the local elite, populated by both old and new money, polo-playing easterners, practical midwesterners, British expatriots, the occasional aristocrat, and their particular Medici, Bernhard Hoffmann, who commissioned the designs for both his own residence, Casa Santa Cruz, and the El Paseo development, and briefly chaired Santa Barbara's Board of Architectural Review.

A widely published expert on the twentieth-century architecture of Southern California, a fine scholar, and a resident of Santa Barbara, Robert Sweeney has produced for the first time an invaluable and exacting chronology of the architectural projects undertaken by both James Osborne and Mary McLaughlin Craig, carefully examining the roles of both client and architect, laying out the development and history of each project, and assessing the nature and success of its design. Erudite and enlightening, it provides a firm foundation for further analysis and study of the Craigs' contributions.

Pamela Skewes-Cox, the Craigs' granddaughter and the daughter of their only child, Mary Craig Skewes-Cox, brings to this project her own passion for the subject and the unique perspective and special insights of a family member with access to personal and business papers and recollections, including those of her mother, family friends, and professional colleagues. From their beginnings in Glasgow, Scotland, and Deadwood in the Dakota Territory, Skewes-Cox brings to life the human dimension of the challenges and achievements of her maternal grandparents and their often extraordinary clients, colleagues and friends. Her research and interviews explore their upbringing, education, personalities, and personal and business relationships,

and reveal Mary Craig's talent and grit as a woman who, without formal training or an architectural license, successfully assumed the reins of her young husband's six-year-old architectural practice and continued it for over three decades.

My involvement with the Craigs' work began in the late 1970s when Mary and Bennet Skewes-Cox first approached the Library of Congress with an offer to donate a large group of the Craigs' architectural drawings. I was immediately taken with the grace, imagination, and beauty of Osborne's drawings, and impressed by their early and accomplished synthesis of many of what were to be the critical elements of the Spanish Colonial Revival. They represented an important development in the history of American architecture largely absent from the library's extensive collection of architectural drawings, and thus were a welcome addition. Over the years there were additional gifts, including one by their daughter Pamela, coauthor of this publication.

For the 2003 opening of Frank Gehry's Walt Disney Hall at the Los Angeles Music Center, I was asked to identify architectural drawings from the collections of the Library of Congress to represent a timeline of Southern California architecture. I chose original drawings by Frank Lloyd Wright, Charles and Ray Eames, Bart Prince, Richard Neutra . . . and James Osborne Craig. Although the work of those first named is far better known, in the long run the architectural contributions of James Osborne Craig may prove to be the more popular, practical, and influential. This long overdue recognition of the Craigs' work is thus most welcome, will make their achievements available to a wide and appreciative audience, and no doubt will inspire new designs in the ongoing development of architecture as a rich and integral part of our national life.

ARCHITECTURE

Robert Sweeney

CHAPTER 1

The Trail from Barrhead

It began November 2, 1888, in Barrhead, a suburb of Glasgow. James Osborne Craig was the second of six sons born to Archibald Craig, proprietor of a textile mill, and his wife Maggie, though, by 1903 only Osborne, his mother and youngest brother survived. And Osborne himself was afflicted with severe asthma. Partly for this reason, he reportedly traveled through southern Spain with a step-grandmother at an early age because of the warm climate, possibly triggering and influencing his later development as an architect.

Craig's formal education consisted of a course of study at The Glasgow and West of Scotland Technical College. He did not, as has been stated previously, attend the Royal Academy in London.[1] He entered the school of architecture at the Technical College in 1904 at age fifteen, identifying himself as an "architect" on his application, possibly indicating that he was working in an architectural firm as an apprentice. At the time, the school of architecture was administered by a joint committee representing the college and the Glasgow School of Art, recently established by Eugène Bourdon (1870–1916), a French architect. The curriculum led to a joint-diploma in architecture to be issued by the two institutions.[2]

Craig did not complete the program at the technical college. He left Scotland in April 1905 on board the British Anchor Line *S.S. Columbia.* The ship's manifest lists Colona, Colorado—where his maternal aunt and her husband had a farm—as his final destination. Colona was located three hundred miles southwest of Denver on a former Indian reservation; Craig's presence was noted in July.[3] The utter remoteness of the place, and Craig's youth, invite speculation. Was there urgency about his health, a need to

escape the industrial pollution of Glasgow? Was the presence of family a happy coincidence, if not a motivating factor, in his decision to go to Colorado? Had he decided to pursue a career in architecture in America?

By 1907 Craig had made his way to Colorado Springs. Established in 1871 at the foot of Pikes Peak in conjunction with the westward expansion of the railroad network, it developed as an affluent residential enclave, a resort and a destination for invalids. Numerous fine Richardsonian Romanesque churches, schools and public buildings were quickly put up.[4] An appropriately grand hotel, The Antlers, designed by the esteemed Boston firm Peabody and Stearns, opened in 1883; the precedent it set is carried on by the Broadmoor today. Craig was listed in the local city directories in 1908, 1909 and 1910, first as a draftsman in the office of architect George M. Bryson (1865–1918). Like Craig, Bryson was Scottish; he reportedly had come to Colorado Springs in 1886 for his health. Little information on his work before 1908 has come to light although he is credited with the design of a Carnegie Library building that was completed in 1904 in Old Colorado City.[5]

Bryson's office was located in the Hagerman Block, built in 1889–1890 at the southeast corner of Tejon and Kiowa streets and extant today. Sometime in 1909 Craig began working for another architectural firm in the building, MacLaren and Thomas. Thomas MacLaren (1863–1928), also a Scot, had practiced in Colorado Springs since 1894 and became the city's best-known architect with a substantial body of work that included civic and commercial buildings, churches and houses. No frontier rustic, he attended the Royal Academy in London and was much premiated for his drawing skills. In 1883 he won the Academy's first prize and silver medal for a set of architectural drawings of "The Two Eastern Bays of the North Cloister of Westminster Abbey." Two years later he was awarded the Academy's Gold Medal and Travelling Scholarship; the Pugin Travelling Scholarship of the R.I.B.A. followed in 1887.[6] Overall his very accomplished travel sketches reveal that he was thoroughly familiar with numerous traditional styles.

MacLaren's partnership with Charles E. Thomas (1876–1957), a former employee, was formed in 1906. Thomas established his own identity with drawings he prepared for Frank E. Kidder's ubiquitous treatise, *Kidder's Architects and Builders' Pocket Book*, first published in 1897.

Two projects, completed before Craig joined MacLaren and Thomas, secured the firm's reputation. Cragmor Sanatorium, the most notable of several residential health care facilities on the outskirts of Colorado Springs, opened in 1905. Claremont, a remarkable house presumably inspired by Rosecliff, Stanford White's 1897–1902 "cottage" in Newport for Hermann Oelrichs which, in turn, was indebted to Marsart's Grand Trianon at Versailles, was completed in 1907. Contemporary projects on which Craig theoretically could have worked include another library funded by Andrew Carnegie and a Masonic temple, both in the prevailing Classical Revival style inspired by the 1893 World's Columbian Exposition in Chicago.[7]

The association with MacLaren and Thomas most likely completed Craig's architectural training. Subsequent work with Sir Aston Webb in London and Carrère & Hastings in New York, mentioned in an

1.01. Rouen Cathedral

obituary and repeated in a later appreciation, is unsubstantiated.[8] One is left wondering about the source of these seemingly inflated published claims about Craig's formal education and professional experience. The truth probably lies in an application for a license he submitted to the Southern California State Board of Architectural Examiners in late January 1919. The application itself has not been located but it can be partially reconstructed from the Board's response, which does survive:

> It appears from Mr. Craig's application that he has had a brief training in a Technical College of Scotland, and the remainder of his theoretical knowledge has been

gained from general reading. It also appears that Mr. Craig has had four and one half years of actual general practice....[9]

It begs credibility to assume that Craig would fail to mention platinum-coated affiliations attributed to him—the University of Glasgow and the Royal Academy, Sir Aston Webb and Carrère & Hastings—had they existed.

Though details are scant, Craig left MacLaren and Thomas and returned to Europe in 1910. One travel sketch survives, possibly depicting the cathedral at Rouen and dated 1910 (Fig.1.01). By 1914 he had returned to America and was poised to begin his independent career in Flagstaff.

Masonic Temple
Flagstaff, 1915 (project)

Osborne Craig's presence in Flagstaff can be traced through entries in ledgers of the Babbitt Brothers Trading Company whose activities as ranchers and merchants drove the local economy. The first entry was posted in July 1914, several months earlier than other documentation suggests. Craig began renting office space from the Babbitts in November and continued through at least July 1916, placing him in Flagstaff for approximately two years.[10]

The earliest project of which there is record—possibly Craig's first independent work—was a design for a new Masonic Temple to be built on San Francisco Street near the courthouse. The drawing is lost but the scheme can be reconstructed partially from an article appearing in the Flagstaff newspaper *Coconino Sun* on April 30, 1915. It describes a two-story building of red sandstone for the first story and white brick or cement finish for the second story. Perhaps prophetically, the article concludes, "...it is hoped that the plans will go through and the building completed this summer." The new temple was still being discussed the following March but, ultimately, Craig's design was not used. The Masons today can provide no information.[11]

Girls' Dormitory, Northern Arizona Normal School
Flagstaff, 1915

Craig never explained the lure of Flagstaff but he probably went there with the prospect of work on the campus of the new Northern Arizona Normal School. The school was founded in 1899 with a student body of twenty-three; fifteen years later, the population had grown to 207. On December 26, 1914, R. H. H. Blome (1854–1923), the president, wrote to the State Superintendent of Public Instruction noting, "... the dormitories are well filled, not a vacant room anywhere. It follows from the above that new dormitories are needed. Two should be provided for during the next two years at an approximate cost of $50,000 each. One should be allowed under the emergency clause to be built immediately and the other later on in the usual way that such things are provided."[12]

The state legislature responded the following year with an appropriation of $8,900 for an addition to the boys' dormitory and, more significantly, $48,000 for the construction and furnishing of a new girls' dormitory. As required by law, the Board of Education advertised for bids from architects to furnish working drawings and specifications for construction. Craig's proposals were accepted and a contract was signed September 17, 1915.[13]

Ground was broken for the new girls' dormitory on September 20. Five weeks later the *Coconino Sun* reported, "Already the foundation has been finished and the red sandstone [is] being erected as fast as it can be cut." The paper followed up in November, "The walls of the new red stone boys' [*sic*: girls'] dormitory are now over half way up and a couple more weeks will see the outside work nearly completed" and again in January, noting "Rapid progress...the girls [*sic*] building to be done in April...." By August 1916 Campbell Hall, as it was then identified, was reported "...filled to its capacity."[14]

Craig's drawings for the building are lost though, surely, the dormitory was completed as he proposed

1.02. Girls' Dormitory, Northern Arizona Normal School, Flagstaff

and the board of education accepted. It stands today, an axially symmetrical, rectangular block with slightly projecting bays at each end and a recessed entry with a portico at the center (Fig.1.02). The foundation is white limestone; walls, as noted, are rusticated red sandstone.

The girls' dormitory was a transition building. Its red sandstone was consistent with Old Main, begun in 1894, and other structures nearby that formed the nucleus of the early campus though without the Victorian and Richardsonian embellishments of the earlier buildings. The portico with its oculus especially signals a new direction but it seems anachronistic; out of place both chronologically and structurally, a classical reference in a frontier environment, albeit rendered in wood. The columns provoked some contemporary discussion. Apparently in response to an inquiry from the state school superintendent, R. H. H. Blome wrote, "The columns that are designed by

the Architect are what is called the 'Tuscan' column —of the classical order. They have a diameter of 17" and are 21 ft. high. According to the Tuscan rules, these should be at least 28" in diameter. Other rules gave them as low at 25", but we think that 28" should be the lowest diameter of these columns."[15] One questions the context of this exchange.

Boys' Dormitory Addition, Northern Arizona Normal School
Flagstaff, 1915

The building as originally constructed was designed by Milliard & Creighton, a Phoenix firm, and completed in 1905 as the first dormitory on campus. It was a two-story brick building with a tri-partite facade and hipped roof; a porch and balcony spanned the width of the projecting center section (Fig. 1.03). In 1914, the State Legislature

1.03. Milliard & Creighton, Boys' Dormitory, Northern Arizona Normal School, Flagstaff

1.04. Milliard & Creighton, Boys' Dormitory, Northern Arizona Normal School, Flagstaff, with addition to west (right) by James Osborne Craig

allocated funds for an addition to the east end of the building. Additional funds were allocated in 1915 for an enlargement at the west end; this work, completed by Craig, added eight rooms, four on each floor. Craig's design strategy was to simply extend the walls and fenestration pattern of the original façade (Fig.1.04). Work essentially was complete by the end of December 1915 and well under budget; some of the excess funds were used for repairs to the original building.[16]

Mohave County Union High School
Kingman, 1915 (project)

Also in 1915, while work on the dormitories was underway, Craig submitted a proposal for a building for Mohave County Union High School in Kingman in response to an initiative by the local board of education. Heretofore, there had been no provision in Kingman for education beyond the tenth grade. Nothing of the nature of Craig's design is known and the project was awarded to a Phoenix firm, Marsh & Wallingford.[17]

Riordan Entrance Gate
Milton, Arizona

While Craig was in Flagstaff he executed another, much more modest project: an entrance gate to the fifty-five-acre residential compound, Kinlichi Knoll, of the very prominent Riordan brothers, Timothy and Michael, in neighboring Milton. The Riordans' two houses—mirror images of each other and the finest in the area—were designed by Charles Whittlesey, architect of El Tovar Hotel at the Grand Canyon, completed in 1904.[18] The houses were linked by a billiard room. The compound included a three-hole golf course that later was enveloped by the campus of Northern Arizona University (Fig. 11.05).

Craig's gate was located on a slight elevation overlooking the golf course and served as a sort of beacon. It consisted of two large piers defining a motor entrance and buttressed by sloping, receding walls terminating in lower piers that in turn provided pedestrian access (Fig. 1.05). The tall piers had shallow niches formed of small stones. Michael Riordan first indicated that the gate was constructed of lava rock; slightly later he described it as "malapais with the green lichens."[19]

Maryland Hotel Cottages
(for Myron Hunt (?), Pasadena, ca. 1916 (project?)

Craig ultimately settled in Santa Barbara but his whereabouts for several weeks in August and September 1916 are unknown; there is inconclusive

Pasadena California

evidence that he spent the time in Pasadena and was associated briefly with the architect Myron Hunt. One signed drawing in Craig's papers for cottages for the Maryland Hotel—Hunt was the architect of record—and an unattributed statement in Craig's obituary support but do not confirm the thesis.[20]

The Maryland Hotel first opened in 1903. The main building and its grounds occupied the city block defined by Colorado and Walnut streets (as Colorado Boulevard was then known) and Euclid and Los Robles avenues. Over the years numerous cottages were added, by 1916 garnering the appellation "bungalowland." More picturesque than informative, Craig's drawing depicts two cottages with pitched roofs but no clarification about the plans or building materials.[21] The drawing is signed; there can be no doubt of attribution, but stylistically it is utterly unlike the drawings he produced a short time later. It is crayon on cardboard, in contrast with the pencil-on-tissue technique he soon adopted, and it has an expressionistic, agitated quality antithetical to the repose seen in later work (Fig. 1.06).

Michael J. Riordan Belfry
Milton, Arizona, 1916–1917 (project)

One other project from this period, a belfry for Michael Riordan, was under discussion before Craig left Flagstaff, although the drawings were completed in Santa Barbara. Riordan reminded Craig of the project in September 1916, writing: "It might be a good time for me (between drinks) to be planning that belfry we spoke about. Better send me a pencil sketch of a contrivance such as we spoke about, and I will be considering, with a view to having you make a plan for the whole structure."[22]

Craig sent a proposal in early 1917. Riordan responded with many suggestions and concluded "... I rather think that it would be better to get away from the Spanish idea for this particular situation.... I ... am ... inclosing [sic] a picture that I cut from a paper showing a tower on a castle in Ireland, the form of which rather takes my eye. Perhaps you could get an idea from this, working in the belfry feature."[23]

Though the drawings for this project are lost, they establish a point of departure, an approximate date, for Craig's exploration of "the Spanish idea." And, in the perceived evolution of Spanish architecture in Santa Barbara, the date is early. Perhaps because of Riordan's unfavorable response—and in spite of several entreaties from him—Craig let the project drop.

1.06. Maryland Hotel Cottages (possibly for Myron Hunt), Pasadena (project)

CHAPTER 2

Santa Barbara

Mr. Craig was a student of early California history in addition to being an architect. He studied the missions of the state, and delved into the reasons for the early architectural development. He found simplicity to be the keynote because the early builders and designers worked with whatever was at hand, and in overcoming the obstacles evolved buildings of enduring beauty and charm.[1]

Osborne Craig was in Santa Barbara by September 1916. Initially he had a transient existence: in January 1917 he was living at Edgerly Court, an apartment house designed by Los Angeles architect Arthur Benton—who also was responsible for the second Arlington Hotel—and constructed in 1913 to accommodate actors and production personnel working at the nearby American Film Manufacturing Studio. The 1917–18 city directory issued in October 1917 indicates that Craig had moved to the Miramar Hotel in Montecito and was associated with "archt J C Pool." In 1918 he lived for several months in a cottage on East Valley Road rented from Miss Helen Sears. On May 18, 1919, the *Morning Press* (Santa Barbara) announced that he had taken a cottage at Siamasia [SIAM asia], a tourist camp on East Valley, "… where he is established for the summer."[2]

Craig's brief stay at Edgerly Court is of special interest. Mary McLaughlin, a young woman from Deadwood, South Dakota, and her friend Mig Bayard took an apartment there in February 1917. Craig and McLaughlin most likely had met at a tea given by Mrs. Alfred Erskine Brush a few weeks earlier; one is tempted to speculate that her decision to move to

Edgerly may not have been pure coincidence. In any case, they were married in November 1919.[3]

Osborne Craig's arrival in Santa Barbara coincided with a period of local architectural ferment. The Mission Revival Style, which flourished between approximately 1890 and 1915, had lost favor and ultimately was supplanted by a loosely defined Spanish or Mediterranean aesthetic. An article entitled "The Renaissance in Spain," that appeared in *Pacific Coast Architect* in June 1914, was a harbinger of things to come. It began with the premise, "The architects of California should feel a great interest in the architecture of Spain" and observed, "No country approaches so nearly our climatic conditions." It went on to define the characteristics of Spanish architecture that resulted from "… the desire of the builders to shelter the occupants from the heat and light. This necessity produced the broad cornice and its transparent purple shadow which, when thrown on a delicate cream colored wall surface, produces a feeling of delicacy and charm which never fails to fascinate." Finally, the article described "… the curious mixing of the Moorish and Christian architecture of Spain … with abundant cream-colored stone, a plentiful supply of iron ore, supplemented by a love of art and form …" that "… produced what is undoubtedly the most picturesque and delightfully delicate inspiration for the architects of the world to profit by."[4]

But the transition was not immediate: in the interim, a World War I–era academic classicism emerged in response to the 1893 World's Columbian Exposition in Chicago, though generally with none of the flourish displayed in the great white city. The earliest and finest example in Santa Barbara is the 1902 Gillespie House, El Fureidis, by Cram, Good-

hue & Ferguson. Looking back to both Greece and Rome, the house is a formal, decidedly severe, symmetrical composition with columns, pediments and an attic story akin to Roman triumphal arches. Though a stylistic enigma to contemporary observers—Gillespie himself characterized the house as "Mediterranean"—it is unimaginable without the influence of the Chicago Exposition. The house was widely published and its influence was palpable. Several houses of the period by the gentleman architect Francis T. Underhill including those for Francisca de la Guerra Dibblee; F. F. Peabody; and Rose Cottage, his own house on Ortega Hill, are variations on the theme. In the same period, distinguished Italianate buildings including the 1903 Santa Barbara Club and 1914 Santa Barbara Post Office, both by Francis W. Wilson, were completed.[5]

In the hands of lesser designers these academic exercises often arrived stillborn. The local YMCA by E. Russell Ray and Winsor Soule, 1918; and Roland F. Sauter's Santa Barbara County Detention Home, 1918, and Alexander Garage, 1919, were without regional relevance and would not have been out of place in any small Midwestern town (Fig. 2.01).[6] Much of Craig's earliest architectural activity in Santa Barbara is revealed in letters written to Mary between 1918 and 1921. He seems first to have been affiliated with J. Corbley Pool, a prolific architectural designer who counted the very prominent Henry Bothin among his clients; he also was active civically. Pool did not develop a unique, identifiable personal style; instead his work mirrored current popular taste. Today his most visible buildings are a remnant of the aforementioned American Film Manufacturing (Flying A) Studio and the Recreation Center. The 1913 Flying A building is a hybrid of Mission and academic revivalism with a theatricality appropriate to its use. The Recreation Center, completed in 1914, was described at the time as "… solidly constructed of brownish red tapestry brick with a red tile roof … built on Spanish lines …," though analogy with the Craftsman aesthetic would have been more accurate. The tea house for Henry Bothin that lives in infamy today because of the 2008 Tea Fire also was designed by Pool.[7]

Pool was working on three projects at the time he and Craig were associated: a hotel and store for Henry Bothin, and an office for the Santa Barbara Abstract Company, all on State Street. Correspondence exchanged after they parted company indicates something of the nature of their working relationship and that the association ended badly. More importantly, it reveals a level of comfort—Craig's freedom to speak candidly—with Bertram Goodhue, by then a nationally prominent architect. Pool's statement, "the time my office force put on some of the jobs which you have since finished up …" implies that Craig did not work for him but rather used Pool's staff to facilitate his own work. And, in addition to unresolved financial issues, Craig accused Pool of sullying his work and integrity, to which Pool responded, "… I have never been on one of your jobs and do not know anything about the merits or demerits." Craig ultimately concluded that Pool and his associate Mrs. Graham "… are a pair of rotters…."[8] Writing again to Goodhue in reference to Pool in December 1918 Craig recalled, "… while our trial agreement was for the period of one year, at the end of six months I got out, his methods, professional pretenses and real personality being too much for me."[9]

2.02. Helen C. Heberton House, Montecito (project)

Helen C. Heberton House
Montecito, ca. 1917 (project)

The conflict with Pool is unlikely to be sorted out but no matter; by the time the association ended, Craig had established a significant client base in Santa Barbara. His first commission may have been for Helen Heberton, a transplant from Ambler, Pennsylvania, a borough north of Philadelphia; she also was a cousin of Craig Heberton who later purchased George Washington Smith's own first house on Middle Road. Craig prepared three schemes for Miss Heberton for a site overlooking the future golf course of the Montecito Country Club. Two of the projects appear to be based on the same plan incorporating a wing projecting diagonally from the central mass. The chief differences are the wall surfaces and roofs. One drawing indicates board and batten siding and a hipped roof over various wings of the building that stops short of a second-story porch. Another may suggest plaster walls; the roof has been extended over the porch and continues without a break over the projecting one-story wing in the English vernacular manner of the architect C. F. A. Voysey.[10]

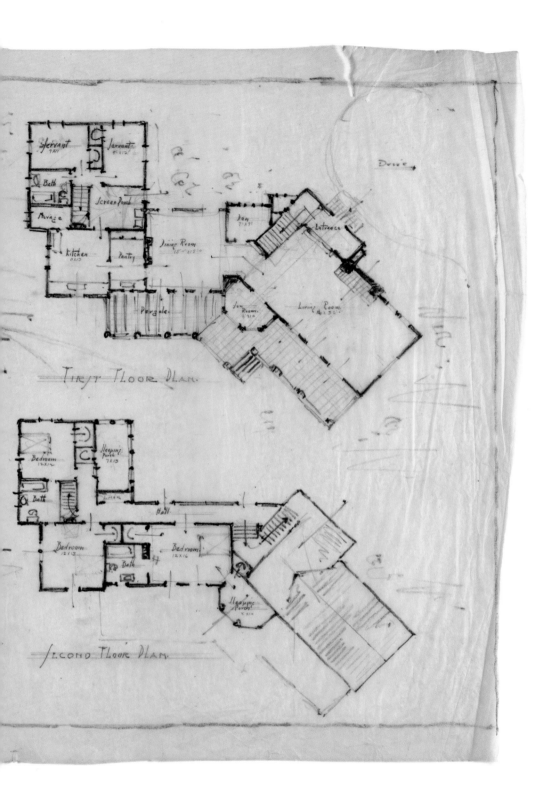

The third scheme, a "tentative sketch," in fact the most developed of the group, was for a two-story house in the nascent Spanish style with smooth, planar wall surfaces and a red tile roof, but it is not a mature statement. The diagonal wing of the other two plans is retained though, containing a double-height living room, in scale and function is no longer a secondary appendage. An octagonal tower serves as a hinge at the point of intersection (Fig.2.02).

The date for this project is speculative but the drawings must have been completed before November 1917, by which time the commission had gone

to Francis Underhill. This conclusion is supported by the drawing for the third scheme. The slightly agitated quality is reminiscent of the sketch for the Maryland Hotel cottages a year earlier, suggesting that both Craig's architecture and drawing technique were in transition.

Writing to Mary McLaughlin in the summer of 1918, Craig mentioned work for Mr. and Mrs. Martin Redmayne and Mrs. Theodore Sheldon; he also indicated that he had been contacted by James Warren, who built the recently opened El Encanto Hotel, though nothing came of this immediately. Later in

1918, Craig was focused on restoration of Mission Santa Inés and a house for Mrs. Charles E. Bigelow in Carmel Highlands. The correspondence also makes clear that this was a period of exploration for Craig: he traveled north as far as Monterey at least twice and wrote eloquently of the experience:

> How pleasing everything is in the county of Monterey and all afternoon was a feast of architectural and natural charm, with the Mission of San Miguel for an "aperitif" and the bay upon which I now look down the "sweet." The coast here is rocky which bespeaks interest and this is no exception.... There are curiously formed little caves which doubtless have been the scene of much smuggling, the whole going to make up one of the most beautiful bits of nature I have yet seen.

Craig followed up a week later:

> I am anticipating even now my next visit to Monterey, this last time I had to get back as quickly as possible, so there was little opportunity to see much of that quaint old town, in many respects the most interesting in California... I was transported by what I saw of old world prototypes; truly it was both pleasing and sad to behold, the simple grandeur of the expression of Spain's influence was satisfying, but what a discordant note is struck in the work since American occupation....[11]

If the classicizing nature of the girls' dormitory at Northern Arizona Normal School reflects the zeitgeist in general and possibly the work of Thomas MacLaren in particular, surely Craig's avowed interest in early California buildings draws on the influence of Michael Riordan. Riordan was well educated, well-traveled and articulate. His interest in Hispanic culture was manifested in the late nineteenth century: he traveled to Mexico several times and expressed a liking for the country and considered establishing a lumber business there. On a visit to Los Angeles in 1900, he gave a talk at the Newman Club, describing "Bypaths of Spanish Padres," "a review of the exploration and settlement of the early missionaries, commencing with the sixteenth century ... and the founding of the missions of California, Arizona and New Mexico."[12] Clearly Riordan found Craig a willing acolyte.

Redmayne House
Montecito, 1918 (project)

Martin Redmayne was identified in the press as "a prominent member of the English colony" in Riverside where he had been affiliated with the thriving citrus industry since 1898; he also had been "... a star member of the Riverside polo team almost since its inception." He seems first to have made his way to Santa Barbara with his new wife in 1917.[13]

First- and second-floor plans are all that remain of this project. Less ambitious than the Heberton scheme, it nonetheless repeats the off-angle wing as a planning strategy. Absent elevations or written descriptions it is impossible to place this house in context of Craig's evolution toward Spanish design.

Sheldon Garage/Gardener's Cottage
Montecito, 1918

The Sheldon garage and gardener's cottage has significance far outweighing its modesty. It was completed in 1918 for Mrs. Theodore Sheldon of Chicago; her considerable wealth derived from railroads and real estate. Edward Sheldon (1886–1946), her son, was a renowned playwright. In 1918 her daughter Mary married Alfred MacArthur, a member of the prominent Chicago insurance family.[14]

More importantly from an architectural perspective, the building is another manifestation of Craig's deep appreciation of early California building, in this case the nearby Masini adobe, to which the design is clearly indebted. Two years after it was completed, *Architectural Forum* made analogy with George Washington Smith's own house on Middle Road, commenting that they "... speak so eloquently of picturesqueness, that it is only necessary to add that in them both is the germ of hope for future Californian

architecture. The former [Sheldon] will eventually have a walled motor courtyard added in front of the two motor doors of the plan. The slope of the ground and the existing, fine large trees had much to do with the arrangement of the plan" (Fig. 2.03).[15]

The local *Morning Press* responded as well with approbation several times, noting the inspiration of the Ortega adobe (as Masini was then identified, owning to its location at the foot of Ortega Hill). In October 1922, the paper described "a charming little house planned from the old Ortega adobe which for years has been a picturesque ruin in Montecito." It followed up twice in 1924. In March it noted—in less than architectural terminology—"… a charming country estate, with an adorable adobe house, with deep set windows and doors and a fascinating little outside stairway leading to a portion of the upper floor. The garden has all the charm of the native foothills, much of it having been left in its natural state." In October the house was interpreted as "… Spanish in type … modeled after the old Ortega Adobe. It was one of the first Spanish houses built here after the revival of inter-

est in this type of architecture. The late James Osborne Craig was the architect" (Fig. 2.04).[16]

Sheldon Garage/Gardener's Cottage Addition; Main House
Montecito, 1918 (projects)

The garage/gardener's cottage built for Mrs. Sheldon was a remnant of a larger development she and her architect envisioned. The overall scope of the project is revealed in two drawings. One depicts an addition to the west of the service building, linked to it by a wall (Fig.2.05). The second drawing includes plans and elevations for a substantial main house (Fig.2.06). The drawings are not dated but surely were completed in December 1918. Craig mentioned in a letter written on the sixteenth that he was "… at present working on commission for Mrs. Sheldon…." (the garage/gardener's cottage was completed in August). He followed up in another letter dated December 29 that he had "… heard nothing, not even an acknowledgment of the drawings and estimates I sent her some ten days since."[17]

2.03. *Mrs. Theodore Sheldon Garage/Gardener's Cottage, Montecito*

FOLLOWING PAGES
2.04. *Mrs. Theodore Sheldon Garage/Gardener's Cottage, Montecito*

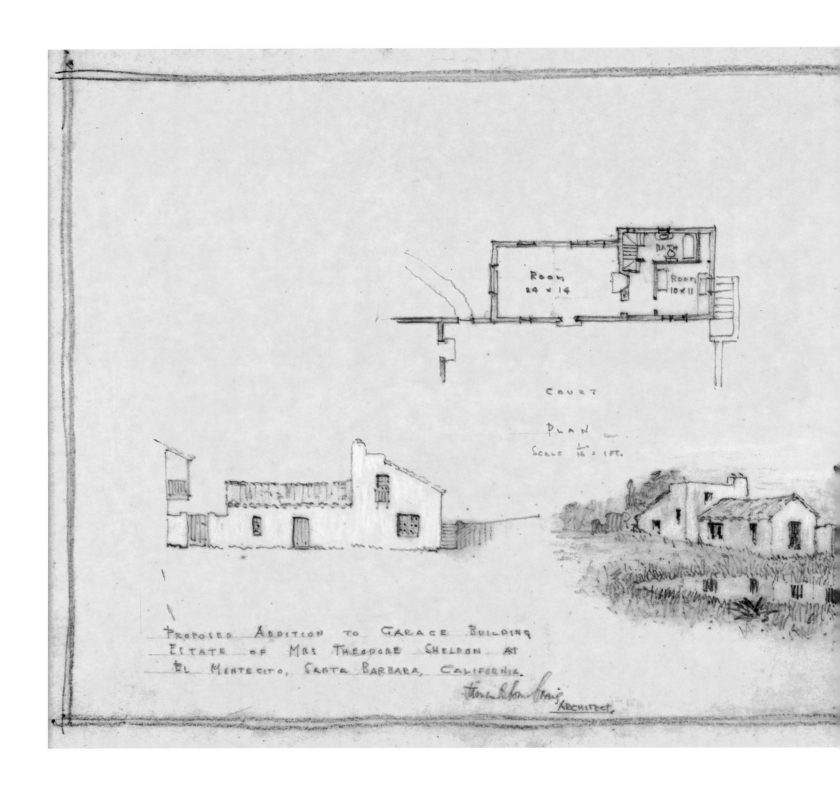

PROPOSED ADDITION TO GARAGE BUILDING
ESTATE OF MRS THEODORE SHELDON AT
EL MONTECITO, SANTA BARBARA, CALIFORNIA.

These drawings are the most convincing statement to date that Craig had hit his stride. The addition to the original cottage is particularly striking: he had made the transition to designs inspired by Andalusian architecture. Entirely self-assured, the large house is irregularly massed with white planar surfaces and the requisite tile roof. The plan encloses a court on three sides; entry is on the central axis and leads to a corridor extending the length of the building, providing clarity of circulation lacking in some of Craig's plans. The success of this project coincides with increasingly sophisticated drawing technique. There is no trace of the expressionistic quality displayed in the sketches for the Maryland Hotel cottages or the house for Miss Heberton.

Neither the addition to the cottage nor the main house was built; the project was abruptly cancelled because of Edward Sheldon's precarious health. In October 1924, referring to Mrs. Sheldon, the *Morning Press* noted, "she has not visited her Montecito home for several years." It was placed on the market and sold in 1925 to Mrs. M. Russell Perkins of Boston.[18]

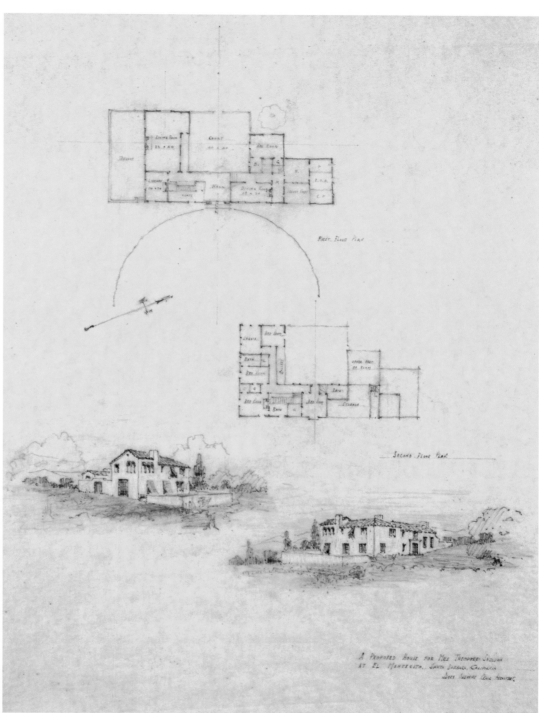

2.05. Mrs. Theodore Sheldon
Garage/Gardener's Cottage
Addition, Montecito (project)

2.06. Mrs. Theodore Sheldon
House, Montecito (project)

AT THE SANTA INEZ MISSION
OCTOBER 1918   JAMES OSBIRNE CRAIG

2.07. Mission Santa Inés, Santa Ynez (project)

Mission Santa Inés
Santa Ynez, 1918 (project)

The nineteenth mission in the chain, Santa Inés was established in 1804; the present building, the second, was completed in 1817. Although never abandoned, it began to decline in the 1850s and by the turn of the century was in ruinous condition. The mission was further compromised by a violent rain storm in 1905. Limited restoration was begun a short time later: a new roof was installed over approximately one-half of the building and the well and windmill were repaired; other projects were completed over time. Crumbling walls were an ongoing concern: as they dried, the adobe disintegrated, leaving numerous cavities.[19]

Nature struck again with greater force in February and March 1911. Rain began February 25 and continued for twelve days; overall, forty inches of rainfall were recorded. Again, the adobe walls of the mission absorbed the water: first, four buttresses supporting the chapel walls collapsed. Then, on March 7, the bell tower fell. Restoration began in June and included reconstruction of the buttresses and bell tower, reconstruction of the roof, and a new foundation along the cemetery side of the building: work continued into 1912. The reconstructed bell tower did not faithfully replicate the original: it was built of concrete and instead of being solid, it was left hollow. Also, there were openings for four bells—instead of the original three—at the top.[20]

Craig visited the mission in 1918 and made sketches (Fig. 2.07). He followed up in a letter to Bertram Goodhue; nowhere is his affinity for early California building expressed more eloquently:

I spent quite a little time about the Santa Inez [sic] Mission ... the new bell tower, the arches of the belfry revealing a concrete wall four inches thick, is cause for regret; from the gentle atmosphere of yesterday, of which the old walls are part, the sudden transition to such modern misconception is harsh and harrowing, and one longs for a development which will make further abuse of this legacy to California impossible. If in my small way I can do anything to advance such an appreciation, or at least prevent greater profanation, it would be a source of unbounded pleasure.

Goodhue responded:

Everything you write about the Santa Inez [sic] Mission I agree with thoroughly.... But as for inducing the Roman Church ... to take any interest in the preservation of their own natural heritage, or even to see the money value of such restoration, seems to be rather hopeless.[21]

The bell tower finally was restored in 1947.

Mrs. Charles E. Bigelow House
Carmel Highlands, 1919

As completed, a house designed for Mrs. Charles Bigelow in Carmel Highlands is an architectural enigma. Its massing is irregular and the location of the entry, at the right-hand corner of the front facade, is a decision hard to justify aesthetically (Fig. 2.08).

Part of the eccentricity may be explained by the site, a precipice overlooking the Pacific Ocean, difficult of access but with a deeply satisfying view framed by cypress trees and rock outcroppings one gets only on the Monterey Peninsula. A more plausible explanation is a chemistry of tangled personal relationships. Craig began work on the project in mid-December 1918. Three weeks later, he was in the area, staying at the nearby Highlands Inn. He met the artist John O'Shea while he was there. During construction, O'Shea took over, at once completing the building and making changes to Craig's design.

John O'Shea (1876–1956) worked in Carmel between 1917 and 1945. He is believed to have had a romantic interlude with Mrs. Bigelow before marrying Mary Shaugnessey in 1922. His role in the house is confirmed by articles in the *Carmel Pine Cone*, June 8, 1922: "John O'Shea supervised the building of Bigelow house," and in *California Southland*, August 1925: "house and garden of Mrs. Bigelow ... started by Mr. Craig, but changed and completed by the owner and the artist, Mr. O'Shea."[22]

2.08. *Mrs. Charles E. Bigelow House, Carmel Highlands (completed by John O'Shea)*

Chesebrough House
Pebble Beach, ca. 1919 (project)

Writing to Mary after returning from one of his excursions to the Monterey Peninsula, Craig indicated the possibility of two new commissions there. One seemed sure: "... I was definitely commissioned to get up sketches for another house ..."; the other was hopeful but uncertain: "... I rather anticipate still another house from the same neighborhood."[23] The definite commission may have been a project for the golfer Edith Chesebrough in Pebble Beach. The site on Seventeen Mile Drive rose above wave-splashed rock outcroppings and the Pacific Ocean, a display of nature upstaging any man-made intrusion.

Craig's response has the additive quality of a true Spanish farmhouse. The surviving elevation drawing depicts a one- and two-story mass with perpendicular wings; a projecting, arched entry and the lean-tos that became a standard feature of Spanish Colonial Revival design. Railed porches overlook the ocean (Fig. 2.09).

The Chesebrough House was not built but comparison with another house nearby that was, designed by George Washington Smith for Mrs. Arthur Rose Vincent, is inevitable. The architects' responses for sites so geographically and physically akin are a study in contrast. Both designs are Spanish, but instead of the provincial inspiration of the Chesebrough project, the Vincent House is a palace, formal and ceremonial, neither more nor less beautiful. It fronts directly on the street. The plan, nearly a square, encloses a central courtyard. Entry is on the central axis and leads through loggias to grand public spaces overlooking the ocean.

HOUSE FROM THE SEA

FROM THE APPROACH

A · HOUSE · FOR ·
MRS · JAMES · OSBORNE · CRAIG ·
AT ·
MONTECITO ·

JAMES · OSBORNE · CRAIG, · ARCHITECT

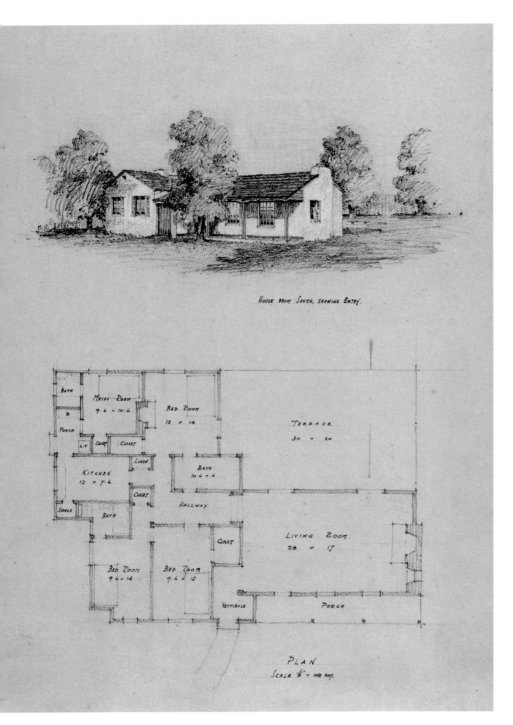

HOUSE FROM SOUTH, SHOWING ENTRY.

PLAN
SCALE ⅛" = ONE FOOT.

Alexander House Remodeling
Montecito, 1919

Historically the client for this commission has been identified as J. B. Alexander; for consistency and to avoid confusion, this appellation has been retained. In fact, the project was an expansion of an existing house purchased earlier by Mrs. C. B. Stewart. By the time work was completed, Alexander and Stewart had married.

Craig enlarged two bedrooms on the front of the building, added a third bedroom and maid's room, and extended the kitchen to the rear. He also designed a fireplace framed with boulders for the living room, bringing the outdoors in and mimicking a design for the Bigelow House. One wants to believe that Craig repackaged the building as well: his published drawing and contemporary photographs show plaster walls and tile roof in the newly fashionable spirit of a Spanish farmhouse (Figs. 2.10, 2.11).

The house was published twice in 1922, first in a memorial issue of *Architect and Engineer* devoted to Craig. The second publication was in *California Southland*, in a propaganda piece promoting the false economy of working with a builder instead of an architect.[24]

2.10. *J. B. Alexander House remodeling, Montecito*

2.11. *J. B. Alexander House remodeling, Montecito*

Brush House
Montecito, 1919 (project)

The project for Mr. and Mrs. Alfred E. Brush, like the houses for Mrs. Theodore Sheldon and Edith Chesebrough, fully demonstrates Craig's facility with the new Spanish style. All the elements are present: asymmetrical massing; planar wall surfaces; arched openings; pitched, red-tiled roofs; the suggestion of an iron grill—*reja*—over the stair hall window; and the ubiquitous lean-to, in this case, the kitchen (Fig. 2.12).

This was a substantial, ceremonial house. The generously proportioned and finely articulated entrance hall led with changes in level and orientation to the public spaces and to an arcaded loggia overlooking the Pacific Ocean in the distance. The bedrooms upstairs are linked similarly by an open gallery over the loggia. Though not grand by Montecito standards, the accoutrements of a lifestyle the Brushes apparently could not afford are evident in the plans. In an obvious moment of pique, Craig wrote to Mary on October 7:

… Brush main drawings are finalized, but I would not be surprised if they put off building as

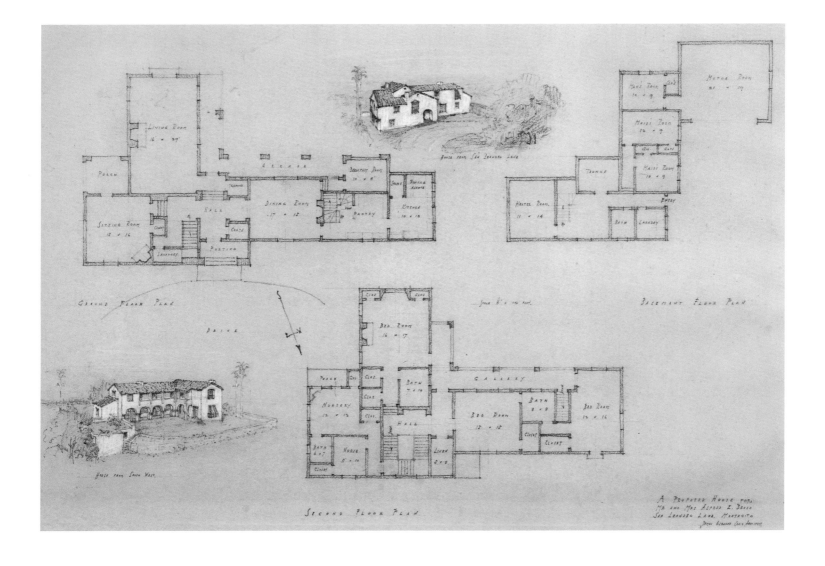

I know it is going to cost much more than they expect, and for some silly reason they will not listen to a smaller house....[25]

Craig's lack of charitableness overlooks the fact that he probably first met Mary McLaughlin at a tea given by Mrs. Brush in January 1917. In any event, he was correct. The house was not built.

Rudolph B. Gring House
Montecito, 1919

A nearly contemporary but much more modest house for Mr. and Mrs. Rudolph Brainard Gring followed. Gring was headmaster of a private boys' boarding school bearing his name in Montecito. The Grings seem to have contacted Craig in September 1919; the plans are dated November and show a simple structure in the Andalusian style. The house was complete in April (Fig. 2.13). In 1924 it was awarded honorable mention as a notable example of architecture by the judges of a Better Architecture Competition.[26]

Oreña Adobe Restoration
Santa Barbara, 1919

A t the end of December 1918 and again two weeks later, Craig indicated to Mary that he needed a place to work. He considered renting space from "Miss Yeoman" and setting it up but noted that the rent was higher than in the San Marcos Building, where he currently had his office. The big break came in October 1919, as he explained to Mary:

Tomorrow the work starts on recreating the old adobe on De La Guerra Street where I will have my digs. There is awfully little money available but I am going to do my best to get a little of the spirit of the day.... Mr. Parshall promised me to take a long lease on a studio in the rear court, which we will build, and it was securing him that made the Rickards willing to go ahead. I have little doubt that all available space will be taken before work is completed and I will be after them to revive the two adjacent buildings which are also old landmarks.[27]

The old adobe to which Craig referred was built by Gaspár Oreña (1824–1903), a member by marriage of the de la Guerra family, around 1858. It served first as the family home and later as commercial space (Fig. 2.14). The Rickard Family Trust owns the property today.

A building permit was issued November 21, 1919; work included restoration of the adobe itself and the new studio to the rear. An article entitled "Orena [sic] Adobe to Be Remodeled as Studio" that appeared in the *Morning Press* on November 22, 1919, described the project in detail:

> The Gaspar Orena home on East De la Guerra street, one of the notable landmarks here, is being remodeled by James B. Rickard who plans to utilize the same as a studio and office building. At the rear of the lot two modernly appointed studios built to harmonize with the lines of the old house will be erected. A court with a fountain is planned between the adobe and the studios. A high brick wall painted white and relieved by plants and shrubs will surround the whole court.… One of the features of the restoration of the old adobe will be a new tile roof.

Oreña Studio
for Doña Acacia Oreña Rickard, Santa Barbara, 1919

The new studio was an unadorned rectangular volume entered through an arch; two large windows at the rear admitted north light (Fig. 2.15). The space was divided internally into two rooms, each with a fireplace. Craig's office on the second floor of the adobe overlooked the studio building and rear court and was his digs until his death.

There is no evidence that Mr. Parshall—père or fils—ever occupied the studio as intended. Instead, in 1920, the building and adjoining courtyard were given a different life as a restaurant. It had its social debut on July 27 with a reading by Marion Craig Wentworth, as announced by the *Morning Press*:

> A reading by Marion Craig Wentworth is an artistic event in which society is interested this evening. Mrs. Wentworth will read "The Women's Town," a delightful comedy from the Spanish of Alvarez Quinterose [sic: Álvarez Quintero], in the charming patio of the recently restored Orena adobe on East De la Gerra [sic] street.…The old adobe has been converted into most attractive studios, which open on a patio and court redolent with the atmosphere of old Spain. Open to the stars and night skies the patio is an enchanting place at evening, and one that is a particular [sic] happy as a setting for Spanish drama.[28]

The Patio Lunch and Tea Room opened with some fanfare the following month, again as recorded by the *Morning Press*:

> Days of yesteryear were recalled last evening when a party of 20 members of old Santa Barbara families, guests of Mr. and Mrs. James B. Rickard were entertained at dinner at Orena Adobe.
>
> It was the opening of the new patio dining room under the direction of Mrs. Christine Holmberg Hall, where luncheon and tea as well as dinners will be served.
>
> The delightful old Spanish court and the patio with its quaint fire place, and the Spanish musicians in costume evoked pleasant memories; and the past lived again for a space.[29]

2.13. Rudolph B. Gring House, Montecito

2.14. Edward Borein in front of Oreña Adobe, Santa Barbara, 1922. Photograph by J. W. Collinge.

Seemingly, The Patio was a success. A cross section of Santa Barbara society came to enjoy its pleasures; their activities were reported regularly in the press. It also received professional recognition. In August 1921 the Southern California Chapter, American Institute of Architects, held its monthly meeting in Santa Barbara. An article in *Southwest Builder and Contractor* recorded the two-day event and mentioned, "Luncheon was served at the 'Patio,' an old adobe residence restored and remodeled into a tearoom by James Osborne Craig, architect." And Rexford Newcomb, the distinguished chronicler of Southwestern architecture, concluded after a visit:

> The house at No. 29 … is especially interesting in its restored condition … but the patio, with its red-tile pavement, its comfortable shelters, picturesque roofs, and garden wall, is the most delightful feature of the place. Tea and cakes are worth twice the price in such surroundings.[30]

By the time Newcomb's comments were published in 1925, the Patio Tearoom was no more. In May 1922, an article in the *Morning Press* revealed that "Santa Barbara natives" intended to purchase The Patio for a club house. The "natives" intentions and the extent of their follow through are unclear but in October Edward Borein took over the space for his studio, fulfilling the original intention.

Gantz House, Crossways Cottage
Montecito, 1920

Crossways Cottage for Beatrice and Harry Gantz—and the Gring house—are as close as Craig came to replicating a true Spanish farmhouse. Certainly the

Sheldon and Brush projects contain stylistic traits consistent with the genre, but they lack the modesty—the utter simplicity which, ultimately, was the appeal—of the prototypes. One needs look no farther than Winsor Soule's book *Spanish Farmhouses and Minor Public Buildings*, published in 1924, to understand the analogy. Craig's presentation drawing—unorthodox but compelling in its depiction of the building from the rear—conveys his affinity (Fig. 2.16).

Dates for the drawing and overall project are loosely established by notices in the press. The January 9, 1920, issue of *Southwest Builder and Contractor* noted, "Lieut. Harry Gantz has sold the major portion of his place in Montecito and will build a smaller fireproof house."[31] The reference was to property formerly owned by Beatrice Gantz's mother and stepfather, Mr. and Mrs. Ferdinand Bain, which extended along Hot Springs Avenue (as it was then known) between Valley Road and Pepper Lane. The substantial Bain House stood to the south near Pepper Lane. Mr. and Mrs. Gantz retained the northern end of the property, across Valley Road from Mt. Carmel Church, for their new house.

The society column of the *Morning Press* followed up on March 30, reporting, "Mr. and Mrs. Gantz are building a house in Montecito near 'The Peppers,' which they will return to occupy this summer." Then on July 8 the column indicated that the house was finished: "Mr. and Mrs. Harry Gantz and their little son, Peter Gantz, who have been living at their ranch hame [*sic*] at Fullerton while their house in Montecito was in course of construction, are expected to arrive most any day, to spend the summer here. The house is on part of the land that formerly belonged to Mrs. Gantz's place, 'The Peppers,' which she sold not long ago, reserving enough of the property for a smaller home. Osborne Craig is the architect."[32]

The house was completed as Craig imagined, an asymmetrically massed, two-story rectangular volume with white plaster walls and red tile roof (Fig. 2.17). The garage projected from the front elevation; originally, the driveway extended diagonally from the corner of Hot Springs and Valley. The modesty of the exterior belies the architect's hand inside: the two-story entry/stair hall extends space vertically and horizontally.

Mr. and Mrs. Gantz occupied the house only briefly. Like many Montecito residents, they were not tethered to one place to live—they had ranches in Santa Ynez and Fullerton—and, in the best local tradition, the house became a rental before it was sold in the early 1920s. Perhaps the most notable tenants were Mr. and Mrs. George Fox Steedman of St. Louis who occupied it in early 1922 before building Casa del Herrero on Valley Road to the east.[33]

Mrs. James Nelson Burnes Cottage
Montecito, 1920

Mrs. James Nelson Burnes was a fixture in Pasadena and Santa Barbara society. Among many references in the social columns, a note from 1916 in the *Pasadena Star-News* seems especially to capture her lifestyle in the two cities: "Mrs. James Nelson Burnes, whose beautiful Italian villa home in Oak Knoll has been, in seasons past, the scene of many delightful social functions, is at Montecito, where she has another charming home the center of much social life."

Myron Hunt designed both of Mrs. Burnes's houses and one wonders about the link between Hunt, Mrs. Burnes, Mary McLaughlin, Osborne Craig, the Maryland Hotel and the cottage Craig designed for Mrs. Burnes at Fernald Point. We will probably never know but Craig's opportunity came

2.16. Gantz House, Crossways Cottage, Montecito

FOLLOWING PAGES
2.17. Gantz House, Crossways Cottage, Montecito

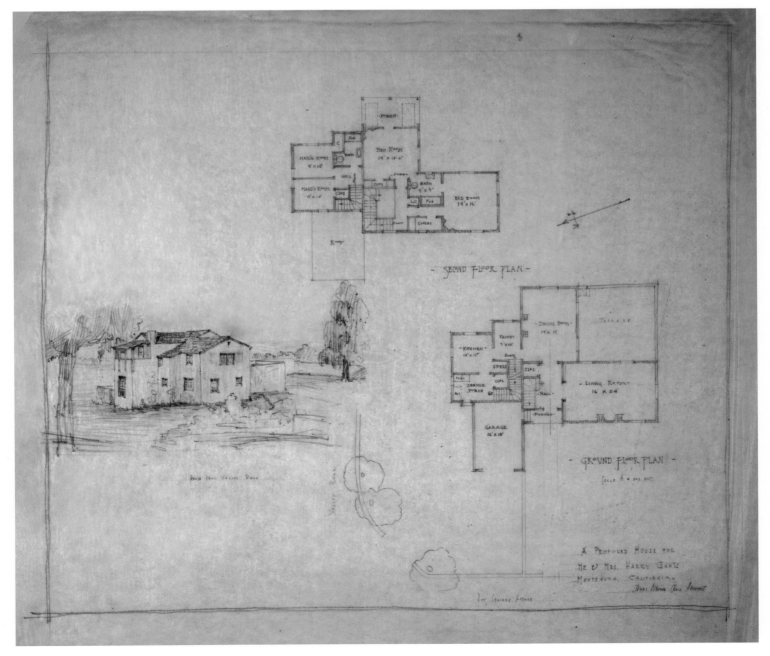

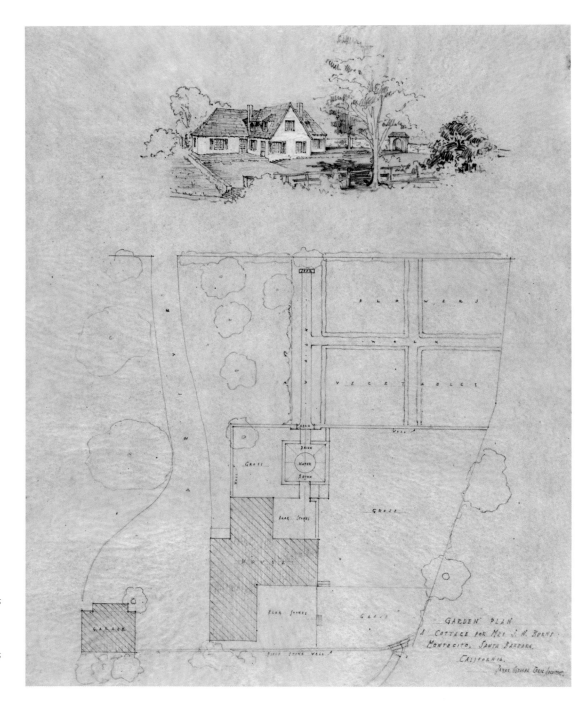

2.18. Mrs. James Nelson Burnes
Cottage, Fernald Point,
Montecito

2.19. Mrs. James Nelson Burnes
House, Fernald Point,
Montecito

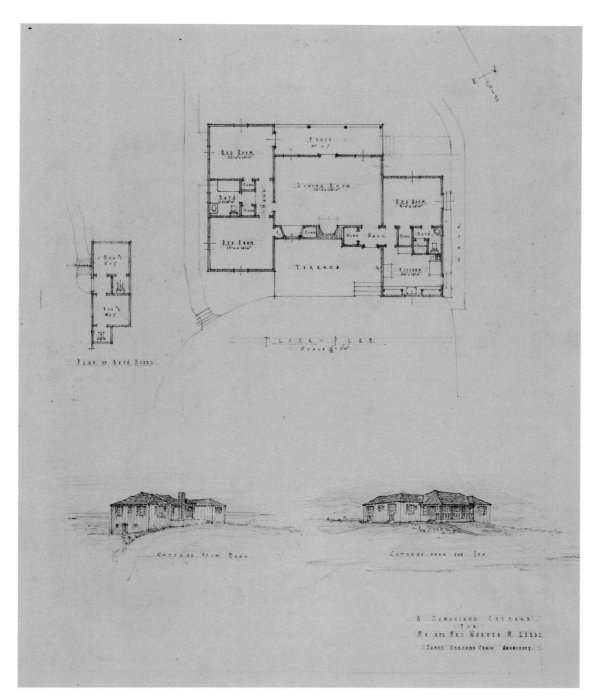

2.20. Leeds Beach Cottage, Sandyland

2.21. Nugent and Chase Beach Cottages, Sandyland

in 1920. On April 25, the *Morning Press* announced: "Mrs. Burnes is building a delightful little Normandie cottage on her Montecito property, plans for which have been furnished by Osborne Craig. The place will be ready for occupancy the latter part of June."[34]

Craig's drawings indicate a two-story dwelling with plastered walls and a steeply sloped roof. A separate garage with two bedrooms above is similarly configured (Fig. 2.18).

The circumstances of this project rival the actual building for one's attention. It represents a distinct—if temporary—stylistic shift for Craig. By this time he was proficient in the accepted "Spanish" style; one wonders what provoked him and his client to change course. No answer is at hand but it may be useful to mention another, coeval, "Normandy" project less than half a mile away. In September 1919 the *Morning Press* reported, "George Washington Smith is drawing plans for a house of French Normandy type, and the work or construction will begin just as soon as the industrial situation will admit of building."[35] This house was for another socially prominent client, Mrs. Norris King Davis. The chronology and physical proximity are too close to ignore. Were these women using their resources to create a new trend, possibly in juxtaposition to a style with which they were not enamored?

While the houses have attributes in common: steeply pitched, shingled roofs and multi-paned windows, in fact, neither is overburdened with characteristics commonly ascribed to domestic architecture in Normandy. They are picturesque, to be sure; but in the case of the Burnes House, the steep roof seems to be the defining feature (Fig. 2.19). An early photograph of the interior reveals a heavy, open-beam ceiling and exposed brick fireplace. The house was completed in September 1920, though Mrs. Burnes had little opportunity to use it. She died two months later at age forty-eight.[36]

Nugent, Chase and Leeds Beach Cottages
Sandyland, 1920

Sandyland, an unicorporated strip of beach framed by a salt marsh on the north and the Pacific Ocean on the south was first developed as an "aristocratic summer colony" in 1915. Not unlike Montecito, individual parcels were irregular in both size and configuration and larger lots were later divided.[37]

Details are scant, but Craig designed three cottages that were built here around 1920 for Daniel Nugent, Harold Chase and Warner Leeds.[38] All were board and batten with hipped roofs. The Nugent Cottage was the largest and the only one to include servant quarters. It was linked to the Chase Cottage by a porte-cochère (Fig. 2.21). The third cottage was for Warner Leeds (Fig. 2.20). All three were ultimately destroyed by winter storms.

University Club
Santa Barbara, 1920 (project)

The University Club of Santa Barbara was incorporated in July 1919. At first there was discussion of establishing headquarters in and possibly purchasing Casa de la Guerra but the directors ultimately concluded that the amount of work and the financial outlay required to make it habitable were excessive. Instead, they rented a house at 25 East Micheltorena Street, fully intending to establish a permanent location later. Winsor Soule chaired several committees charged with locating an appropriate site and generating designs for a new building.[39]

In December 1919 Soule reported that the 1880 Lacy house at the southeast corner of Santa Barbara and Sola Streets "... was considered the most favorable ..." but because of the price, "... consideration of this property has been dropped." Between January 1920 and May 1922 the group retained an option to purchase a site on Carrillo Street adjacent to the Recreation Center owned by David Gray, a club member. Winsor Soule reported in February 1920 that his committee "... had examined six or seven sites and they regarded the Carrillo Street property ... as the best...."[40]

The issue of developing plans for a new building on Carrillo was addressed in June: a committee consisting of Winsor Soule, Chair; J. F. Murphy; E. K. Lockard; W. A. Edwards; E. W. Neff and O. H. Schaaf was formed to establish a program. The committee met twice and presented a "tentative" program to the board on August 2. The new building was to be two stories, "... of an informal type following the general lines of Spanish architecture" and was to "... be developed with the idea of providing for future expansion with the growth of the club." Each of the six committee members was asked to prepare a rough sketch which "... then will be criticized by the committee as a whole and as a result of this criticism a final scheme will be developed by the cooperative efforts of the committee and presented to the directors."

Though the minutes are silent on the circumstances, Osborne Craig was added to the committee in August and, by default, was handed the tentative program already established.[41] He quickly formulated a proposal for a Spanish-style building, domestic in scale, extending to the south and opening to a garden, tennis court and servant cottages. The entry hall gave access to corridors leading to a library, lounge, game room and dining room that in turn enclosed an outdoor terrace and court on three sides (Fig.2.22).

Craig and the others met on September 1 to discuss the preliminary plans. The consensus was that the guidelines presented to the architects were too ambitious and the program was revised. By November, the committee had formulated a new plan but there was no further action until May 1922. By then the club had received a new offer on the Lacy property at Santa Barbara and Sola Streets. The directors decided to purchase the house and remodel it for club purposes.[42] Soule, Murphy & Hastings completed the work, stripping the exterior of Victorian excess and rendering it in the current Spanish style.

Craig's participation in the designing of a new clubhouse was a credit to his talent. The University Club was founded by and for college graduates and students; junior college students were not admitted. Nor would Osborne Craig have been.

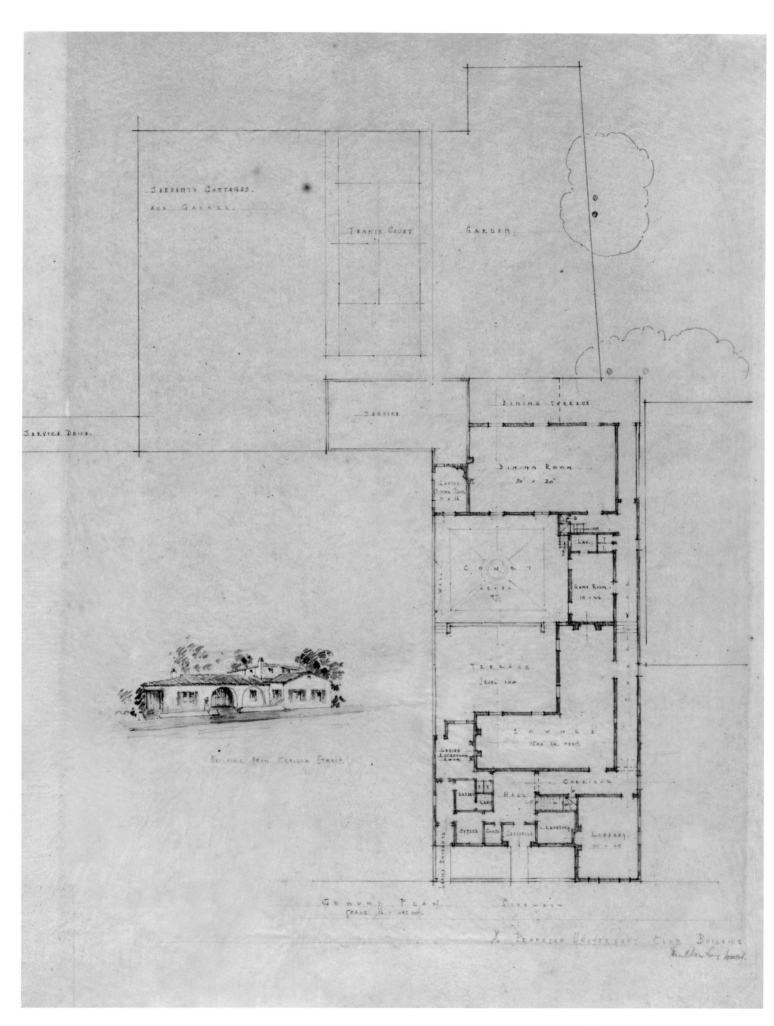

SERVANT'S COTTAGES.
AND GARAGE.

TENNIS COURT   GARDEN

SERVICE DRIVE.

SERVICE

DINING TERRACE

DINING ROOM
50' × 30'

LADIES
DINING ROOM
17 × 16

COURT
LEVEL
97'

LAV.

GAME ROOM
14 × 24

TERRACE
LEVEL 100

LOUNGE
1500 sq. feet

LADIES
RECEPTION
ROOM

CORRIDOR

LADIES
LAVA.

HALL

OFFICE   COATS   VESTIBULE   LAVATORY   LIBRARY
20 × 25

COTTAGE FROM CABRILLO STREET.

GROUND PLAN
SCALE 1/16 = ONE FOOT

X PROPOSED UNIVERSITY CLUB BUILDING

49

CHAPTER 3

Irene and Bernhard Hoffmann

3.01. Hoffmann House,
Santa Barbara, south
elevation

Irene and Bernhard Hoffmann first came to Santa Barbara in November 1919 from Stockbridge, Massachusetts, to spend the winter. Within a year they had settled in. Bernhard Hoffmann explained:

> We decided to move to California because of the health of a member of the family.... We have friends and relatives in various cities, San Francisco, Pasadena, San Diego and elsewhere. It would have been pleasant to live in any of those cities....
>
> We were impressed by two places in California—Ojai and Santa Barbara....
>
> But we saw the beginnings and possibilities here, and the fact that this city is on the ocean persuaded us to come here.
>
> We had read "Two Years Before The Mast," and we knew the story of Cabrillo and we were immensely interested in the De la Guerra house and the Carrillo adobe and the other old buildings, and all they implied and all their history meant.
>
> Perhaps it was because we were newcomers—in reality this is Mrs. Hoffman's [sic] dream,—that we saw the possibilities of restoring some of the oldtime [sic] beauty and picturesqueness, and preserving what we already have.[1]

It is tempting to speculate that the Hoffmanns met Osborne Craig at Siamasia in Montecito, where they all stayed in 1919. A more tenable explanation is that they first crossed paths after Craig established his office in the Oreña Adobe. Irene Hoffmann was taking Spanish lessons from Delfina de la Guerra, who was still living in the adjacent ancestral home, and Hoffmann reported seeing The Patio and being impressed.[2] No matter. The Hoffmanns had a vision

and the financial resources to carry it out. They became Craig's Medici.

Hoffmann House, Casa Santa Cruz
Santa Barbara, 1921

> There are many beautiful and well-appointed modern homes in Santa Barbara, but none more beautiful and appropriate to its charming family life that that of Mr. and Mrs. Bernard Hoffman [sic] of Massachusetts and California. Set high above Mission Canyon and appropriating its natural beauty, the handsome house, designed by James Osborne Craig and carried to completion by Carlton M. Winslow, looks out over the city and its incomparable setting as though gravely considering its future problems.[3]

In May 1920, the *Morning Press* reported that Mrs. Hoffmann, who with her husband had occupied the Dalliba cottage on East Valley Road in Montecito for several months, had leased the McCalla house on upper Garden Street and would take possession in June. Five months later, Mrs. Hoffmann purchased the property from Mrs. McCalla.[4] Though one might question the choice of Santa Barbara instead of more fashionable Montecito, the site at the edge of Mission Canyon with a precipitous drop off—and corresponding view across the canyon—was undeniably appealing and the house was set well back from the street, assuring privacy.

The house was constructed in the late nineteenth century; an early photograph shows it to be large and unlovely (Fig. 3.02). The layout was conventional: the entrance hall was roughly in the center of the plan with the living hall, morning room and library to the left or west; the dining and service rooms were

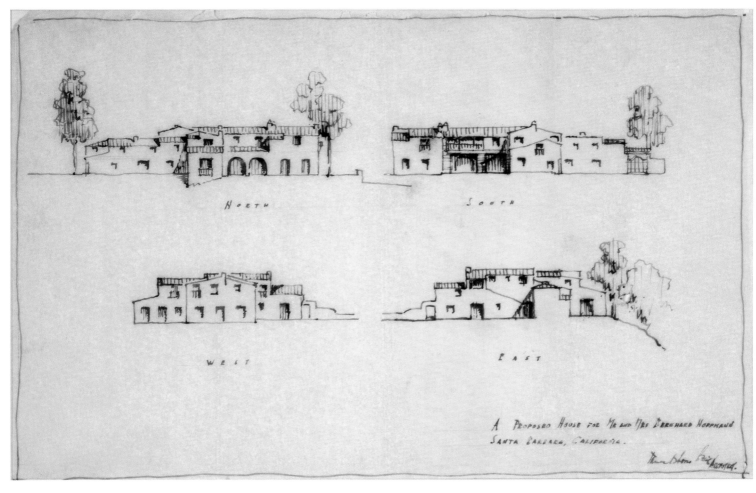

A PROPOSED HOUSE FOR MR AND MRS BERNHARD HOFFMANN
SANTA BARBARA, CALIFORNIA.

to the east. Almost immediately the Hoffmanns commissioned Craig's office to generate measured drawings of the existing first and second floor plans, signaling their intention to make improvements.

By December, Craig had completed drawings indicating substantial modifications to the McCalla house though essentially within the existing footprint: the seeds of the final house are here. Most significantly, the plan was bisected by an open loggia replacing the living hall; the smaller rooms to the west were combined to create a new living room. A new dining room—the only major addition—projected to the north and the old space was divided into a reception room and office. The scope of the changes notwithstanding, overall the new layout was less important than the obvious interest in recreating the building in the nascent Santa Barbara style. In addition to the loggia with its arched openings, the perimeter walls were greatly thickened and had smooth planar surfaces; a *reja* was indicated over the dining room window.

Undated pen-and-ink sketches signed by Craig show further development: the main entry has been moved to the east elevation, and the reception room and office have been extended to the south (Figs. 3.03, 3.04). In the similarly undated fourth and final incarnation, the open loggia was replaced by a library but otherwise the plan remained essentially

as drawn earlier; i.e., a reworking of the McCalla house, albeit with extensive reconfiguration (Figs. 3.04, 3.05).

Craig's presentation drawings of the final scheme reveal the dramatic transformation. The house has the additive quality of a Spanish farmhouse with the new dining room and reception room/office wings projecting from the main mass, the dining room in the form of a lean-to. Arched openings and the irregular red tile roof—alternately gabled and hipped—reinforce the effect. The undeniable potency of the composition results from bold, simple forms utterly absent the Italianate or vaguely "Mediterranean" flourishes prevalent in so much contemporary Santa Barbara architecture.

Before reconstruction work—and it was from the foundation up—on the house began, an existing service building a few feet to the northeast was remodeled to Craig's specifications as a two-bedroom servant cottage. The permit was issued May 20, 1921. Ten months later, on March 31, 1922—two weeks after Craig's death—the permit to transform the late-Victorian McCalla house into a paradigm of Spanish Colonial Revival architecture was issued; the estimated cost was $90,000. Carleton Winslow, Craig's successor architect, carried out the work as Craig intended. Snook and Kenyon, builders of numerous Santa Barbara landmarks, were the contractors.

OPPOSITE, TOP
3.02. McCalla House, Santa Barbara

OPPOSITE, BOTTOM
3.03. Hoffmann House, Santa Barbara, elevations

ABOVE
3.04. Hoffmann House, Santa Barbara, plans

FOLLOWING PAGES
3.05. Hoffmann House, entrance court

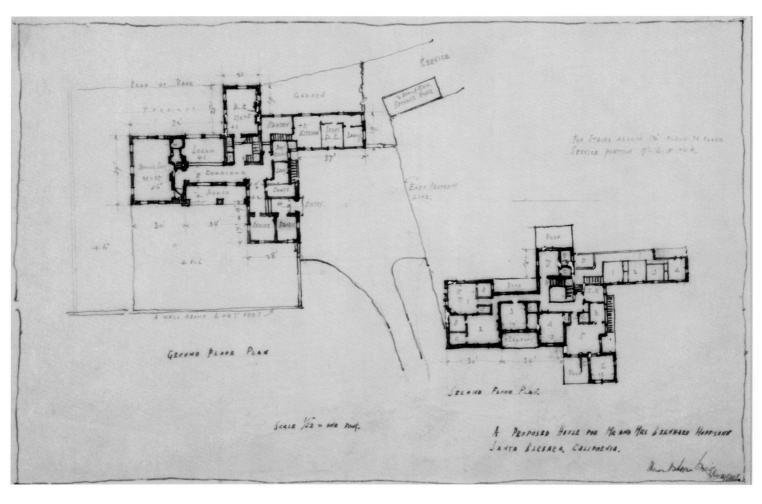

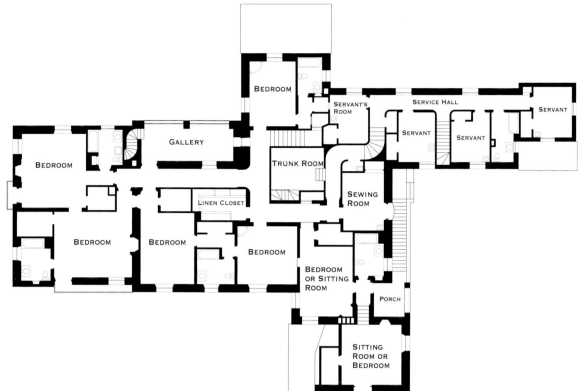

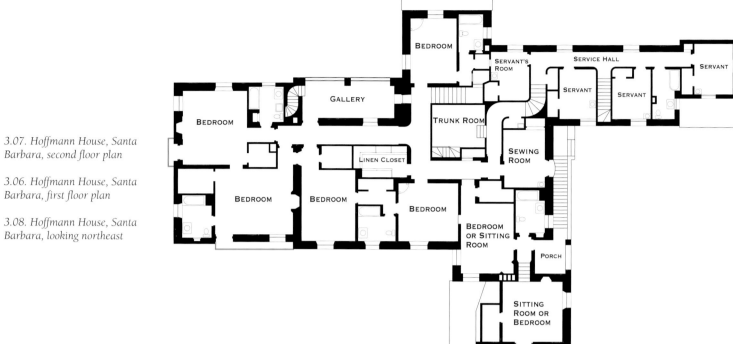

3.07. Hoffmann House, Santa Barbara, second floor plan

3.06. Hoffmann House, Santa Barbara, first floor plan

3.08. Hoffmann House, Santa Barbara, looking northeast

BEDROOM

SERVANT'S ROOM

SERVICE HALL

SERVANT

GALLERY

SERVANT

SERVANT

BEDROOM

TRUNK ROOM

SEWING ROOM

LINEN CLOSET

BEDROOM

BEDROOM

BEDROOM

BEDROOM OR SITTING ROOM

PORCH

SITTING ROOM OR BEDROOM

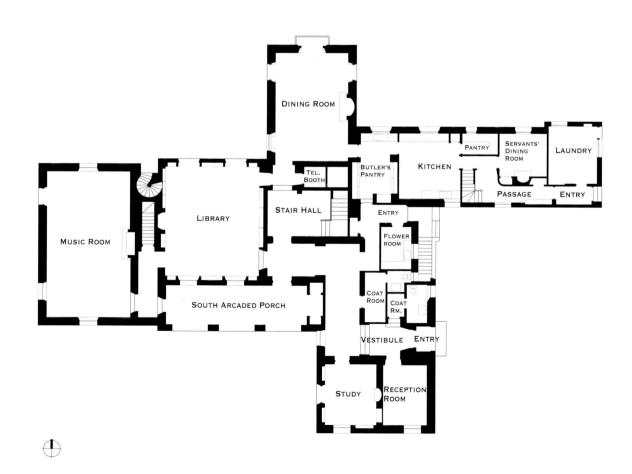

DINING ROOM

PANTRY

SERVANTS' DINING ROOM

LAUNDRY

TEL. BOOTH

BUTLER'S PANTRY

KITCHEN

LIBRARY

STAIR HALL

ENTRY

PASSAGE

ENTRY

MUSIC ROOM

FLOWER ROOM

SOUTH ARCADED PORCH

COAT ROOM

COAT RM.

VESTIBULE

ENTRY

STUDY

RECEPTION ROOM

3.09. Hoffmann House,
Santa Barbara, south
elevation

3.10. Hoffmann House,
Santa Barbara, south
elevation

3.11. *Hoffmann House, Santa Barbara, stair hall*

3.12. *Hoffmann House, Santa Barbara, stair hall*

3.13. Hoffmann House, Santa
Barbara, music room

3.14. Hoffmann House, Santa
Barbara, library

3.15. Hoffmann House, Santa
Barbara, dining room

The house was complete by August 1923. Comparison with the work of George Washington Smith is inevitable, yet the scale, massing and absence of classical detailing and symmetry distinguish this as a work of Osborne Craig. Few devices were used to mitigate the size of the building or its visual weight; tension is created by the push and pull of irregularly juxtaposed forms (Figs. 3.01, 3.05, 3.08–10). No attempt was made to create ceremonial axes: rooms are entered at corners suggesting diagonal circulation (*see* Fig. 3.06).

This is a house of corridors. None of the main public spaces—music room, library or dining room—is accessible directly from the entrance vestibule but instead by halls providing shifts in direction and an air of mystery and slight disorientation. The main stair occupies its own self-contained space and is approached similarly (Figs. 3.11, 3.12). The two main terminuses—added by Craig—are high-ceilinged, ceremonial spaces: the music room with its fine sixteenth-century fireplace and the dining room overlooking Mission Canyon (Figs. 3.13, 3.15). The library between, with a low vaulted ceiling and walls lined with bookcases is more intimate (Fig. 3.14). Similarly, the second floor is something of a maze with its family bedrooms, guestroom and servant quarters. A separate apartment with a small kitchen was provided for the Hoffmanns' daughter Margaret, who was diabetic, and her nurse; the outdoor stair on the front elevation leads to this. The house has multiple fireplaces, each a study in sculptural simplicity (Figs. 3.16–3.21).

Critical architectural response was immediate and positive. In February 1924 the house was included among the "city's most beautiful homes and gardens." In March it received honorable mention as a notable example of architecture. Two years later, *California Southland* published an article on the garden designed by Florence Yoch (Figs. 3.24, 3.25).[5]

Casa Santa Cruz has a checkered history. The Hoffmanns moved out around 1936, leaving the house vacant until 1943 when they sold it to the neighboring St. Anthony's Seminary. It then entered a long period of decline. The seminary used it for both administrative and residential purposes; between roughly 1949 and 1951 it served as a Franciscan Brothers School. Over time, it was reduced to a near ruin; at one point, the certificate of occupancy was revoked by the city. The seminary offered it for sale in 1989; the current owners, Tanny Keeler and Kent Hodgetts, acquired it in 1999. Restoration has been ongoing since. Tanny Keeler has commented especially on

3.16–21. Hoffmann House, fireplaces

3.22. *Hoffmann Guest Cottage,*
Mission Canyon, Santa Barbara

the effect of light in the house, observations possible
only after intimate exposure over time:

> Windows and doors are so placed in this house, that
> one could actually live here without electricity if one
> had to, for Craig captures the first rays of dawn and
> traps natural light in dark halls until the sun sinks fully
> in the west. If there is a moon, half to full, it floods into
> the west side of the house, both floors. Dozens and
> dozens of adjustments made because of the sun's path
> or the moon's arc. But these are things only the house
> dwellers can know.... It is the numerous subtleties that
> make the house alive.[6]

3.23. *Hoffmann Office, Mission Canyon, Santa Barbara, with Osborne Craig*

Hoffmann Cottages and Office
Mission Canyon, Santa Barbara, 1920–1921

In short order, Osborne Craig became the de facto house architect for Irene and Bernhard Hoffmann. While plans for their house were being formulated and grand schemes for civic improvement were on the horizon, Craig undertook three smaller domestic projects for his clients: the chronology is dizzying. All were constructed in Mission Canyon below the main house and reached by foot bridges (Fig. 3.24).

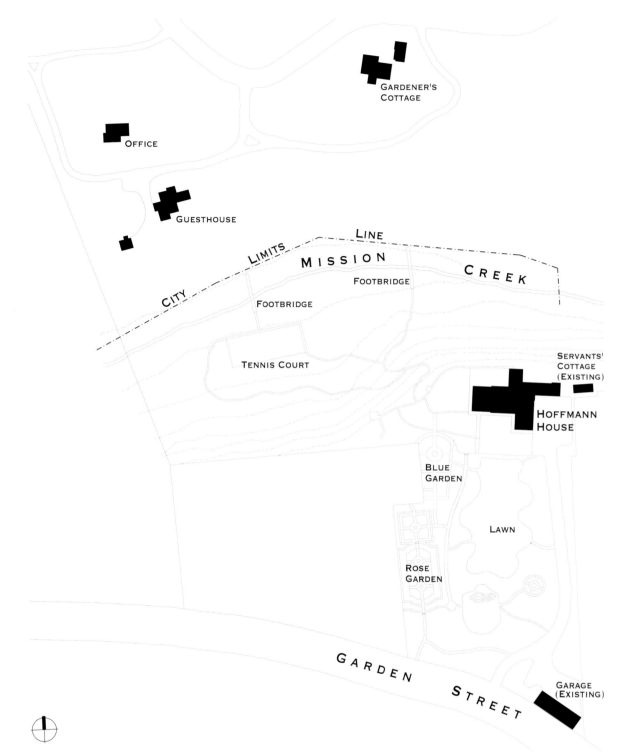

GARDENER'S
COTTAGE

OFFICE

GUESTHOUSE

CITY LIMITS LINE

MISSION CREEK

FOOTBRIDGE

FOOTBRIDGE

TENNIS COURT

SERVANTS'
COTTAGE
(EXISTING)

HOFFMANN
HOUSE

BLUE
GARDEN

LAWN

ROSE
GARDEN

GARDEN STREET

GARAGE
(EXISTING)

3.24. Hoffmann site plan,
including garden designed by
Florence Yoch and Lucile
Council

3.25. Hoffmann House garden,
designed by Florence Yoch and
Lucile Council

First was a guest cottage; the Hoffmanns occupied it while the big house was underway and they returned after they left Casa Santa Cruz. The preliminary drawings are dated October 1920; they were revised in August 1921. Craig designed the structure to conform to the sloping site, resulting in a plan on multiple levels with the maid's room in front being partially below grade (Fig. 3.22). The living room projects mid-point from a two-story central volume; stairs lead down to the dining and service rooms, up to the bedrooms. A gardener's cottage followed; the drawings are dated March and April 1921. The third building was described on site plans as an office and while no drawings have been found, Craig was photographed at the site during construction (Fig. 3.23).

3.26. *St. Anthony's College additions and alterations, Santa Barbara (project)*

St. Anthony's College Additions and Alterations
Santa Barbara, December 1921

The McCalla site on Garden Street shared its eastern property line with St. Anthony's College, established in 1896 by Franciscan Friars at old Mission Santa Barbara as a school for young men interested in becoming Franciscan priests. In December 1921 Bernhard Hoffmann was working with Craig on drawings to redevelop the original stone building designed by a German Franciscan brother, Adrian Wewer, and built between 1898 and 1901. The earliest reference to the project is a December 2, 1921, diary entry in *The House Chronicle of St. Anthony's Seminary, 1897–1922*:

> Rev. Rector and Sub-rector spen[t] the evening at Hoffmann's. We propose a plan of future development of St.

Anthony's Seminary which Mr. Hoffmann sponsors to have drawn out in full by his architect, Mr. James Osborne Craig.

Three subsequent entries in December indicate that Craig was at the site and plans were being made. One of his drawings has the note "A Proposed Development of St. Anthony's College"; another is labeled "Proposed Additions and Alterations to St. Anthony's College" (Fig. 3.26). Neither drawing clarifies the work that was intended, whether the existing stone building was to be remodeled in the Spanish style or if additional construction were contemplated.[7]

El Paseo/De la Guerra Plaza Restoration
Santa Barbara, 1921–22

… The neo-Sevillian architects were summoned, and back of the old manor house of the town's Spanish social leaders, the de la Guerra family, there sprang up, about paseos, plazas and patios, a group of white-stuccoed, tile roofed studio apartments. The artists, the sellers of oriental art objects and Hungarian glasswares, the male and female weavers of inflammatory art fabrics, knowing the value of atmosphere, all moved in. Nearby, semi-ruinous edifices dating back to the early American occupation were repaired to house an exotic book-shop and one of those expensive tobacconists who encourage you to invent your own mixture. Montecito [sic] thus acquired a shopping district fit to match Washington Square or middle Fifth avenue.[8]

El Paseo was the defining moment in the career of James Osborne Craig and, to a large extent, the architectural legacy of Santa Barbara. A complex of shops, offices, artists' studios, apartments and a restaurant, it was completed posthumously and faithfully to Craig's designs. It was the result of the initiative of Irene and Bernhard Hoffmann.

With the exception of Mission Santa Barbara, Casa de la Guerra, the nucleus of the Hoffmanns' initiative, is the most important architectural remnant of Santa Barbara's Hispanic past. It was built between 1818 and 1827 by José de la Guerra (1779–1858), comandante of the Santa Barbara Presidio and who, Rexford Newcomb concluded, "wielded an influence out of all proportion to his military position." On the death of Don José, the house passed to four of his sons: Francisco, Pablo, Miguel and Antonio. In 1870 Miguel purchased the southernmost two rooms in the west wing, legally dividing the house. Finally, in 1904, the larger portion was inherited by Pablo's children Francisca, Carlos, Delfina and Herminia.[9]

Though still in family hands, the building by 1910 had accrued Victorian embellishments and was in disrepair, the result of decline that began in the 1870s. Francis T. Underhill, whose name appears everywhere one looks in early twentieth-century Santa Barbara, if one goes looking—in 1906 he married Carmelita Dibblee, Francisca's daughter—renovated the house in 1910–11. The intended work was described in a contemporary newspaper account:

Work will be commenced today on the old De la Guerra mansion which will be restored to its original picturesque appearance....

All modern additions to the residence will be removed and the mansion will be in keeping with the style of architecture of the period which it represents ...

The tiles will be removed from the roof which will be braced with new timbers and covered with shingle over which the tiles will be placed. The boards will be removed from the ends of the building on De La Guerra street, which were placed there to protect the adobe, and will be replaced by plaster. The old porch will be torn down around the court and a new one built.

Work proceeded in two phases. The central and northeast wings were reconstructed in 1910; the southwest wing in 1911. In the process, Underhill altered the building formally as well as structurally. His most visible changes were unification of the roofs of the house itself and the porches lining the three sides of the front elevation into one continuous slope, and the enclosure of the street ends of the porches to create small rooms. He also removed the Victorian flourishes and at least the upper portion of a two-story, tower-like structure at the rear (Fig. 3.27). This was the house as Craig knew it.[10]

By September 1921, the Hoffmanns' goals were clear. The Morning Press reported that they intended to restore the de la Guerra house as a historical nucleus and had purchased property immediately to the north and east to erect additional structures. The western portion of the house not occupied by the family was to be placed in rentable condition. The new buildings were to be arranged around an inner court "which will give the effect of a quaint little street in the south of Spain" and were to include shops, offices and apartments. Osborne Craig had been commissioned to do the work.[11]

Three months later, the Morning Press announced that the project had been enlarged, that the Hoffmanns had acquired an adjoining parcel to the northeast, the Carrillo property, which roughly doubled the area available for development and allowed access to Canon Perdido Street to the north. The article continued, "For many weeks James Osborne Craig, architect, has been working upon sketches of buildings.... It is declared that in quaintness and artistic grouping, this series of buildings can only be matched in the old cities along the Mediterranean." With the acquisition of the additional property, Craig modified the plans to include a second enclosed court or patio that would house a restaurant, "also reminiscent of the Old World."[12]

Soon enough, the Hoffmanns' vision became even grander: they set their sights on De la Guerra Plaza, immediately across De la Guerra Street to the south. Details come from an account of a special session of the Santa Barbara City Council held on February 4, 1922, published in the Morning Press. A group including the Hoffmanns had purchased two properties in the plaza still in private hands and offered to re-sell them to the city at cost, creating a contiguous parcel with land already owned by the city. The plaza was laid out in 1853 and a building combining city hall and firehouse was erected there in 1875. A half-century later, the goal was to restore the plaza and construct a new city hall. With the new properties under the city's jurisdiction, Raffour House, a hotel and restaurant constructed in the plaza around 1887 but that extended halfway into De la Guerra Street, could be removed, an issue that had been lingering since at least 1910. The group of supporters petitioned the city to create a bond initiative to pay for the improvements.[13]

Santa Barbara Daily News followed up a day later, hailing the initiative as "The re-creation of Santa Barbara the beautiful; a return to the olden days of warm, colorful Spanish architecture; and the fashioning of this city into a shrine which will draw lovers of the quaint and the picturesque from over the whole wide world...."[14]

The February 6 Daily News also included an unsigned editorial, surely written by the publisher,

The De La Guerra House.

3.27. *Casa de la Guerra, Santa Barbara*

3.28. *El Paseo, Santa Barbara, entrance to Street of Spain from de la Guerra Street. The Oreña Adobe is at the far right.*

3.29. *El Paseo, Santa Barbara, court looking northeast*

3.30. *El Paseo, Santa Barbara, court looking northwest*

On De La Guerra Street

Thomas M. Storke, that was effusive in its praise of the proposed project. Titled "That Wonderful Thing," it began,

"The most wonderful thing in the history of Santa Barbara!"

This is the feeling of many citizens of Santa Barbara today, in fact, of practically everyone, as they discuss the proposed plan to restore the past of the community in architecture....

As explained elsewhere in this issue, the plan is to remove the city hall from the De la Guerra plaza; to remove the Raffour House, thus widening East De la Guerra street; to build a new city hall on the plaza, De la Guerra and Anacapa Streets, strictly in keeping with ancient traditions; to preserve the De la Guerra house, rich in history and legend; to construct a house which will be ideally complimentary, immediately in rear of it; and to restore De la Guerra plaza to its former status as a park in which the citizen and sojourner may rest while they hear good music, or listen to nature's music, the splash of a fountain.

Nor are these plans all. For it is also proposed, as a corollary, to widen Anacapa street for several blocks, so that Santa Barbara's present one-business-street arrangement will broaden into a more compact and convenient shopping center....

From every standpoint the plan is indeed worthy of enthusiastic support and of carrying through to a triumphant and artistic fruition....

THE PATIO

NORTH WEST CORNER OF COURT.

In behalf of Santa Barbara the Daily News wishes to express sincere gratitude for the public-spiritedness, and the appreciation for beauty and for the traditions of the past which Mr. and Mrs. Bernard Hoffman [sic] are showing. Though but comparative newcomers, they have proven that they belong in Santa Barbara by right of their understanding of the history of Santa Barbara and their keen sympathy with its finer aims and ideals.

They have made the re-creation of Santa Barbara as a typical Spanish city of more than a century ago something more than a subject for academic discussion. They are well on the way, with the help and co-operation of the council and the other residents who know and love Santa Barbara, toward translating a splendid vision into a striking and permanent reality.[15]

As Storke observed, the February 4 city council meeting was *ex post facto* to the planning process: James Osborne Craig already had been appointed to design both the new city hall and improvements to the plaza. His drawings were presented at the meeting. They show a combination of new construction and existing buildings that were to be remodeled in the Spanish style for consistency.[16] A square pavilion punctuates a central lozenge-shaped area. City hall is shown as a three-story building at the northeast corner of the plaza, with a two-story wing to the south (Figs. 3.31, 3.32).

Commenting on the project, Craig concluded,

It must be understood, of course, that there cannot be a return to the conditions exactly as they were in an

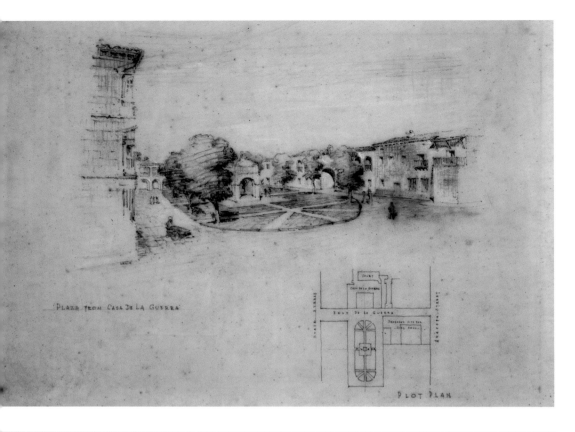

"PLAZA FROM CASA DE LA GUERRA"

PLOT PLAN

PLAZA FROM McKAY BUILDING.

THE PATIO

Prior to his early and regrettable death a few weeks ago, James Osborne Craig had been working for a period of about one year on the plan of the "Street in Spain." Added to the solid equipment of the well-trained architect he added the imagination of a poet and the soul of an artist.

The sketches shown in these pages are his. The realization of Santa Barbara's wonderful dream of a restoration of the more than century-old Spanish-California town will suffer by his passing.

How famous old Lobero Theatre, built nearly fifty years ago, and recently purchased by Community Arts Association, will look when remodeled.
—Sketch by George Washington Smith, Architect.

3.31. City Hall Plaza restoration, Santa Barbara (project)

3.32. City Hall Plaza restoration, Santa Barbara (project)

early day…. They used to have bullfights in the plaza in those days, but I hardly think it would be advisable to resurrect that form of diversion today. Also, much of the work of the early Spaniards was crude, owing to a lack of materials and workmen. What we will strive for is an effect that will reveal the early Spanish influence expressed in a manner that will harmonize with present day conditions. It is to be regretted that we have largely neglected to pay any attention to this matter in our building in the past, but if we can carry out the plans we have in mind with reference to the new city hall and the restoration of the plaza we shall have taken a long step toward a change in these conditions.[17]

James Osborne Craig's death six weeks later, on March 15, significantly altered the dynamics of the work in Plaza de la Guerra. Posturing by the architectural community began almost at once. The break in continuity—the politics—became apparent after Hoffmann presented Craig's drawings informally to the city council on April 12. He wrote the next day to William Templeton Johnson, a San Diego architect whose most familiar building today is La Valencia Hotel in La Jolla:

You will see from the enclosed cutting that the P. & P. [Plans and Planting] Committee has another job thrust upon it.

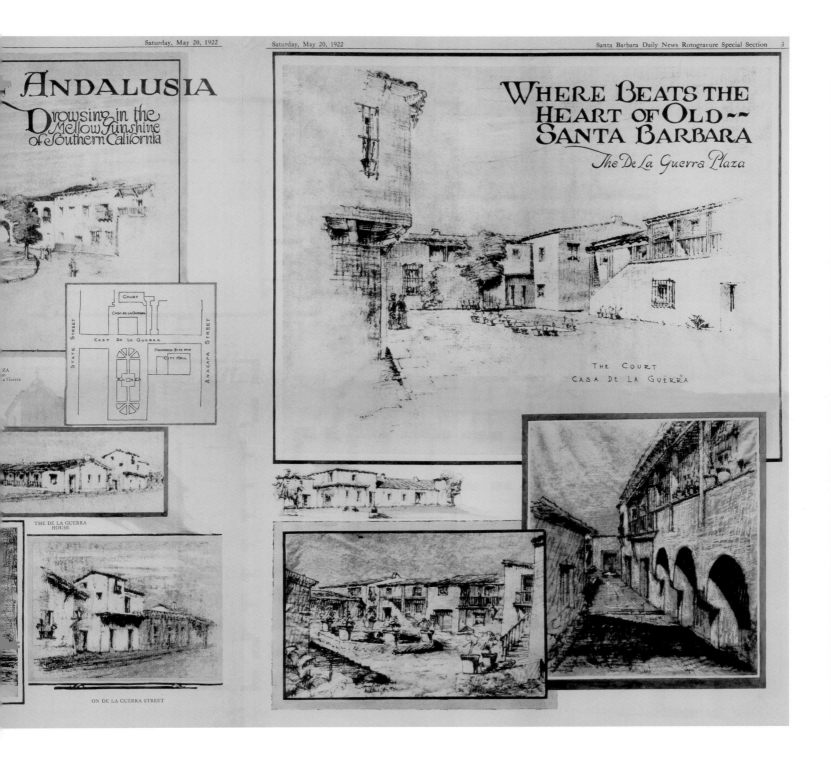

ANDALUSIA
Drowsing in the Mellow Sunshine of Southern California

WHERE BEATS THE HEART OF OLD ~~ SANTA BARBARA
The De La Guerra Plaza

THE COURT
CASA DE LA GUERRA

THE DE LA GUERRA HOUSE

ON DE LA GUERRA STREET

We are very glad as a matter of fact, because it was a question of what the City Manager might do with the plan, and we are only advisors.

If attractive sketches of the building and Plaza could be arranged, it is less likely that the actual work done by the City will fall short of the possibilities.

Mr. Baxter and I talked it over this morning, and we feel that if Mr. Winslow would complete the sketches that Mr. Craig started, or would carry the sketches as far along as he could with the notes available, it would be quite likely that Mr. Craig's suggestions would be treated with considerable consideration.

In fact, the Community Arts Committee was asked by the city council to prepare new sketches though Craig's proposal was not immediately forgotten. It was featured prominently on May 20 in a special rotogravure section of the *Santa Barbara Daily News*, though the plans were ultimately abandoned (Fig. 3.33).[18]

Work on El Paseo, fully under the Hoffmanns' control, went forward as a glorious remnant of the larger project. Craig's final plans are dated January 19, 1922, and indicate four contiguous buildings. One parallels the east wall of Casa de la Guerra and creates the passageway identified as Street in Spain. It has shops below and apartments above. Second is the row of shops backed up to the north wall of the casa. The open-air restaurant is third; the two-story

3.33. Santa Barbara Daily News, May 20, 1922, roto-gravure section. Courtesy of the late Patricia Gebhard.

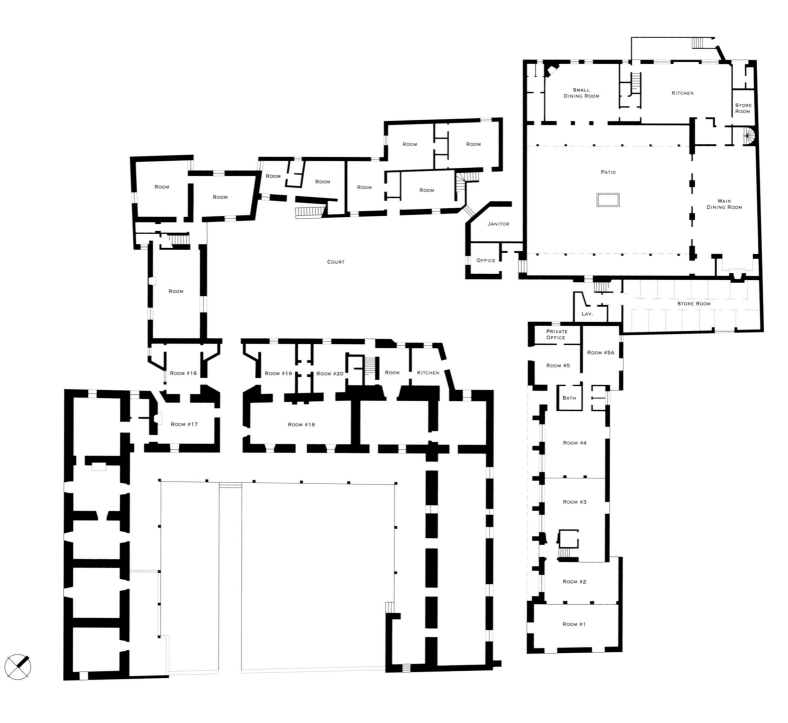

3.34. *El Paseo, Santa Barbara, second floor plan*

3.35 . *El Paseo, Santa Barbara, first floor plan*

space is framed by balconies on the north and south that in turn lead to four apartments. The fourth is the L-shaped structure that encloses the north and west sides of the patio behind the Casa; it contains shops on the ground floor and apartments and an office above (Figs. 3.34, 3.35).

Craig also completed several elevation sketches that show his vision as complete, self-assured and compelling. He was at his best. The drawings leave no doubt as to the processional route he had in mind. One depicts the intended entry from De la Guerra Street and relates the new construction to Casa de la Guerra (Fig. 3.28). The soul of El

Paseo—the sanctuary—is the court behind Casa de la Guerra. The buildings framing the court are additive in the best Spanish sense: they seemingly could have been constructed over a long period of time (Figs. 3.29, 3.30). The off-angle geometry especially, seen on the plan, suggests the ad hoc planning and construction of the imagined prototypes. Numerous alterations over the years—though in a perfect world regrettable—have not seriously diminished the quality of the composition.

After Craig's death, oversight passed to Carleton Winslow who redrew the plans with very minor revi-

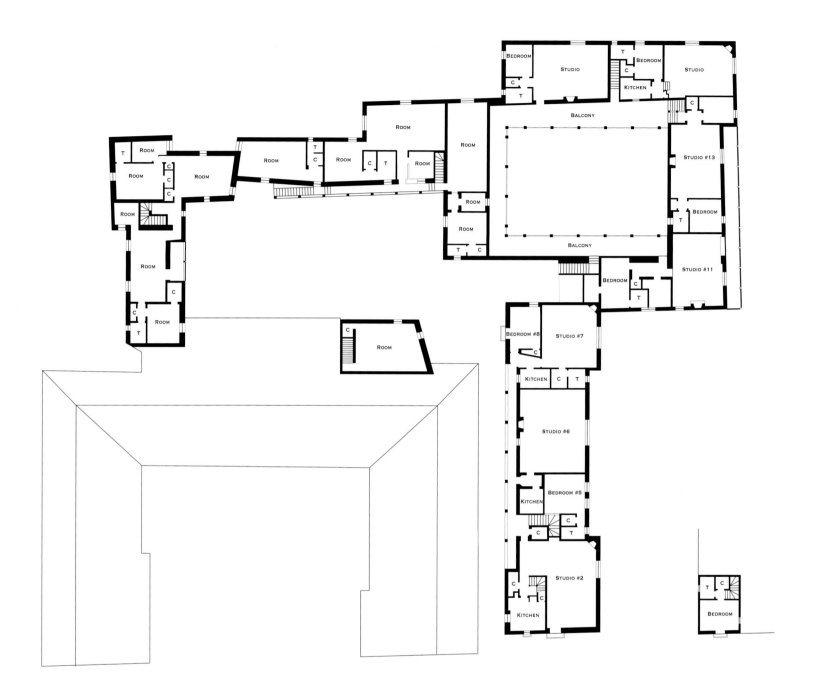

sions; he also completed working drawings and details. On the first floor, an entry passage leading to the restaurant from Anacapa Street was specified. Upstairs, fireplaces were added to each of the apartments. Otherwise, Winslow's drawings were faithful to the original concept.

Preliminary work on the site began in July 1922 when a house east of Casa de la Guerra, being used as a hardware store, was moved to 1036 Alfonse Avenue. Surveyors began driving stakes for excavation on October 24, the same day Hoffmann signed a contract with Snook & Kenyon, builders of many of Santa Barbara's prominent landmarks.[19]

El Paseo was completed in stages. Permits for the first units, Street of Spain and the row of shops along the north wall of Casa de la Guerra, were issued in November 1922. The permit for the third unit, the restaurant, was issued in February 1923 and the permit for the fourth unit, the offices enclosing the north and west boundaries of the court behind Casa de la Guerra, was issued the following November. The apartments in Street of Spain, the first unit of El Paseo, were ready for occupancy in July 1923; the restaurant opened in October.[20] The fourth unit was completed by early 1924.

3.36. El Paseo, Santa Barbara, court looking west. Photograph by J. W. Collinge.

3.37. El Paseo, Santa Barbara, court looking northeast. Photograph by J. W. Collinge.

3.38. El Paseo, Santa Barbara, patio restaurant. Photograph by Jessie Tarbox Beals.

3.39. El Paseo, Santa Barbara, main dining room. Photograph by J. W. Collinge.

FOLLOWING PAGES
3.40. El Paseo court

A chemistry of impeccable scale, formal variety and asymmetry led to the transformation of a neglected "back yard" into a welcoming urban space unequalled, then as now, in Santa Barbara. Early photographs taken by J. W. Collinge reveal buildings as Craig intended them (Figs. 3.36, 3.37). If one misses the sunken rectangular pools he sketched, one also longs for the removal of the outsized and stylistically inappropriate baroque fountain now in place.

The restaurant was designed to "embody the atmosphere of old Spain," with "outdoor service in the spacious patio, under Moorish awnings" (Fig. 3.38). An enclosed main dining room (Fig. 3.39) and a small dining room opened from the patio. The rooms were "lighted with electric lights hung in lanterns of Colonial Spanish type, emphasizing the Castilian architecture and interior decoration of the entire structure, which will house so many artists in

the studios above."[21]

El Paseo was designed to house a variety of tenants: artists, small shopkeepers, residential occupants; there also were several offices. Soon after the first units were completed, stores selling antiques and art goods opened and, in 1925, Alice Millard, who lives in history as chatelaine of La Miniatura, the house in Pasadena designed by Frank Lloyd Wright, opened a store selling fine rare books. The local businessmen Max Fleischmann, F. F. Peabody and Bernhard Hoffmann himself all took office space there.

The building has a complicated history: alterations, many of them minor, began almost immediately.[22] The most significant change occurred in 1928. *Southwest Builder and Contractor* announced in May that Carleton Winslow was preparing plans for an addition to the El Paseo complex; it was to be constructed on a parcel fronting on Anacapa Street immediately to the east of the restaurant that Bern-

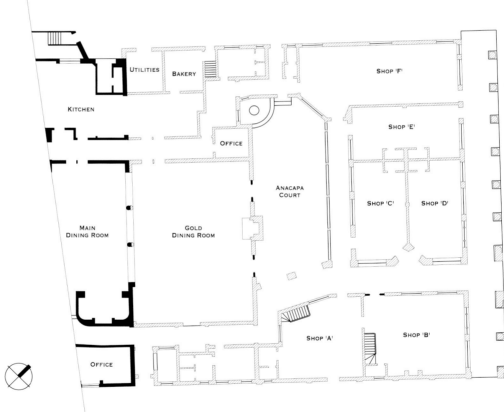

3.41. Carleton Winslow, El Paseo Anacapa addition, Santa Barbara

3.42. Carleton Winslow, El Paseo Anacapa addition, Santa Barbara

hard Hoffmann acquired in 1923 but never developed. The *Morning Press* followed up in June stating, "Plans have been discussed ... for ... building stores in the rear of the place to face Anacapa street; also to make a new, artistic entrance from Anacapa to the restaurant."[23]

Initially, the addition included a large dining room abutting the original El Paseo building and a wing extending perpendicularly to Anacapa and containing two shops in tandem. The street elevation comprised an arcade of two bays fronting the easternmost shop and a sort of triumphal arch capped with a Spanish baroque pediment and precast urns—the "new, artistic entrance"—that gave way to an arcaded corridor leading to the new restaurant space and ultimately connecting with the passage added by Winslow in 1922. A perspective drawing of this scheme was published in the *Morning Press* on September 27 with the

caption, "Since the plan was drawn, it has been decided that the arcade will be extended along Anacapa the full width of the property and it is possible that another shop will be built in what would be the right corner of the picture" (Fig. 3.41). Another article published in November confirmed the intentions: "All the frontage on Anacapa street ... will be taken up under the present plans."[24]

Drawings for the enlarged Anacapa addition indicating four shops to the north of the arcaded corridor and the fully extended arcade along the street were completed in October 1928. A patio was created in the open space between the new restaurant and shops (Fig. 3.42).

Although the source material is silent on the matter, one of the reasons for the addition was clearly the need for increased seating for the restaurant. While numerous period photographs show the large

3.43. Carleton Winslow, El Paseo Anacapa addition, Santa Barbara

open-air patio well populated, in truth it was an optimistic gesture inconsistent with Santa Barbara's cool evenings. The two enclosed dining rooms opening from the patio proved inadequate early on and a third space, designed by Winslow and replacing a storage room across the corridor south of the patio, added in 1925, did not solve the problem.[25]

Today, Carleton Winslow's 1928 dining room is physically and organizationally distinct from the original El Paseo restaurant. This was not originally the case. As designed, the west wall opened to Osborne Craig's main dining room through three arches. Though diminished by the closing of the arches, the space with its ceiling decorated with stenciling by Albert Herter, remains one of the most beautiful in Santa Barbara. To paraphrase Rexford Newcomb, a meal there is worth twice the price in such surroundings. Happily, the court between the new dining room and the shops is used today for outdoor dining as originally intended.

Still, additions to existing buildings are always challenging. Winslow's enlargement of El Paseo, in many ways extremely satisfying, speaks a different language than Craig's building. In the few short years separating the two designs, architecture had evolved. The arcade especially, with its Spanish Renaissance embellishments suggests urbanity and contrasts emphatically with the largely unadorned village simplicity of the original structure (Fig. 3.43).

Unlike the debut of the original El Paseo, the Anacapa addition was greeted with considerable fanfare. The premier opening, December 28, 1928, was billed as "A night of nights ... By special arrangement, Ruth St. Denis has been engaged for the evening, coming direct from New York for the occasion. Miss St. Denis will give four dances, presented here for the first time" (Fig. 3.44). A "jubilee dinner dance" followed the next evening and a New Year's Eve party was scheduled for December 31.[26]

Slightly later, the *Morning Press* looked commented favorably on the building: "The Anacapa street addition with its long arcade, smart shops, rambling passageway and tiny patio of charming irregularity, is sure to become a popular means of entering the older group of buildings and should serve as an inspiration and model for further development."[27] The following year, the Community Arts Association awarded the addition first place for buildings completed in 1929, describing its "... well lighted shops and picturesque small patio" and concluding that it was "An interesting development of the type of building which helps to make use of the interior of the block."[28]

Hagiography for a Building

Critical response to El Paseo was immediate and positive and Osborne Craig was given full, posthumous, credit. Early in the construction process, *Santa Barbara Community Life* supported the overall initiative to tap Santa Barbara's Hispanic roots and observed, "Architecturally speaking, the adobes of early days—missions, dwellings, and trading cen-

ters, were one of the irresistible magnets which drew travelers west." It also published several of Craig's drawings for El Paseo with the conclusion:

Art in Santa Barbara received a serious setback through the passing of James Osborne Craig early in 1922. But his personality is nevertheless indelibly stamped in the architecture of the city. His contemplated work is being carried on by others, and the summer of this year will mark the completion of one of the noteworthy projects which he started....[29]

In February 1924, the judges in a Better Architecture Competition selected El Paseo as one of the "ten most notable examples of architecture in Santa Barbara...." They explained:

El Paseo is notable for the informal novelty and interest of its plan; the incident and charm of its various parts. These buildings as a group embody to an unusual degree the romance and quality of the architectural tradition associated with the early years of California, one well adapted to this arid climate with its bright sunshine and deep shadows. There is an inspiration here that should have a great effect in the development of a truly Californian architecture.[30]

California Southland published an article in April 1924 in which the author, M. U. Seares, declared, "The fine, old California town of Santa Barbara has been saved from the commonplace by the character of the citizens who live there. Restoration of the early Spanish buildings has come just in time to rescue its beauty from oblivion."[31]

Henriette Boeckman, writing in the *Los Angeles Times* in September 1924, noted Craig's "gifted architect's hand" and described "... the inner court located in the rear of the old de la Guerra house. Max Reinhardt never arranged a more effective setting for any stage than that court presents by night. Perfect peace and yet how dramatic is the scene! Usually only one lone, iron-banded lantern over near an awninged niche furnishes light." Boeckman also noted the "... quietude and the picturesque beauty of the Street in Spain, whose dominating quality is that great art which this country is fast losing, simplicity" and concluded, "No matter what is demanded of the Little Street in Spain by those who would establish themselves within its confines, it rises to the effort with surpassing success." The patio restaurant with its pool was "... sheltered by great awnings of striking Venetian sailcloth, which undulate in the breezes two stories overhead."[32] Boeckman didn't use the words, but she was describing mystery and atmosphere, key elements in any great work of architecture. Nowhere did Craig better demonstrate his mastery.

Pacific Coast Architect, published in San Francisco, devoted its March 1925 issue to El Paseo. Essentially a photo essay of images by J. Walter Collinge, a distinguished local photographer, the introduction by Harris Allen, an architect, paid due homage and concluded, "Mr. Hoffman [sic], in building what is virtually a monument to James Osborne Craig, has given something to Santa Barbara beyond money and beyond price."[33]

3.44. *Denishawn Dancers, El Paseo, December 28, 1928. Photograph by J. W. Collinge.*

Even the lofty Garden Club of America took notice. A visit to El Paseo was included in the itinerary of the group's storied Thirteenth Annual Meeting, held in Santa Barbara in April 1926. Members, women at the height of social trajectory, arrived from points east aboard a thirteen-car New York Central Railroad "Garden Club of America Special." They stopped first in Pasadena, then drove over the Santa Susana Pass to Santa Barbara encountering "… the Missions, the Mountains, the Sea … the ravishing gardens, the eucalyptus trees, the sunshine, [and] the fiesta at El Paseo…."[34]

In 1928, while additions to the complex were being considered, the *Morning Press* published an effusive appreciation entitled "De la Guerra House Glorious Landmark of Early California":

> … This interesting old house has become the nucleus of an artistic renaissance since 1923. At this time the late James Osborne Craig, a gifted young architect, envisioned an artistic and community center. His original sketches were adopted and the vision took form. Quaint, though modern shops and studios have been architecturally welded. There is a mellow romance to an "Old Street in Spain," with its grass-edged stones; an ever green and refreshing inner court and the delightful El Paseo. Along the "Street" are tile insets to commemorate the visits of Dana and titled visitors from Spain.
>
> While the de la Guerra studios and patio awaken delightful memories and furnish a thrill, this thrill and delight are doubled by the El Paseo. Verily, this dining place is beyond compare. Skirted by balconies of the Spanish motif, here and there a mysterious doorway, canopies above drawn over to shade the patio from the high noon sun, mosaic stone floors, occasional old wrought iron lamps—here is a bit of the Old World. El Paseo, while a part of the everyday life of Santa Barbara, is a lasting and pleasant memory for the visitor.[35]

In 1929, after the Anacapa Street addition was completed, both the *Santa Barbara Daily News* and *Morning Press* published full-page tributes with banner headlines. On March 23, the *Daily News* gave a history of the development of El Paseo and concluded:

> The ramifications of the idea are to be seen through the entire business district of State street in the uniformity of California architecture. For it was from the building which started first with the restoration of the Orena studios and then the growth of the de la Guerra group that the conception of a business district with a uniform and appropriate architecture first sprang when the earthquake of 1925 made its application possible.

PATIO ENTRANCE FROM DE LA GUERRA STREET.

Another article in the same section had a more global perspective: "The execution of this project gave Santa Barbara one of the most beautiful and unique attractions of any Californian—or American—city."[36]

G. A. Martin, writing in the *Morning Press*, followed up in the same vein. His article, headlined, "El Paseo Inspired City's Renaissance," concluded:

> Though the talented architect did not live to see the culmination of any portion of the work he planned... the first of the studios and shops of El Paseo served as an incentive to Santa Barbarans to recreate here a city of Andalusian beauty in keeping with the history and traditions of the place.

Martin continued:

> The accomplishments along the line of his plans resulted in the charming group known as the "de la Guerra Studios." Their construction resulted in such prompt and ready appreciation here and throughout the state that this may be said to be one of the most notable contributions toward the popularity of Spanish Colonial architecture which has now become not only of local, but of international acclaim.[37]

Finally, in 1930, the *Los Angeles Times* published an appreciation of El Paseo, calling it "... a picturesque colony into which the world pours the varied art treasures of the past and present ... potteries, textiles, paintings, jewels, metal work, glassware, flowers and shrubs, furniture and fashions of the whole wide world." The article continues:

> It is Mr. Hoffmann's belief that this successful restoration of an early California hospitality center [Casa de la Guerra] will result in the entire State awakening to the historic treasures that abound within its borders, and that each community will begin to preserve and to restore the many historic shrines that are now neglected and in ruins; Los Angeles having already fulfilled his prophesy in the opening of the picturesque Paseo in Olvera street, which in a few years will no doubt rival the famous Santa Barbara colony.[38]

If architectural fine points and evocative historical allusions are the primary reasons for its staying power today, historically the real contribution of El Paseo was civic. It established a vibrant public space in an area that previously was no more than the slovenly back yard of Casa de la Guerra, and completion of the addition accelerated the expansion of the business corridor east to Anacapa Street, as anticipated by Thomas Storke in 1922 (Fig. 3.48).

Before the addition was constructed, El Paseo turned its back on Anacapa Street. Since approximately 1920, the area immediately to the east, defined by Anacapa, De la Guerra, Canon Perdido and Santa Barbara Streets, had been a rough-and-tumble warren of Chinese and Japanese shops, gambling halls and tenements.[39] This began to change when the new Lobero Theatre, designed by George Washington Smith and Lutah Maria Riggs, at the corner of Canon Perdido and Anacapa, was completed in 1924. Although there was development on Anacapa to the north—Julia Morgan's Margaret Baylor Inn was competed in 1927 and the Santa Barbara County Courthouse in 1929—the leap immediately across from El Paseo to the east occurred later, near the end of the Depression. The splendid new post office building, designed by Reginald Johnson, diagonally across the intersection of Anacapa and Canon Perdido from the Lobero Theatre, was completed in 1937 and replaced "a Chinese restaurant and other disreputable establishments located on that notorious corner."[40] El Presidio, by Edwards and Plunkett, at the corner of Anacapa and De la Guerra, was completed much later, in 1945.

Consistently in the literature discussing El Paseo the references are to Spanish architecture. In March 1929, the *Santa Barbara Daily News* observed:

> While born in Scotland, Craig had spent much of his youth in the south of Spain where he soon learned to love the low-white-walled buildings of the peasant type. In Santa Barbara he found the opportunity to re-create this type of architecture as the foundations for a native California type springing from the mother-Spanish which had been laid by the builders of the old adobes.[41]

Certainly the buildings of Andalusia with their white plastered, planar walls and red tile roofs cannot be discounted. Still, in Craig's designs for El Paseo, it is Spanish inspiration filtered through Mexico that prevails. This thesis is supported factually by one Mexican reference and theoretically by another. The structure to the east of Casa de la Guerra that defines Street of Spain most certainly derives from an arcade in Cuernavaca. The similarities are too pronounced to ignore. A photograph of this arcade was published

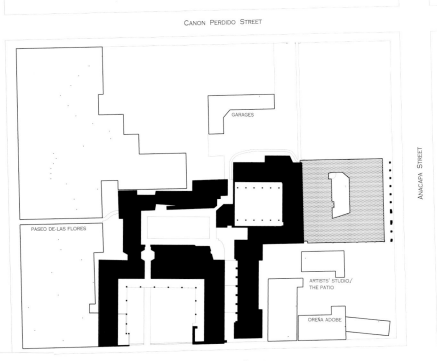

3.48. El Paseo site plan

CANON PERDIDO STREET

GARAGES

ANACAPA STREET

PASEO DE-LAS FLORES

ARTISTS' STUDIO/ THE PATIO

OREÑA ADOBE

DE LA GUERRA STREET

in 1915 by Louis La Beaume, a St. Louis architect, in his book *Picturesque Architecture of Mexico* (Fig. 3.45; compare with Fig. 3.47).[42] Although Craig is not known to have owned this book, there is no reason to suppose he did not have access to it. His rendering, all sepia ink and white chalk, terminates the axis with the entrance to the restaurant instead of the bridge shown in the prototype (Fig. 3.46).

Another Mexican building, El Convento de Monjas Dominicas de Santa Catarina, completed in Pátzcuaro in 1747, also bears striking formal similarities to El Paseo. Both buildings are comprised of series of rooms arranged irregularly around courtyards, a layout traced by George Kubler to southern Spain "… with its Moorish and Roman antecedents …" and that, in both Spain and Mexico, was "… associated with the privileges of wealth." There are strong analogies as well in elevations and materials (Fig. 3.48).[43]

Evidence that Craig was aware of the convent is at once speculative and provocative. A possible source of information was Anna Louise Murphy

Vhay (1881–1964), an artist who moved to Santa Barbara in 1920. Her studio was listed at 11 East De la Guerra Street, two doors west of Craig's office, in the 1922 city directory; they must have met. Confirmation of her travels in Mexico before January 1923 comes from a letter Bernhard Hoffmann wrote to her discussing an exhibition of "Mexican pictures." Two decades later, she and her son, David, published a book, *Architectural Byways in New Spain, Mexico*, that includes brief discussion of Pátzcuaro. They conclude, "In Patzcuaro [sic], perhaps more than anywhere else in Mexico, one is conscious of a pervasive sense of antiquity."[44]

Whether Craig used El Convento de Monjas Dominicas de Santa Catarina as a prototype is unlikely to be resolved. He did, however, extract the essence of Pátzcuaro and its buildings as defined by the Vhays. With a sensibility that seems anticipatory today, Craig captured and reused the past with perfect pitch in El Paseo.

Two schools of thought come to mind concerning the Hoffmanns' initiative in incorporating Casa

3.49. El Convento de Monjas Dominicas de Santa Catarina, Pátzcuaro. Photograph by Isrrael Fuentes.

3.50. El Paseo, Santa Barbara, Street of Spain, looking north from de la Guerra Street

3.51. El Paseo, Santa Barbara, Street of Spain looking south

de la Guerra into the El Paseo complex. One would have protested the accretions to the historic house and the loss of context. The other would have demolished the building and developed the property. The end result was a justifiable and happy compromise, foreshadowing today's historic preservation ethos. By 1922 the house had had long ceased serving its original purpose as a political and social mecca in Santa Barbara. In 1911, Josefa de la Guerra leased the two rooms in the west wing her father had purchased in 1870 to Katherine and Margaret Burke (familiarly known as the Misses Burke) for use as a curio shop. A philosophically controversial move at the time, it established a precedent for the Hoffmanns' conversion of the west wing into office space.

Succeed, the Hoffmanns did. Sadly, today, their vision, given three dimensions by James Osborne Craig, has been compromised by changes in ownership, occupancy and agenda. The buildings today are in good condition and enlivened by citrus trees and flowering vines (Figs. 3.50, 3.51). But the vibrancy imparted by artists and small shopkeepers has been muted by hedge funds and financial consultants who use the spaces as offices. The analogy is imperfect but the effect is not unlike multiple banks on a streetscape; in 1967 Ada Louise Huxtable made sardonic reference to "suffocating dullness." Still, the architecture of El Paseo remains. Bill Mahan, Santa Barbara architect, offered his twenty-first century perspective:

> I was first introduced to El Paseo in 1961 by my boss and mentor, Robert Ingle Hoyt. "She's the best we have.... And she has a lot to teach you...." Her patio was full of people eating and talking and enjoying the pleasant atmosphere of her warm sunny architecture....
>
> It's all so human and that's because its scale is human. Its orange trees reach to its roof line and its doors and windows are cozy in size....
>
> Recently, on my way back from State Street, headed for City Hall, I decided to cut through El Paseo. There is a walkway that leads from State Street to a lovely little atrium patio.... From the atrium patio there are two archway entrances into El Paseo's main patio.... To the left is a very small archway, a passage that gives real meaning to the term *human scale*. I chose that one....
>
> And then I was in the main patio. There was an explosion of blue sky and sunlight filling this open space that is so handsomely defined by the white and simple one and two story architecture of rural Andalucia. The flowering vines, the manicured shrubs, the sun drenched flagstone, the fountain gurgling. It was all there.... Except the people—there were no people. There was only silence, almost a religious science like an empty church after the service has ended....
>
> Robert Hoyt was right: she's the best we have and she has a lot to teach us. But, when her patio is empty and silent, is anyone listening?[45]

Why equivocate? El Paseo is not a great Santa Barbara building. It is a great American building.

CHAPTER 4

Final Works

Cowles Reservoir
Montecito, 1921

By early 1921, after fewer than five years in Santa Barbara, Osborne Craig had established an extraordinary client base. William H. Cowles, owner of the *Spokesman-Review* in Spokane, was among the most substantial. He and his family began coming to Santa Barbra in 1909, staying in temporary quarters. In 1914 they built a very large house designed by Kirtland Cutter on 156 acres on Eucalyptus Hill in Montecito (Fig. 4.01).[1] The reservoir Craig designed for them seven years later was in response to the inadequate water supply in Montecito. Water towers—tanks on skeletal wooden supports—were common solutions, though they were disfiguring intrusions on the landscape.

Cowles approached the problem differently, commissioning Craig to design a reservoir on his property. Work was underway by March 1921, though a month later Craig told Mary that Cowles was <u>not</u> going to complete the project that year. He followed up two days later that Cowles had "… kept me wandering about that damned hill of his until nearly seven…." Finally, Craig told Richard Pitman in an undated letter that Cowles was "… now a bit disgruntled over the cost." The reservoir must have been completed by March 1923 when the minutes of a meeting of the Montecito County Water District noted, "W. H. Cowles submitted letter containing protest against the inclusion of his Montecito property in the … Water District."[2]

Although a solution to a pragmatic need, Craig's reservoir nonetheless was a thing of beauty. Enormous in scale, it was laid out within easy access of the house and originally overlooked the mountains in the distance (Fig. 4.02). Framed by low sandstone walls and with its brick paving and benches, it clearly was intended to be a place of contemplation. Charles Gibbs Adams was credited with the garden design and planting.[3] Today, residential development and lush landscaping have altered the setting (Fig. 4.03).

Armstrong House
Pasadena, 1921

The 1921 marriage of Mary Katherine Burnes and Lionel Armstrong was a surprise to readers of the Santa Barbara society columns. Miss Burnes, daughter of Mrs. James Nelson Burnes, was sixteen. Soon after returning from their honeymoon, the Armstrongs announced their intention to build a house and gave the commission to Osborne Craig. The site in Pasadena was flat with few distinguishing characteristics; Craig responded with two distinct schemes. The drawings are not dated but were completed between October 1921 and Craig's death in March 1922. The more successful proposal was an English cottage, medieval in spirit with an open pitched ceiling in the living room (Fig. 4.04). The Armstrongs settled on another design with a similar floor plan but Spanish overtones (Fig. 4.05). The house was completed in 1922; Carleton Winslow was supervising architect.[4]

Mrs. William L. McLaughlin Cottage
Pasadena, 1922

Craig's drawing for this cottage for his mother-in-law is undated but there can be no doubt that it

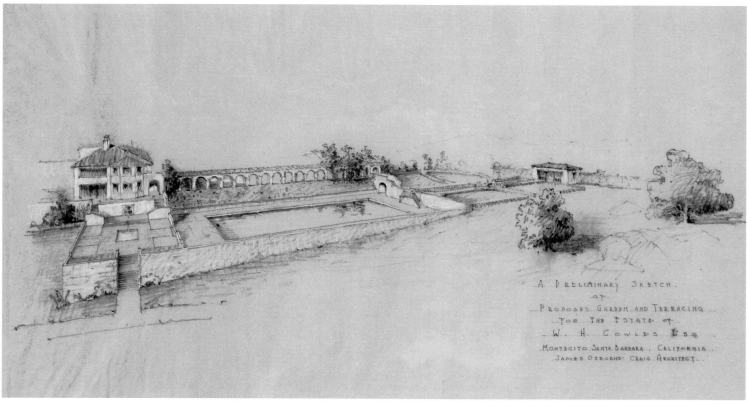

A PRELIMINARY SKETCH
OF
PROPOSED GARDEN AND TERRACING
FOR THE ESTATE OF
W. H. COWLES ESQ
MONTECITO SANTA BARBARA, CALIFORNIA
JAMES OSBORNE CRAIG ARCHITECT.

A PROPOSED HOUSE FOR
MR. AND MRS. LIONEL ARMSTRONG
PASADENA, CALIFORNIA.
JAMES OSBORNE CRAIG, ARCHITECT.

HOUSE FROM SOUTH EAST.

LIVING ROOM.

4.04. Armstrong House,
Pasadena (project)

4.05. Armstrong House,
Pasadena

4.06. Mrs. William L.
McLaughlin Cottage,
Pasadena

4.07. Mrs. William L.
McLaughlin Cottage,
Pasadena

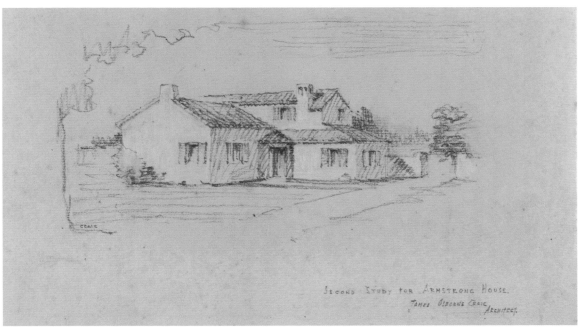

SECOND STUDY FOR ARMSTRONG HOUSE.
JAMES OSBORNE CRAIG, ARCHITECT.

was designed in early 1922. Very modest, it recalls generic Spanish farmhouses composed of seemingly additive units with tile roofs, gabled and shed (Fig. 4.06). The most notable aspect of the plan is the wing containing the maid's room and garage, which is rotated a few degrees off axis. The house was published immediately, a tribute to its obvious appeal (Fig. 4.07).[5]

Mrs. McLaughlin's cottage replaced an earlier house on the site. Unlike the original building, it was positioned at the rear of the lot, creating a park-like expanse at the front and ignoring the standard setback on the street. It was constructed between July and December 1922, although surviving documentation leaves key questions unanswered. The building permit describes an "addition" at an estimated cost of $1,600. Tax assessor records, dated December 8, 1922, indicate a cost of $2,731, suggesting more than an addition.

Lugo Adobe Fireplace
Santa Barbara, 1922

The Lugo adobe was constructed in the nineteenth century. Bernhard Hoffmann purchased the property, by then derelict, in 1922 and began immediately to restore the building; according to the *Morning Press*, "The chimney and fireplace were made from a design by the late James Osborne Craig (Fig. 4.08).[6] The adobe became the studio of the artist Ernest Dielman; he called it "Mi Sueno."

Craig's Death

He was so quiet and reserved that few of us realized how much he had done.[7]

His passion for architecture aside, the defining aspect of Craig's persona has to have been his health. He had been afflicted since childhood with severe asthma. The earliest written documentation of Craig's frailty is a series of letters from Michael Riordan written in the summer of 1917. In the first, Riordan expressed sorrow that Craig had "… not been up to your usual form for a while." He followed up a week later, "I am sorry to know from your note of the fifteenth that you are going to take a vacation in the hospital. I trust that the ordeal that you are to undergo will be not at all serious and that you will really have a vacation." Though the ordeal was not specified, a third letter written in September indicates that Craig had had surgery. Riordan wished him well: "I fancy that the lay-off, even though the operation was a slight one, was not as pleasant an experience as a fishing trip to Oak Creek, but even this likely depends to a large extent on the way one looks at it."[8]

Craig's own references to his physical wellbeing were frequent and ominous. He apparently was a victim of the Influenza Pandemic of 1918, writing to Mary McLaughlin in December that he was "…feeling beastly." Four days later, he reported "I have not even been out of bed and was quite light headed with fever; thank God it is less high today but I feel and

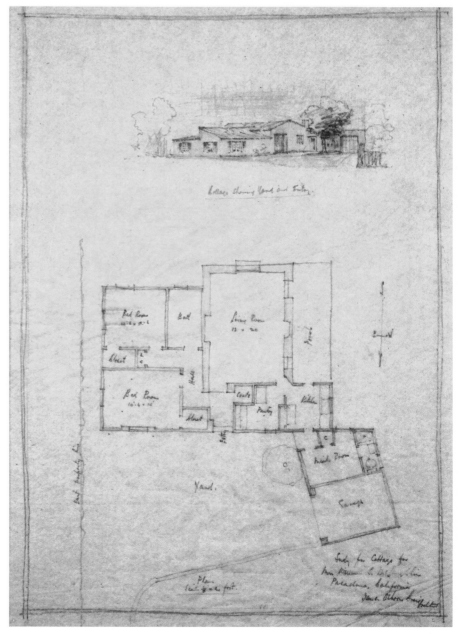

look like the proverbial something which the cat might have hauled in."[9]

The possibility that Craig had tuberculosis was ruled out in 1919: before their marriage, he wrote to Mary in Philadelphia, "You may put your mind at rest dear as far as my being tubercular; Dr. Campbell spent much time when he first took me in hand looking for such traces in every possible channel....When free from asthma I can walk, ride and do things which one with such an infection could never with impunity do." But instead of finding relief, the asthmatic attacks became both more serious and more frequent. He wrote again later in the month that he had had pneumonia.[10]

In late November 1920 Osborne sought relief from his asthma in Palm Springs. Within days he reported, "By next Thursday I will have my mucus membranes pretty well dried up again, as I should say reduced to a normal condition, which I hope I can keep after I come home." He followed up in a second letter the written the same day, "I am...better so I have decided to stay another week...if I can only get decently over my asthma here, perhaps I can keep it away after I get back by taking continual care...."[11]

4.08. Lugo adobe fireplace

Although the optimism continued, there were relapses when he returned to Santa Barbara. Ultimately, Craig retreated to Palm Springs three times. First he stayed at the Desert Inn. Later, Mary and their new daughter, also Mary, joined him in a rented house. They returned to Santa Barbara in early April 1921.

Eleven months later, on January 25, 1922, the *Morning Press* reported, "Mrs. Osborne Craig came over from the Ojai, where she is spending the winter, and passed the day here Monday." Osborne, accompanied by his two Marys, had once again sought relief in a dryer, warmer climate. They were living in a rented house designed by Myron Hunt, extant today though rebuilt after a fire in 1917. James Osborne Craig died there of bronchial pneumonia, age thirty-three, on March 15.[12]

To the Santa Barbara community, Craig's death was sudden and unexpected. To his wife, it could have been neither. A month later, *Southwest Builder and Contractor* announced that Carleton Winslow had taken over Craig's office at 29 East De la Guerra Street and would complete "... all the work Mr. Craig had underway at the time of his death. After completing the work Mr. Winslow will retain the office, to be used in connection with his Santa Barbara work."[13]

James Osborne Craig's considerable accomplishment was acknowledged during his lifetime and, to an even more extraordinary degree, posthumously. A groundswell of interest after his death caused one observer to note the "gratifying response" and the "far reaching effect of [his] work."[14] In short order, a retrospective exhibition of his drawings for De la Guerra Plaza and El Paseo was organized; a memorial fund was established; and a special issue of *Architect and Engineer* was devoted to his work.

The exhibition took place at The Patio the last week of April 1922 and led to the commemorative issue of the magazine. The *Bulletin* of the Community Arts Association Plans and Planting Committee explained:

The Library and Exhibit committee recently arranged and held an exhibition of the work of the late James Osborne Craig. The interest aroused by this exhibit was so widespread that the Committee felt warranted in responding to the many requests that this Exhibit be put in more permanent form. As a result, the material was submitted to "The Architect and Engineer," and an article on the exhibit and other recent Santa Barbara projects appears in the August number.[15]

The somewhat obtuse essay by Irving F. Morrow, a San Francisco architect who, with the engineer Joseph Strauss, went on to design the Golden Gate Bridge, begins with an approving nod to architectural historicizing—as opposed to archaeology—resulting from "... broadened knowledge [of the past] ... that should be welcomed as the basis for a more intelligent choice and synthesis." He envisioned a new "... California architecture...coming under the influence of a group of designers possessed of a vivid sense of beauty and a fresh and buoyant outlook." Morrow termed Craig's death "... a loss to the cause of architecture in California ..." and concluded, "... although his work is of a personal and reticent nature ... it is work which will quietly but surely insinuate itself into the spirit of our awakening architecture, and become a potent if unobtrusive influence."[16]

Mary Craig followed up with her own tribute, "The Heritage of All California," published in *California Southland* in September. She struck a not dissimilar tone: though written in the first person, the article clearly draws on Osborne's passion for Early California building. Mary took what she had absorbed and built a case for what today continued Morrow's argument for regionalism in Santa Barbara architecture.

Is not respect and emulation of work well done a great thing? In countries where this is most observed we find the greatest culture; for so is the best in each generation preserved and transmitted. But here, do we really care? I think one only has to travel the length of our highway and look at the Missions, for the most part in their deplorable state of decay, to have this question answered....

It is a very creditable thing that in Santa Barbara, even though it be in a small way, there is a real concerted action to do this thing—to preserve in a dignified, unaffected manner the architectural beauty that is the heritage of all Californians....

Nature has been so lavish in creating our background: the early Spanish-Californians have left us the beautiful prototype, and we are become an unthinking group if we will not profit by it.[17]

This article established the guidelines for Mary's emergence as a designer in her own right a year later.

CHAPTER 5

Mary Craig, Architect

After Osborne's death, Mary Craig and Mary, her daughter, initially had a gypsy existence. The house on Buena Vista had been rented while the family was in Ojai; after they returned they stayed at Daniel Nugent's cottage in Sandyland and with Bob and Grace McGann at Ca' di Sopra in Montecito. Later they spent several months in Philadelphia, returning to Santa Barbara in January 1923.[1]

Soon enough Mary decided to become an architectural designer, to pick up where Osborne left off. Shortly after returning from Ojai, she established an office in an outbuilding on the site of the Hoffmann House, then under construction. She confirmed her intentions a short time later, joining Carleton Winslow in Craig's office at 29 East De la Guerra and, in 1923, hiring Ralph Armitage, a licensed architect working for Winslow, to work with her as well.

Paseo de las Flores for Santa Barbara Seed Company
Santa Barbara, 1923

Mary's first project was a passageway connecting El Paseo and State Street, the principal commercial corridor in Santa Barbara.[2] As originally built, El Paseo was accessible only from De la Guerra, Canon Perdido and Anacapa Streets, a design decision surely forced by the abutting Malis Building on State. The new eight-foot-wide corridor through the Malis Building was added during construction of the last unit of El Paseo, the building enclosing the patio behind Casa de la Guerra to the north and west (*see* Fig. 3.48). It was called Paseo de las Flores, in recognition of the client and owner of the building, Santa Barbara Seed Company. As chaste as El Paseo itself, the proportions, contrast between solid and void and fine detailing reveal that Mary had learned Osborne's lessons well (Fig. 5.01).

This modest commission was an auspicious start for Mary Craig. In January 1924 the *Santa Barbara Daily News* trumpeted the new corridor as "a revolutionary development in business construction." Two months later, it received honorable mention as a notable example of architecture. There was a telling aside, however. Henriette Boeckman, writing in the *Los Angeles Times* on the "scheme to re-Spanishize Santa Barbara from an architectural standpoint," drew a contrast between

> … home-builders [who] have admirably stepped in file with the idea…and…the average business man [who] is uncannily conservative about the front of his shop and State Street, Santa Barbara's one grandiloquently long thoroughfare …, shows but few followers as yet of effective new-old design in building.
>
> The most delightful bit is shown in the new front on a florist shop. This florist told the writer he had carried out the change against the wishes of his father not to speak of the opposition of many business men.[3]

Mary's successful architectural debut was followed almost immediately by an exhibition of her designs for small houses sponsored by the Plans and Planting Committee and held in June 1924. The show comprised "… about fifty drawings of the Spanish type for which her work is noted and included "plans, interiors, and details of construction." The *Morning Press* praised the work, concluding:

Skill in handling architectural problems of construction, distinctiveness and an unusual atmosphere of authenticity combined with a charming quality of seeming to be adapted exactly to the location in which they are placed, make Mrs. Craig's house designs, as shown in the exhibit now on view particularly notable here where so much attention must be given to type.

Simplicity is probably the outstanding feature of all the houses shown and through strict adherence to the principal of unbroken expanses of wall, purity of line and cutting away of cluttering detail a far more typical effect has been obtained in these small houses than in many large ones where niches, shelves, cornices, variegated color schemes and ornamental carvings detract from the fundamental impression desired.[4]

Canby House
Montecito, 1924

A house for a member of Mary's inner circle, Mrs. M. Waterman Canby, née Margaret Waterman, followed in 1924. As a young girl, Miss Waterman had lived in the first grand house in Montecito.[5] After their marriage in 1917, she and her husband James Canby built a house on Mesa Road designed by George Washington Smith. The Canbys divorced in 1924 and she, seemingly in reduced circumstances,

commissioned Mary Craig to design the smallest house she had ever lived in.

Urbanistically, Montecito is a study in contrasts, a result of its happenstance development. The substantial houses on vast acreage, on which the community's reputation rests, stand shoulder-to-shoulder with utterly modest cottages of a different era and social stratum. Over time, most of the large parcels have been subdivided, in some cases into postage-stamp lots. Mrs. Canby's site on Lingate Lane was an example.

Mary Craig responded with a design for a two-story, three-bedroom house that was sited with almost no setback from the street (Fig. 5.02). The exterior conformed to the conventions of the time: planar wall surfaces and tile roof; inside the layout was straightforward with no opportunity for the ceremony to which Mrs. Canby was accustomed (Figs. 5.03, 5.04).

Mrs. Canby lived in the house only intermittently until her untimely death in 1932. In the parlance of the time, the house was "taken" by several noteworthy tenants including William A. Slater, Jr., who lived there while his house on Buena Vista, also designed by Mary Craig, was being completed; and H. Philip Staats, who collected and edited the material for the book *Californian Architecture in Santa Barbara*, published in 1929.[6]

5.01. Paseo de las Flores for Santa Barbara Seed Company. Photograph by J. W. Collinge.

5.02. Canby House, Montecito

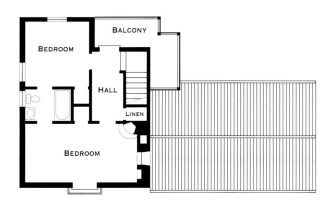

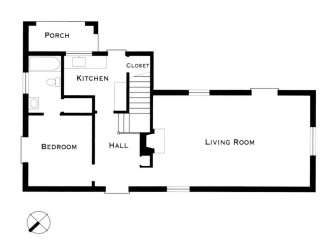

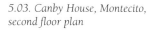

Speculative House, Hermosillo Court
Montecito, ca. 1924

While Mary Craig's social connections were critical to her success as an architectural designer, she also had an instinctive entrepreneurial streak that surfaced on call throughout her career. The first example was a house, probably built speculatively, on newly developed Hermosillo Court in Montecito. Laid out in 1923 on a ten-acre tract of land between Hot Springs Avenue and Coast Village Road, the subdivision comprised fifty-four building lots approximately fifty feet wide and 130 feet deep. The tract was bisected north to south by Park Drive—in fact, a boulevard with landscaped islands—entirely too grand for the modest parcels and incongruous with existing rural roads in Montecito.[7]

5.06. Hodgson Prefabricated
Buildings, Campbell Ranch,
Goleta. Photograph by Mary
Craig.

Mary's role in the construction of this house is as opaque as the date of completion. She did not design the building. Instead, she either reused the plans for her mother's house in Pasadena designed by Osborne in 1922, or provided the plans to the developer. The house was occupied by July 1924, though no official records have been located confirming the actual date it was finished.[8]

This clone of the McLaughlin house is today much closer in original appearance than the prototype in Pasadena, which has been drastically altered. The most important space is the living room with its high, pitched ceiling (Fig. 5.05).

Campbell House
Campbell Ranch, Goleta, 1924

At the opposite end of the spectrum were two very large contemporary houses: one for Mrs. Colin Campbell in Goleta; the other for Emmor J. and Beatrice Miley in Montecito, for which Mary Craig received commissions in the mid-1920s. Their chronologies overlap; however, Colin Campbell was first to express his intention to build: in 1920, he acquired an oceanfront site in Goleta, as reported by *Southwest Builder and Contractor:*

> Col. Colin Campbell has purchased 265 acres of the Henry P. Balcom ranch on the Coast highway, and it is reported he will spend more than $1,000,000 on a residence and buildings and on improvements to the grounds. A water system is now being constructed and a lake is being dredged.

The scale of the project is underscored by a small village of Hodgson prefabricated buildings that was quickly put up (Fig. 5.06). Other preliminary work included miles of roads, numerous telephone lines and the beginnings of two polo fields.[9] This was to

be a working ranch, a hands-on enterprise for the Colonel and his family.

Colonel Colin Campbell served in the Central Indian Horse Regiment in India and Afghanistan and fought in the siege of Chitral, Pakistan, in 1895. Later, as Lord George Curzon's administrator, he played a significant role in organizing the 1903 Durbar near Delhi, which celebrated the coronation of King Edward VII and Queen Alexandra as Emperor and Empress of India. Nancy Campbell was a member of the very progressive Leiter family of Chicago who with partner Marshall Field dominated the local dry goods and department store business between the Civil War and the end of the nineteenth century. Two commercial structures in Chicago, the First and Second Leiter buildings, commissioned by her father, Levi Z. Leiter, and completed in 1879 and 1891, live in the history of the tall building as exemplars of the transformation from wall bearing to skeletal construction.[10]

The Craigs' link to the Campbells dates to Mary's school days in Washington, D.C., when her friend Juliette Williams married Joseph Leiter, Nancy Campbell's brother. By 1920, Osborne and Mary were seeing the Campbells socially in Santa Barbara and Osborne was anxious for the commission. Justifying a trip to Palm Springs to rest, he told Mary with emphasis, "I do not want them to feel that I would not be up to undertaking their work should they really be considering me."[11]

Campbell and his wife Nancy do seem to have offered the commission to Osborne Craig after discussion with other architects who, according to Mrs. Campbell, had proposed "... such expensive plans, $191,000 and on to that the architect gets 15 percent, and so we wrote and said that we did not want a palace, we wanted a plain living house...."[12] Nonetheless, the house as finally built contained

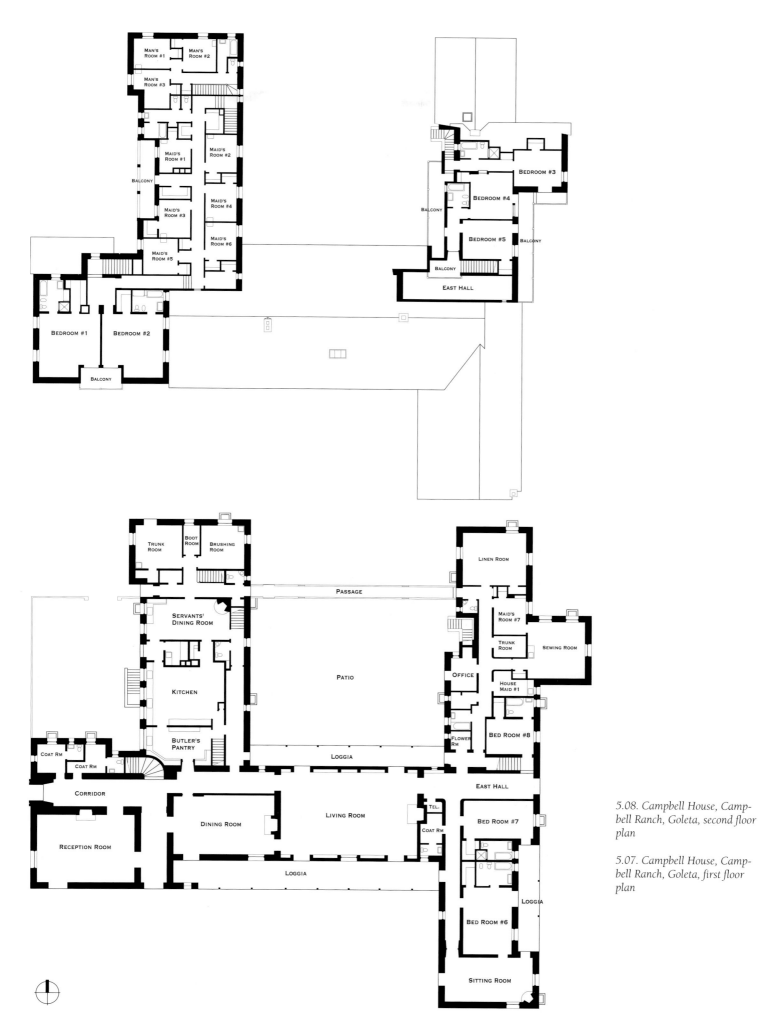

MAN'S ROOM #1 MAN'S ROOM #2
MAN'S ROOM #3
MAID'S ROOM #1 MAID'S ROOM #2
BALCONY
MAID'S ROOM #3 MAID'S ROOM #4
MAID'S ROOM #5 MAID'S ROOM #6

BEDROOM #3
BALCONY BEDROOM #4
BEDROOM #5 BALCONY
BALCONY
EAST HALL

BEDROOM #1 BEDROOM #2
BALCONY

TRUNK ROOM BOOT ROOM BRUSHING ROOM
PASSAGE
SERVANTS' DINING ROOM
LINEN ROOM
MAID'S ROOM #7
TRUNK ROOM SEWING ROOM
KITCHEN
OFFICE HOUSE MAID #1
PATIO
BUTLER'S PANTRY
FLOWER RM BED ROOM #8
COAT RM COAT RM
LOGGIA
CORRIDOR
EAST HALL
TEL.
RECEPTION ROOM DINING ROOM LIVING ROOM COAT RM BED ROOM #7
LOGGIA
LOGGIA
BED ROOM #6
SITTING ROOM

5.08. Campbell House, Campbell Ranch, Goleta, second floor plan

5.07. Campbell House, Campbell Ranch, Goleta, first floor plan

105

approximately 18,000 square feet; only the most jaded would have considered it plain.

There is no evidence that Craig prepared drawings for the house. His death in March 1922 was followed by Colin Campbell's fourteen months later, in May 1923; their widows saw the project through to completion. The result is an architectural anomaly. The expansive layout, indicating a ceremonial lifestyle that would have been familiar to Nancy Campbell, is juxtaposed with the method of construction, adobe, one of the most rudimentary building materials though well suited to the house's location on a ranch.

Mary Craig completed preliminary plans and drawings in September 1923; the finished plans are dated April 1924. A central wing positioned west to east contains the public spaces—reception, dining and living rooms laid out sequentially—and terminates in a perpendicular wing. Bedrooms for Mrs. Campbell and her son extend to the south; service rooms are to the north. Additional family bedrooms occupy the partial second floor. A second perpendicular wing extends to the north and contains service rooms on both floors. The main entry is at the west end of the principal mass; a circulation axis extends through the house to the east ending in a secondary, two-story entrance hall. This entry allowed family members access to the parts of the house in which they actually lived—two daughters' bedrooms were upstairs—without passing through the public areas (Figs. 5.07, 5.08).[13]

By this time very old fashioned, the layout conforms to the well-tested logic of an Edwardian country house in which a retinue of servants was the norm—service areas of the Campbell house occupy roughly a third of the square footage—and pay homage to a Victorian conceit of a room for every purpose that continued into the Edwardian era. There is provision for seven maids and three menservants; however, their proximate living quarters are carefully segregated and reached by separate flights of stairs or, as Clive Aslet put it discussing another house, "…needless to say there was no way through from the men's to the maids' bedrooms…."[14] A passage on the ground floor links the two wings extending to the north—and completes the enclosure of the patio—obviating the need for domestic help to pass routinely through the family rooms.

The house was completed in early October 1924. Its resemblance to an unidentified drawing by Edward Borein found in Mary's papers is unmistakable and it is impossible not to wonder if this was her point of departure (Fig. 5.09).[15] The considerable mass of the building is relieved by projecting and receding balconies and loggias and deep-set window voids (Figs. 5.10, 5.11). The only real elaboration is the articulated surround at the main entrance (Fig. 5.12). Extensive landscaping further mitigated the overall bulk.

A note in the *Morning Press* indicates that Mary Craig also planned the interior decoration. The effect was a hybrid of a southwestern hacienda with open-beam ceilings and tile floors, and furnishings befitting British aristocracy; Colonel Campbell's big game

5.09. Unidentified drawing attributed to Edward Borein

5.10. Campbell House, Campbell Ranch, Goleta, southwest elevation

5.11. Campbell House, Campbell Ranch, Goleta, south elevation

5.12. Campbell House, Campbell Ranch, Goleta, main entrance

trophies also were in evidence (Fig. 5.13). Most of the objects came from the Campbells' former residence, a castle at Port Regis near Broadstairs, a coastal town about eighty miles east of London. The *Los Angeles Times* gushed about their fabulousness, describing "Half a million dollars' worth of rare paintings and household effects …" that arrived "… in steel vans of five to ten tons each, and requiring ten trucks and trailers to haul it to Goleta." Outstanding pieces included a Georgian lacquerwork break-

front; sixteen eighteenth-century English Chippendale dining room chairs and a seventeenth-century Elizabethan cupboard (Fig. 5.14); and an eighteenth-century Chippendale mantel mirror (Fig. 5.15). There also were a large quantity of English silver and many sets of vermeil flatware.[16]

As a resplendent social mecca, Goleta had never seen the likes of the Campbell House: British nobility and royalty were entertained. In 1925 Edward William Bootle-Wilbraham (1895–1930), third (and

last) Earl of Lathom, a staunch financial supporter of a young, impecunious Oscar Wilde, was a guest. Three years later Prince George (1902–1942), younger brother of Prince Edward, who served briefly as King Edward VIII, attended a dinner-dance for forty-six people given by Mrs. Campbell. He was a member of the Royal Navy and arrived in California on board the *HMS Durban*. He had a penchant for motion picture celebrities and the day after Mrs. Campbell's party he went to Hollywood with William

A. Slater where Mary Pickford and Douglas Fairbanks gave a dinner in his honor at Pickfair. Guests included Charlie Chaplin, Greta Garbo and Gloria Swanson.[17]

Many other gatherings at the Campbell Ranch—some including Mary Craig—were documented in the society columns. But the spell was short: Nancy Campbell was there only about six years; she died in England in 1930. Her son Colin and his family lived there for several years before the house was offered for sale and the contents auctioned in June 1941,

though the house itself did not sell until later. It remains today in a ruinous and defaced state, since 2007 a property of the University of California.

The university has an opportunity to preserve a critical—if temporarily forgotten—West Coast monument of American history. The house cannot and should not be recreated as a museum—the furnishings have been dispersed and, even if located, would be prohibitively expensive to acquire—but as a living component of university life.

5.13. Campbell House, Campbell Ranch, Goleta, living room

5.14. Campbell House, Campbell Ranch, Goleta, dining room

5.15. Campbell House, Campbell Ranch, Goleta, reception room

Emmor J. Miley House I

Montecito, 1924

Mary Craig received two commissions from Emmor and Beatrice Miley in late 1924: a comparatively modest house on San Leandro Lane in the Ivydene Tract and a far grander residence with outbuildings on a large site at the north end of El Bosque Road. The strategy was that the Mileys would live in the smaller house while the larger one was under construction.

The house on San Leandro was one of several flat-fronted, plaster-skinned projects that Mary designed in the twenties and early thirties. Like so many buildings in Santa Barbara the house, though grounded in the spirit of Andalusia, is a riff on its sources. Essentially linear in composition—the second floor is expressed only intermittently in elevation—a cross axis is established off center by a gabled, two story mass containing the entry framed with sandstone blocks and surmounted by an iron balcony in the best Spanish tradition (Fig. 5.16).

Emmor J. Miley House II

Montecito, 1924

In October 1924, as the Campbell House neared completion, the *Morning Press* announced that construction would soon begin on a new house for Emmor and Beatrice Miley on property directly in front of San Ysidro Ranch; Mary Craig was the designer. The commission seems to have come to her with few financial constraints: the Mileys had oil money and needed a house to display their windfall though, at approximately 14,000 square feet, it was smaller than Mrs. Campbell's adobe palace.

The two-story plan wraps around a central patio overlooked by a balcony (Figs. 5.19, 5.20). The entrance hall leads to the stair hall, library and music room on the right. The dining room and service wing are to the left. Though this is a house of considerable pretention, analysis of the layout leads to several inevitable conclusions: overall, there is less than full resolution. An axis is established from the front door to a door across the entrance hall leading to the patio, yet the patio itself is entered off axis. A cross axis extends from the library though the entrance hall to the dining room, creating a fine enfilade (Fig. 5.30). Conversely, the music room, the largest and most ceremonial space in the house, is reached through a secondary corridor, dark and narrow. In the patio, the columns supporting the balcony are positioned irregularly and the beams overhead are awkwardly resolved.

The full weight—physical as well as visual—of this house with its rusticated Santa Barbara sandstone cladding is apparent on arrival: the west (front) and south (side) facades are seen simultaneously (Figs. 5.17, 5.18). The effect is amplified by stone lintels and windowsills, and ironwork. Both eleva-

5.16. Miley House I, Montecito

FOLLOWING PAGES
5.17. Emmor J. Miley House II, Montecito, west or front elevation

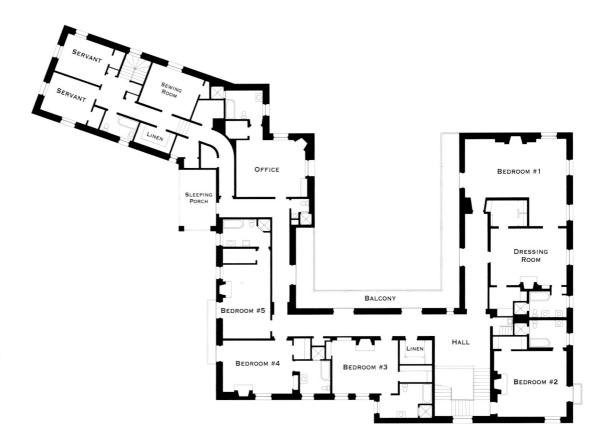

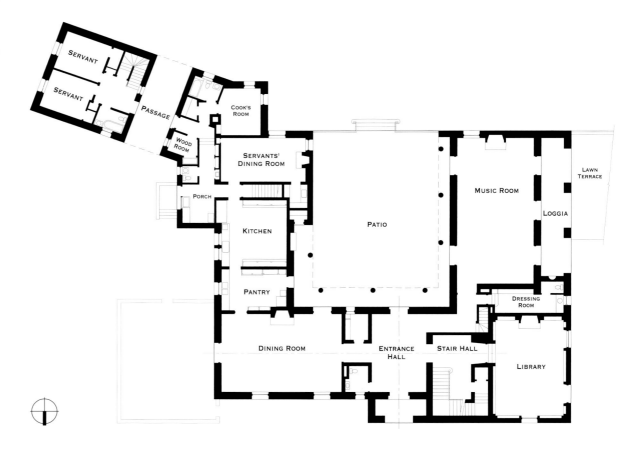

PREVIOUS PAGES
5.18. Emmor J. Miley House II, Montecito, south elevation

THIS PAGE
5.20. Emmor J. Miley House II, Montecito, second floor plan

5.19. Emmor J. Miley House II, Montecito, first floor plan

OPPOSITE
5.21. Emmor J. Miley House II, Montecito, west or front elevation, looking north

SERVANT
SERVANT
SEWING ROOM
LINEN
OFFICE
SLEEPING PORCH
BEDROOM #1
DRESSING ROOM
BALCONY
BEDROOM #5
HALL
LINEN
BEDROOM #4
BEDROOM #3
BEDROOM #2

SERVANT
SERVANT
PASSAGE
COOK'S ROOM
WOOD ROOM
SERVANTS' DINING ROOM
LAWN TERRACE
MUSIC ROOM
LOGGIA
PORCH
KITCHEN
PATIO
PANTRY
DRESSING ROOM
DINING ROOM
ENTRANCE HALL
STAIR HALL
LIBRARY

5.22. Emmor J. Miley House II, Montecito, balcony looking west

5.23. Emmor J. Miley House II, Montecito, patio looking north-west

FOLLOWING PAGES
5.24. Emmor J. Miley House II, Montecito, patio looking west

tions are essentially flat; the front is relieved by the arched entry porch and *rejas* (Fig. 5.21). The side elevation has greater articulation with its arcaded loggia and differing roof angles. The patio at the back, with its white plaster walls, is more in the spirit of contemporary "Californian" architecture in Santa Barbara (Figs. 5.18, 5.23, 5.24).

The two-story stair hall is embellished with a finely detailed iron railing, one of the truly remarkable features of the Miley House (Figs. 5.25-5.27). The drawings, however, are unsigned and cannot be attributed to Mary with certainty; the ironwork may have been designed by Chester Carjola and added by a later owner. The library with its paneling, bookcases and stone fireplace is the most intimate space in the house (Fig. 5.28). The music room with its scored stone walls is overlooked by a musicians' balcony; it opens on one side to the patio, on the other to a loggia and distant ocean view (Figs. 5.29, 5.31, 5.32). And the enfilade linking the library and dining room, indicated on the plan, is expressed in three dimensions as stone arches (Fig. 5.30).

Even though mass is the defining quality of this house, there are fanciful moments, particularly the fine ironwork of the stair railing, the *rejas* and the brackets supporting a balcony on the north elevation (Fig. 5.33). And each of the chimneys has a unique sculptural stone cap.

This house was to be the trophy of an oilman who suddenly won big but it was not unique: other contemporary wildcatters were guilty of similar architectural grandstanding. Among many examples, it may be useful to make specific analogy with a house built by E. W. Marland in Ponca City, Oklahoma. The similarities are striking. Marland's house was designed by John Duncan Forsyth (1886 or 1887–1963), an architect based in Tulsa, and completed between 1925 and 1928. Like the Miley House, it was built of rusticated masonry though at 44,000 square feet it was more than three times as large. Both houses have an overwhelmingly solid, masculine presence with their stonework, open beam ceilings and wrought iron embellishments and both have playful chimneys, though the Marland house seems to be a more personal statement.[18]

The houses have something else in common. Neither Marland nor Miley had the financial wherewithal to sustain his grandiose vision. Marland's economic reversals began in 1928 and in the early thirties he and his wife moved to a smaller building on the property.

5.28. Emmor J. Miley House II,
Montecito, library

5.29. Emmor J. Miley House II,
Montecito, living room as furnished by second owners

5.30. Emmor J. Miley House II,
Montecito, enfilade

5.31. Emmor J. Miley House II, Montecito, musicians' loft

5.32. Emmor J. Miley House II, Montecito, grill detail

5.33 Emmor J. Miley House II, Montecito, north elevation

FOLLOWING PAGES
5.34. Cramer House, Montecito

Construction work on the Miley project ended in March 1928, before the building was complete. In July Snook & Kenyon filed suit to recover $36,385.07 for labor and materials. Four years later the house was purchased by John T. de Blois Wack (1901–1992) and his wife Ethel du Pont Barksdale (1898–1974) who commissioned Chester Carjola, a Santa Barbara architect, to complete the work.

Cramer House
Montecito, 1925

A house for Mrs. Ambrose Cramer represented a shift from the Hispanic prototypes Mary had turned to earlier. Vaguely Mediterranean in spirit, a contemporary account described it as "… an adoption of the Italian farm-house type" (Fig. 5.34).[19]

One wonders about the catalyst for the design of this house. There is refinement both in the exterior symmetry and interior details that do not suggest a farmhouse and that Mary had not pursued previously. The answer surely lies with the client and her family. Grace Meeker Cramer was the daughter of Arthur Meeker, the meat-packing titan from Chicago, and his wife Grace. In 1915 she married the architect

5.35. Plaza Rubio, Santa Barbara, site before develop-ment

5.36. Plaza Rubio, Santa Barbara, site plan

Plaza Rubio Subdivision for Mrs. Joseph A. Andrews
Santa Barbara, 1924–26

In the end, it was not the grand houses for Nancy Campbell and Emmor Miley, representing a lifestyle sustainable by very few, that secured Mary Craig's reputation. Another much more populist project, a group of seven houses built on a tract of land facing Mission Santa Barbara, was Mary's key to the pantheon of Santa Barbara architecture. The significance of this undertaking is enhanced by Mary's association with the very entrepreneurial Margaret Andrews. Mrs. Andrews probably first visited Santa Barbara as a widow, Mrs. Charles Forsyth of Milwaukee, in early 1920. Within three years, she had decided to settle: in November 1922, *Southwest Builder and Contractor* announced that Floyd Brewster, architect of the recently-completed Hazard Memorial/Museum of Comparative Oology in Mission Canyon—later the Santa Barbara Museum of Natural History—had completed plans for a ten-room house for her to be erected on Mission Ridge Road.[21] Mrs. Forsyth became Margaret Andrews in March 1924 on her marriage to Dr. Joseph Andrews, an ophthalmologist.

Mrs. Andrews began acquiring real estate soon after her arrival in Santa Barbara: quickly and perspicaciously she assembled a portfolio to be reckoned with. Most to the point was a tract of land directly across from Mission Santa Barbara that was put together in December 1924 by Henry L. Hitchcock and Frances H. Lingham, local real estate developers (Fig. 5.35). A tract map published in March 1925 shows the land

Ambrose Cramer who in turn was associated with David Adler, a designer whose adaptations of traditional styles made him the architect of choice for much of North Shore Chicago. In the teens and twenties, Adler—in tandem with his sister Frances Elkins, who worked as an interior designer—provided his extremely affluent clients an aura of "good taste" antithetical to the contemporary innovations of Frank Lloyd Wright and his school. In giving the commission for her house to Mary Craig, Grace Cramer was pointedly casting aside the services of her estranged husband though his influence—direct or implied—seems palpable. Five years later, less than persona non grata, Ambrose Cramer completed the famous Meeker house, Costanza, nearby on Valley Road.[20]

5.37. Plaza Rubio, Santa
Barbara, perspective drawing

subdivided into twenty-three lots bordered on the east
and west by Emerson Avenue and Laguna Street and
on the north by a new street, Plaza Rubio, named in
memory of José González Rubio (1804–1875), a priest
who played a significant role in the turbulent nineteenth-century transition of Alta California from Mexican to American sovereignty, especially in Santa
Barbara. An extension of East Padre Street connecting
Laguna and Emerson divided the development internally (Fig. 5.36). The map indicated that Mrs. Andrews
had acquired eight parcels from Hitchcock and Lingham including seven of the eight lots fronting on Plaza
Rubio; the eighth was owned by Leon Levy, an insurance agent. Mrs. Andrews also purchased a lot at the
corner of East Padre and Emerson and, later in the year,
another at the corner of East Padre and Laguna.

Leon Levy was first to build; the permit for his
house at number 420 was issued in December 1924.
There is scant evidence that Mary Craig was some-
how involved. On December 2, Alexander MacKellar, a building contractor, wrote to her about
unspecified changes to the "plans of residence to be
erected for Mr. and Mrs. Leon Levy."[22]

Two days later, on December 4, Mary wrote a letter to Mrs. Andrews stating that she was "… proceeding with drawings for group of houses." Work was
far enough along by mid-February to get construction estimates; initially only three houses were contemplated. Estimates received February 11 were in
the $27,000 range, an amount clearly within Mrs.
Andrews's budget; a few days later, a fourth house
was added. A perspective drawing of the project that
must have been completed at this time shows the
four houses in thematically consistent Spanish style

(Fig. 5.37). Though relatively modest, all are two-
story structures with two or three bedrooms (Figs.
5.38–5.41). On February 14 Mrs. Andrews signed
an agreement with Davidson & Maitland to construct
the four houses for a total of $36,374.00. Permits
were issued March 2.[23] The houses were published
soon after completion (Fig. 5.42).

Barely were the four houses completed when Mrs.
Andrews expanded her building campaign, again
enlisting the design assistance of Mary Craig. On
June 2, 1925, Mrs. Andrews was issued a permit for
a fifth house at the corner of East Padre and Laguna
streets. Stylistically consistent with the original four,
it was unique in having only one story (Figs. 5.43,
5.44).

Slightly earlier, in April 1925, Mrs. Andrews purchased an existing house across Emerson Avenue to
the east. Constructed in 1906, it was badly damaged
in the June 1925 earthquake. Mary Craig was given
the task of repairs; a permit was issued in August. In
the course of reconstruction, the house was trans-
formed into the Spanish style.[24]

Mary's final house in the group, 408 Plaza Rubio,
was begun in January 1926; it was intended for Mrs.
Andrews's sister, Elizabeth Knight (1871–1959). It
was completed in May as noted in the *Morning Press*:

> Miss Elizabeth Knight and Miss Frances Mooers are
> returning to Santa Barbara at the end of May from Mon-
> rovia where they have been living for the last three
> months, to take possession of the house which Mrs. J.
> A. Andrews is having built for them. The house is near-
> ing completion and is in the group of Spanish houses
> Mrs. Andrews has had built just below the Mission
> Santa Barbara and facing it.[25]

*5.38. 434 Plaza Rubio,
Santa Barbara, second
and first floor plans*

*5.39. 430 Plaza Rubio,
Santa Barbara, second
and first floor plans*

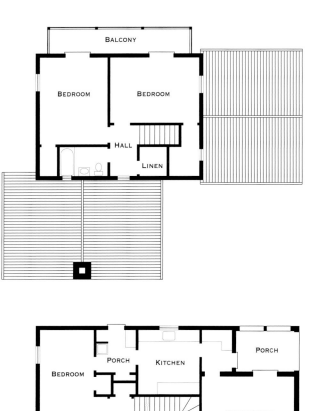

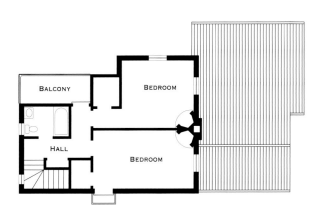

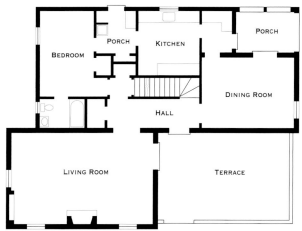

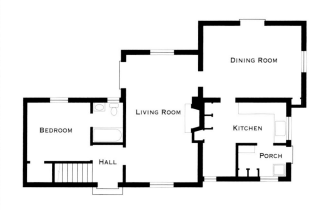

*5.42. Plaza Rubio
from street*

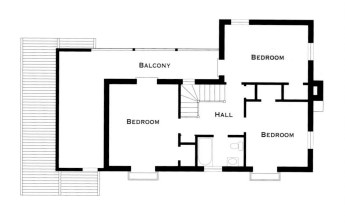

BALCONY

BEDROOM

BEDROOM

HALL

BEDROOM

BEDROOM

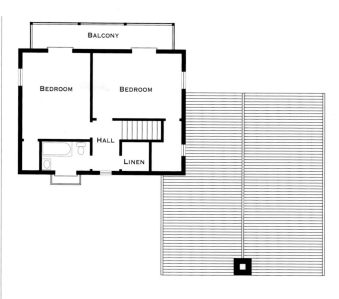

BALCONY

BEDROOM

BEDROOM

HALL

LINEN

5.40. 424 Plaza Rubio,
Santa Barbara, second
and first floor plans

5.41. 402 Plaza Rubio,
Santa Barbara, second
and first floor plans

KITCHEN

PORCH

BEDROOM

DINING
ROOM

HALL

LIVING ROOM

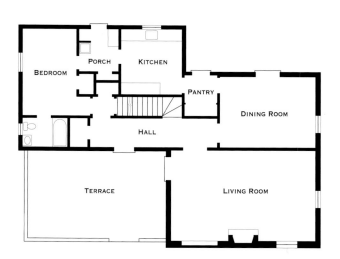

BEDROOM

PORCH

KITCHEN

PANTRY

HALL

DINING ROOM

TERRACE

LIVING ROOM

5.43. 2100 Laguna
Street, Santa Barbara

Mary Craig's work at Plaza Rubio was accorded extraordinary civic recognition. Photographs of the first four houses were published in the *Morning Press* in January 1926 with the note that they had been "Awarded 1st prize, Class 3, *Morning Press* photographic Competition." *California Southland* followed up in June, paying tribute not only to Margaret Andrews and Mary Craig, but also to the memory of Osborne Craig:

> Near the Mission Santa Barbara, and circling around its wide fields before the beautiful south front, is a group of houses lately built in the most approved Santa Barbara methods. All the charm of color and old world detail which Santa Barbara has lately learned to use in her buildings has been drawn upon to make a delightful neighborhood in this choice situation.
>
> Unwilling to leave this, the most Californian of the city's residence sections, to be spoiled by careless building, the owner of the property ... planned a group of houses to be up-to-date in every particular and engaged Mrs. James Osbourne [sic] Craig to make the designs.
>
> When two such women consult to make houses which people will want to live in we may be sure of the success of the project. Mrs. Andrews, the owner and builder has studied house keeping [sic] conditions in Santa Barbara and has embodied in these livable houses the results of years of experience in beautiful home-making. Mrs. Craig has carried on the traditions of California's colonial houses so well understood and expressed by Mr. Craig in his short career as the architect who started the Santa Barbara renaissance.[26]

The fifth house, at East Padre and Laguna, was awarded second prize for five-room houses in the 1927 "Better Houses week competition." The jury explained:

> This house ranks very high. It is excellent in design and compact in plan. It has a large number of exterior units, such as bays and gables for so small a building. The least attractive feature is that the windows of the kitchen open onto a screened porch and not directly to the outside, so cutting off some light.[27]

Like its siblings, the house at 408 Plaza Rubio received second prize in the seven-room class in a "Better Houses week competition." The jury felt it was "... a comfortable house of substantial dignity. The overhang at the front and the balcony outside the upper windows relieve the barenness [sic] and cast interesting shadows on the white stucco walls."[28]

Not unlike Osborne Craig's El Paseo, Plaza Rubio had urban implications taking it well beyond mere building. The twenties was a period of civic expansion in Santa Barbara; development of unoccupied land was inevitable though, admittedly, the last vestiges of the rural setting original to the Mission were lost. Still, it is hard to imagine the challenge of building across from Mission Santa Barbara and impossible to imagine a finer solution. The houses on Plaza Rubio neither intrude on the mission nor are upstaged by it. With near pitch-perfect planning, they are far enough away to remain deferential yet close enough to embrace the mission in a framed composition (Figs. 5.45–5.50).

PREVIOUS PAGES
5.44. 2100 Laguna Street, Santa Barbara

5.45. Plaza Rubio, Santa Barbara

5.51. Logan's Garage, Santa Barbara

5.52. Logan's Garage, Santa Barbara, reconstructed arcade

Open Air School for Santa Barbara Board of Education
1925

A project for a school building for the Santa Barbara Board of Education is among the most enigmatic of Mary's career. Even the name is confusing: although it is identified most frequently in the source material as the "Open Air School," it also is referred to as a "Health School" and the "Santa Barbara fresh air school." The project can be dated to May 1925 when the philanthropist and school board president Frederick Forest Peabody wrote to Mary that the

board expected to go ahead with the building on which she had been working. Peabody continued that he had recommended her as the architect and that the board had approved.[29]

The site was on the southeast corner of the intersection of Santa Barbara and De la Guerra streets. Mary's drawings have not been found but were far enough along for *Southwest Builder and Contractor* to report on September 18 that she was preparing plans for a one-story frame and stucco building to accommodate twenty-five pupils. The scheme was approved ten days later.[30]

Contradictorily, the project seems already to have been abandoned by this time. Bernhard Hoffmann, writing in August to William Templeton Johnson, suggested that the school board had been unable to continue with the new building after the June 29 earthquake. This supposition is supported by a report in the *Morning Press* on October 13 that the open air school would open later in the week in the manual training room of the Franklin School. The school board met on November 19 and formally recommended that the Health School be discontinued at the end of the month. At the same time, final payment to Mary Craig for her services was authorized.[31]

Mrs. Joseph A. Andrews Automobile Showroom and Garage for W. C. Logan
Santa Barbara, 1925

The chemistry of female designer and female developer proved efficacious: Plaza Rubio was the first of several commissions Margaret Andrews awarded Mary Craig. In short order, while the houses were

5.53. *La Hacienda Carrillo, Santa Barbara*

under construction, Mrs. Andrews underwrote a new commercial garage building for W. C. Logan on Carrillo Street and a restaurant next door to the west.

The seeds of the Logan project can be traced to the decision by the Catholic Church to sell the property Logan was leasing on State Street. Anticipating the move, Logan purchased a site nearby, as described by *Southwest Builder and Contractor* in December 1923: "W. C. Logan has purchased a lot of 70 ft. frontage, on E. Carrillo St. He will build a modern garage and sales bldg., with grease and wash rack dept. Dodge Automobile Agency will lease the bldg."[32]

Logan's existing lease on State Street was in effect for two more years; Mary's ledger indicates that she began work on the project in July 1925; plans were ready in August. The distinguishing feature was the arcaded, covered walkway paralleling the street (Fig. 5.51). Arcades were proposed for the reconstruction of State Street after the earthquake and although a few were built, including Rogers Furniture Store and Johnston's Cafeteria, many merchants resisted because they felt their storefronts were obscured. They are a feature of Hispanic architecture in the New World that can be traced to Philip II's Laws of the Indies, guidelines established by the Spanish crown in 1573 for building in colonies outside Europe, chiefly in the Americas. To wit: "Around the plaza as well as along the four principal streets which begin there, there shall be arcades, for these are of considerable convenience to the merchants who generally gather there...."[33]

The Logan Building and other examples in Santa Barbara only hinted at the full potential of The Laws of the Indies as a planning strategy. One needs only to go to Morelia, Michoacán, Mexico, a planned, sixteenth-century colonial city, to understand the glories that were possible. Nonetheless, the Logan Building was recognized on completion in January 1926 as "...one of the finest examples of the application of Santa Barbara architecture to a business building in the downtown district...." Two months later, in a city sponsored competition, it received Second Award. Recognition came a third time in 1928 when it was awarded "Second Prize Among the Best Examples of Civic and Commercial Architecture Erected in Santa Barbara ... in 1926."[34]

The garage was demolished in 1979. Although it was replaced by a larger building serving a different function, Mary Craig's arcade was replicated from the original drawings by Michael Towbes, owner of the property (Fig. 5.52).

Mrs. Joseph A. Andrews Commercial Building, La Hacienda Carrillo
Santa Barbara, 1925

Seemingly insatiable in her desire to build, Margaret Andrews undertook a unique project coinciding with construction of Logan's Garage on a site immediately to the west: a commercial building constructed of reused adobe bricks. *Southwest Builder and Contractor* announced in August 1925 that Mary Craig was preparing the plans; permits were issued in October and November. A central patio was enclosed by a two-story structure with a balcony at the rear of the property and two projecting side wings (Fig. 5.53). Various businesses were housed there including a restaurant, an Oriental rug shop, and an Elks Club.[35]

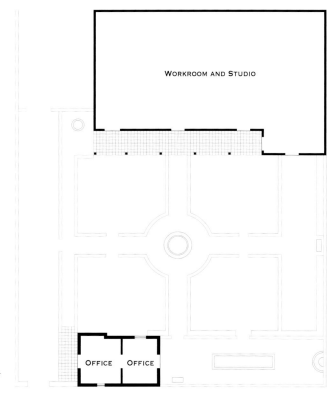

and Santa Barbara Junior High School. By 1927 he reportedly employed twenty-five assistants.[36]

In 1926, perhaps imbued by his initial success and overly optimistic, Von Waldt-Hausen commissioned Mary Craig to prepare drawings for a new office and studio. The site, 100' x 225' , was on Milpas Street, then as now a commercial strip less gentrified than downtown Santa Barbara. Mary Craig's scheme—based on an earlier, unidentified project by her husband—is in effect a fully internalized, walled compound that turns its back on its surroundings (Fig. 5.54). Two structures—a double office fronting on Milpas and a much larger combined workroom and studio at the back of the lot—open to an enclosed patio in the center of the space. Entry from the street is through double wooden gates leading to a driveway that extends the length of the property (Fig. 5.55).

This project has an air of refinement worthy of Bernhard Hoffmann's ambitions. The street facade is essentially an unadorned planar surface with a tile roof. The wall is penetrated by the entry gates and by one window with an iron grill. Immediately behind the wall is a second, smaller walled court with a pool and fountain. The processional aspects the designers clearly envisioned begin inside the walls—other than the gates, there is no direct, contaminating entry from the street—and pass through the offices, each with fireplace, into the smaller court and then through the larger court to the workroom and studio, the creative center of gravity of the plan.

Mary Craig's scheme is complete and specifications were prepared but the building was not constructed. Permits issued in January and February 1928 indicate that von Waldt-Hausen finally developed the vacant lot with a stucco office building with a composition roof and a shed with galvanized roof, costing together less than $1000.[37]

Von Waldt-Hausen Studio
Santa Barbara, 1926 (project)

5.54. James Osborne Craig, unidentified drawing

5.55. Von Waldt-Hausen Studio, Santa Barbara

Herman Von Waldt-Hausen (1882–1961) was a manufacturer of architectural ornament; he worked variously in stone, staff and concrete. Born in Germany, he arrived in Santa Barbara in 1923, possibly with the promise of work on the Granada Theatre. Within a few years he had embellished several local landmarks including the Lobero Theatre

5.56. Mary Craig House, One Acre, Montecito, with wall added by Osborne Craig in 1920

5.57. Mary Craig house before remodeling

Mary Craig House, One Acre, Remodeling and Additions

Montecito, 1926

On the heels of the work for Mrs. Andrews, Mary Craig began various improvements on One Acre, the Montecito property she purchased in 1918. Over time, she doubled the size of the original house and added several cottages. By the time of her death One Acre had become a compound of structures protected from the street by the wall Osborne designed in 1920 (Fig. 5.56).

Set close to the street, the main house originally was a warehouse for fruit; it had been remodeled as a dwelling before Mary bought it (Fig. 5.57). Interior photographs reveal low, lath ceilings supported by exposed beams and whitewashed adobe walls befitting the building's humble origins (Fig. 5.58). She expanded it with a wing to the south containing a new living room, two bedrooms and a bath; she also designed a tiled sink for the pantry (Fig. 5.63). The original entry was unchanged; it led to a loggia linking existing and new construction (Fig. 5.59). The enlarged plan enclosed a central, brick-paved patio on three sides (Fig. 5.61). At the same time, she replaced the board-and-batten siding of the original cottage with smooth plaster and also converted the garage Osborne built in 1918 into living space (Fig. 5.62).

Though entirely modest by Montecito standards, One Acre had a magical setting with mountains as a backdrop; it was embellished with tile purchased in Spain, a neoclassical marble mantle and chintz (Fig. 5.60). Photographs of the house by Jessie Tarbox Beals were published in *House Beautiful* in 1930. The title of the article was "The House in Good Taste," the term used so often in reference to Mary Craig.[38]

5.58. Mary Craig House,
One Acre, original living room
(identified as dining room in the
enlarged plan), Montecito.
Osborne Craig's architectural
books on the shelves are now
in the possession of his granddaughter, Pamela Skewes-Cox.

5.60. Mary Craig House,
One Acre, living room

5.59. Mary Craig House,
One Acre, plan as enlarged

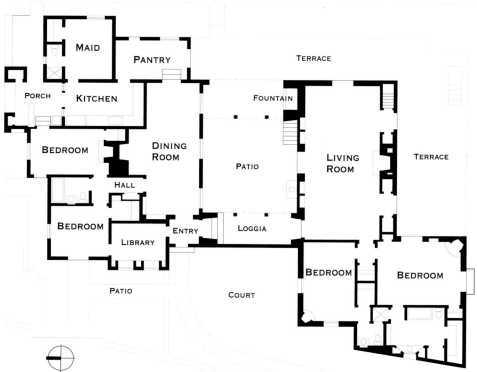

MAID

PANTRY

TERRACE

PORCH

KITCHEN

FOUNTAIN

BEDROOM

DINING
ROOM

PATIO

LIVING
ROOM

TERRACE

HALL

BEDROOM

LIBRARY

ENTRY

LOGGIA

BEDROOM

BEDROOM

PATIO

COURT

5.61. Mary Craig House,
One Acre, Montecito, patio

5.62. Mary Craig House,
One Acre, Montecito, north
elevation

5.63. Mary Craig House,
One Acre, Montecito, tiled
sink

J. P. Jefferson Service Cottages
Montecito, 1926–1927

Mary Craig worked on three service cottages sited linearly on the Montecito property of Mr. and Mrs. John Percival Jefferson in 1926–27. She designed one—the third building to the right—for the Jefferson's chauffeur (Fig. 5.64). Slightly later, she remodeled the other two, most significantly adding fireplaces in the living rooms (Figs. 5.65, 5.66).[39] As a group, the cottages are modest. Though each is a distinct design, their similar size and consistent materials—cement plaster walls and tile roofs—convey stylistic unity.

Alma S. Urmston House
Pebble Beach, 1927

The site for the Urmston House, arguably the finest of Mary Craig's career, comprised just over one-and-a-half acres on a wooded bluff overlooking the Pacific Ocean. The house was placed high on the property, a few feet from the road above. Vaguely reminiscent of early vernacular building in neighboring Monterey, so admired by Osborne Craig, the Urmston House has a balcony overlooking the view. Dormer windows, whose unique form defies architectural terminology, are the distinguishing feature (*see* pp. 10–11). Another pair of recessed windows

has an outsized header articulated with dentils (Fig. 5.67).

Downstairs, the interiors of this house appear to anticipate the Colonial Revival aesthetic that took hold in the thirties, especially the dining room with its wooden paneling. Similarly, the living room fireplace alcove seems rooted in some unnamed New England prototype (Fig. 5.68). Upstairs, the bedroom ceilings are in fact the exposed skeletal undersides of the roof structure (Fig. 5.69). Though hardly an attic, if this photograph was in black and white, and if Betty Katz were standing there, Edward Weston's 1921 Attic Series would come powerfully to mind.

One wonders in general about possible influence and in particular about Mary's awareness of a slightly earlier project in Monterey. In 1920 Frances Elkins acquired Casa Amesti, an early nineteenth-century adobe, and with her brother, David Adler, shored up the crumbling building structurally and reimagined the interiors. Though not specifically American colonial, an argument could be made that Elkins created a West Coast prototype that had a decisive influence on Mary and countless other designers as well.[40]

Mrs. William A. Slater and William A. Slater, Jr., House
Montecito, 1927

A house designed in 1927 for Mrs. William A. Slater of New York and her son, William A. Slater, Jr., represents a new direction for Mary Craig. Not small—though it pales in comparison with the Campbell and Miley houses—it has a refinement of scale lacking in these grander houses and invites analogy with the contemporary work of George Washington Smith. By the mid-twenties, Smith had enlarged his vision of the Spanish farmhouse from contained, rectangular volumes to expansive plans that often were focused on interior patios. Two houses: one for Mrs. Arthur Rose Vincent, Pebble Beach, 1924; the other for Mr. and

5.69. Alma S. Urmston House,
Pebble Beach, bedroom

5.68. Alma S. Urmston House,
Pebble Beach, living room

5.70. *Slater House I, Montecito*

5.71. *Slater House I, Montecito, front elevation. Photograph by Jessie Tarbox Beals*

5.72. *Slater House I, Montecito, living room. Photograph by Jessie Tarbox Beals.*

Mrs. Peter Cooper Bryce in Santa Barbara, designed two years later, illustrate the evolution. The Vincent house is essentially square in plan; its footprint belies the amount of space devoted to the central patio. A loggia on three sides of the patio provides the basic path of circulation. The Bryce house is less regular in outline and has three sequential patios; interior corridors replace the open loggia.

The Bryce plan surely was the prototype for the one worked out for Ellen Slater and her son Will. Mary Craig was tight socially with the Bryces and had access to their house. Will saw it when he and Mary had lunch there while formulating their own plans, strengthening the argument.[41] Though not a clone, the layout of Slater nonetheless shares unmistakable characteristics with the Bryce plan. Both feature sequential patios—Bryce has three; Slater, two—and both use prominent trans-

verse corridors paralleling the patios as a circulation strategy. Both houses terminate in wings at the rear enclosing a patio open on its fourth side (Fig. 5.70).

Plans for the Slater House were developed in early 1927; the evolution can be traced in correspondence between Mary Craig and Ellen Slater. On March 31, Mary wrote to Mrs. Slater about Will's wish to have her wing "... distinct and separate from the part of the house in which he lives." She continued, "We have been working over some preliminary plans but have not done anything very definite and will not do so until the property is actually yours." Two weeks later, Mary sent preliminary plans for the house, explaining that Will had worked with her "... over the mass and roof lines...."[42]

From the street, the Slater House is seen from a slight elevation: the site on Buena Vista, like Mary Craig's property a short distance to the south, slopes

downward. A graveled court separates the house from the street. The front elevation is an amalgam of asymmetrical masses unified by conventional attributes of planar, white plaster surfaces; *rejas*, and red tile roofs (Fig. 5.71). An axis through the house is established at the main entry and leads through two patios: one at the center, the other overlooking the Pacific Ocean in the distance. The extremely civilized plan accommodates both ceremony and privacy. A cross-axial corridor leads to the living room in one direction, dining room on the other. Mrs. Slater's bedroom is at one end of this corridor; other private spaces open onto the second patio (Figs. 5.72, 5.73).

The Slater House is one of Mary Craig's finest and it comes with an added reward. Mary rarely explained her design philosophy but in this case she did in a letter to Mrs. Slater:

> While there is not a great deal of space in the house it covers a large area and there are many wall surfaces. Of course, an entire two story house, or a house more compact, would be cheaper but not so charming or adaptable to this climate. In spreading out the design we have, of course, done it with an idea of making the most of all views. Every room except the kitchen have [*sic*] charming glimpses of sea and mountains. Your rooms particularly look out to that nicest view of the mountains with views to the south of the sea and the point of land that juts out to the west.[43]

Concerned about the cost of the house, Mrs. Slater asked Mary to make adjustments. Mary complied, eliminating a few rooms and reducing the size of all that remained. She also commented that Will "… clings to the present plan and prefers to have it smaller than change it…." In the end, the overall scheme remained intact. The house was constructed by Snook & Kenyon; work began in October 1927 and was completed in mid-April 1928. Many of the wooden doors in the house were purchased by Mary during a trip to Spain in the summer of 1927.[44]

Montecito Water District Administration Building
September, 1926, 1929

The Montecito Water District administration building standing today on San Ysidro Road was completed in 1929. It was designed and reworked over a period of years corresponding to the fits and starts of the organization itself and ultimately can only be seen as a greatly compromised version of the designers' intentions.

The Montecito Water District was born of the need to provide water to Montecito; its history can be traced in newspaper articles and minutes from

5.73. *Slater House I, Montecito patio. Photograph by Jessie Tarbox Beals.*

5.74. *Slater House I, Montecito], corridor. Photograph by Jessie Tarbox Beals.*

5.75. *Montecito Water District Administration Building, Montecito (project). Drawing by Ralph Armitage.*

5.76. *Montecito Water District Administration Building, Montecito. Photograph by Jessie Tarbox Beals.*

meetings of the board of directors. Preliminary discussion began in early 1922; several months later, the ubiquitous Francis T. Underhill became president. At first, meetings generally were held in Montecito Hall on East Valley Road. Only in May 1923 is there mention in the minutes of the need to secure an office. The board considered purchasing a two-and-one-half acre site on the northwest corner of the intersection of Valley and San Ysidro roads but the price, $15,000, ultimately was deemed prohibitive.[45]

A solution, for the site if not the office, presented itself three years later. The minutes of July 13, 1926,

report "… a communication from Mr. A. E. Bingham offering as a gift to the District a very desirable piece of land on San Ysidro Road in case the Directors should decide to use it for the benefit of the District." Bingham's offer was accepted and the board followed up in due course:

Director Jameson reported for the Committee on Office Building that arrangements had been made with Mrs. J. O. Craig to furnish sketch plans for the building making it conform as closely as possible with the ideas expressed by Mr. Bingham in connection with the gift

5.77. *Slater House II, Montecito, front elevation. Photograph by Wayne McCall.*

5.78. *Slater House II, Montecito, front elevation*

FOLLOWING PAGES
5.79. *Slater House II, Montecito, hall*

5.80. *Slater House II, Montecito, entrance hall*

of the property on which it is to stand. Mrs. Craig is making good progress and will shortly have the plans ready to submit to the Directors.[46]

The plans were signed by Ralph Armitage and dated September 18, 1926. They show a structure comprised of three wings enclosing a patio. A covered walkway extends the length of one wing. Walls were white plaster; roofs—hipped and shed—were tile. The overall composition had the additive quality of a Spanish farmhouse (Fig. 5.75).

The board's response was quick and decisive: a special meeting was called on September 29 "... to consider the tentative plans and cost estimates submitted by the Architect for the proposed office building.

After consideration it was moved ... that ... (a) The Architect be instructed that the limit of cost of the building has been fixed at Sixteen thousand dollars ($16,000.00) which sum is to include plumbing, electric wiring and fixtures for heating...."

Mary Craig and Armitage followed up with a modified scheme dated October 27, 1926. The covered walkway was eliminated and the roof plan was simplified. The patio remained, laid out with four pools positioned axially and defined by planting; there also was a wall fountain. These plans were accepted by the board, "... subject to such minor modifications and changes as were suggested...." Bids were solicited from five contractors; the estimate of $17, 792.50 submitted by Davidson and Maitland was approved. Then, at a subsequent meeting on December 26, 1926, the board decided against spending the District's funds on an office building and the president was authorized to suspend for the present all such operations.[47]

More than two years passed before the board readdressed the issue of an office building. Finally, on March 12, 1929, Ralph Armitage presented drawings for an entirely new design. The plans were approved and a bid of $10,611.00 from Thompson and Banks was accepted. The building was completed in July.[48]

As constructed, the building is considerably less ambitious than the earlier proposals. It is a simple rectangular mass with a recessed porch on the front elevation, plaster walls and hipped tile roof (Fig. 5.76). None of the amenities first envisioned: patio, pools, wall fountain, were included. Nonetheless, it was awarded third place by the Community Arts Association for buildings completed in 1929. It was described as "Well proportioned and in keeping with surroundings and residential neighborhood."[49]

Mrs. William A. Slater, Sr., House
Montecito, 1929–1930

Two years after completing the house for Mrs. William A. Slater and her son Will on Buena Vista, Mrs. Slater commissioned Mary to design another house nearby on Valley Road. A two-story Mediterranean design with a flat facade, the most extraordinary feature is the full-height entrance hall (Figs. 5.77, 5.78, 5.80). The plan has characteristics in common with the earlier house: a cross corridor running the length of the building and a central patio (Fig. 5.79). The patio is paved in Spanish fashion: pebbles are laid vertically (Figs.5.81, 5.82).

Vision and Reality in the Twenties

The 1920s was the formative decade in the Santa Barbara we know and revere today: a small town with an exceptional number of extraordinary buildings. In addition to many fine houses not generally accessible, there is stylistically coherent civic and commercial architecture: Meridian Studios by George Washington Smith and Carleton Winslow; the Brobdingnagian but nonetheless eye-popping Santa Barbara County Courthouse by William Mooser of San Francisco; the Santa Barbara Biltmore Hotel, Reginald Johnson's masterpiece; Edwards and Plunkett's Arlington Theater with its extravagant forecourt—

where in the history of movie theaters does one find a processional route like this?—and its "Spanish village" interior.

The fervor for architecture based on Hispanic or Mediterranean sources lasted for approximately a decade-and-a-half, 1915 to 1930. In Santa Barbara at the end of the twenties, the accomplishment was celebrated with numerous accolades in the press. At least one went beyond mere superlatives. Ella Winter, perceptive if ever able to detect subversive motives in any endeavor, overcame her "Englishwoman['s] prejudices against America" after observing "the number of experiments, social and artistic, going on in the United States," especially "... the number of communal undertakings that exist in this

commented, "... the Storkes are playing their usual contemptible role. I wish that I were an advertiser so I could have the satisfaction of withdrawing any connection with the paper."[51]

The implication was that Hoffmann and the Community Arts Association, of which he was president, were force-feeding their ideas and goals, however high-minded, on the citizenry. In late 1925, Bernhard and Irene Hoffmann sought the advice of an outsider, Stuart Lake, concerning public opinion of the Association's activities. Lake's findings were reviewed by the board in late January, as recorded in the minutes of two sessions:

There was general discussion as to the differences frequently developing between the community service

5.81   *Slater House II, Montecito, patio detail*

5.82   *Slater House II, Montecito, patio detail*

"individualistic" nation. She found "communism" in California, a "... unique and most interesting experiment in achieving civic beauty ..." spearheaded by Bernard Hoffman [*sic*] who was able "not only to fit buildings to their environment, but to make citizens like it and want to do it themselves.[50]

Ella Winter got it wrong. The natives were not happy; rumblings of discontent can be traced to the design community's assertiveness concerning Craig's designs for De la Guerra Plaza following his death in 1922. After the 1925 earthquake, Hoffmann seized the opportunity to reimagine Santa Barbara architecturally on a much grander scale than before but he and his supporters also realized the need "... to influence as far as possible public opinion...." Hoffmann followed up similarly in September, soliciting the support of Myron Hunt in "... the arousing of public interest in architecture." Also, Hoffmann did not immediately enjoy the support of the press. In a letter to T. Mitchell Hastings written in November he

ideal and that of "High art" and it was generally agreed that the Association suffered loss in community support when the latter ideal was pushed without sufficient consideration of the average persons [*sic*] point of view, knowledge and wishes.[52]

In other words, the townspeople either could not or would not make the distinction between art and profit.

A short time later, in March 1926, the Architectural Advisory Committee was discontinued. Finally in late 1927 Hoffmann resigned both as president and director of the Community Arts Association and as chairman of the Plans Committee. Something of the turmoil is revealed in a letter from another director, William G. Paul, who mentioned "... clash of individual minds and methods ..." but nonetheless praised Hoffmann's administration as "... one of continuous development...."[53]

Though he had lost his grip, Hoffmann continued to trumpet his accomplishment. In February 1929, on the occasion of his being made an honorary member of the Southern California Chapter of the American Institute of Architects, he gave a talk describing work in Santa Barbara after the earthquake:

> I take it to be an expression of satisfaction and appreciation of a larger movement—a cooperation of many people and agencies—to bring about what seems to have been a notable step in the application of the art of architecture, and the principles of community integration and planning.

Discussing the organizational structure rapidly put into place—the Architectural Advisory Committee; the Board of Review, organized by Charles Cheney, best remembered for his work as a city planner in

> ...that distinctive style which for several decades has been successfully growing up in this State, deriving its chief inspiration directly or indirectly from Latin types which developed under similar climatic conditions along the Mediterranean, or at points in Mexico and California.

He also paid homage to Bertram Goodhue who, "In the design of the J. Waldron Gillespie [house]...in Santa Barbara...first developed a new and appropriate design based on historic precedent and existing climatic conditions."[55]

Referring to "the El Paseo group"—Cheney meant Osborne Craig's work; the Anacapa Street addition was not yet complete—among other build-

Palos Verdes; and the Community Drafting Room—Hoffmann observed the cold reality:

> Apparently our public is not ready yet for the type of community co-operation which can be so well brought about by an organization of the type of the Board of Review....
>
> In this commercial day, the layman's interest seems to center more on the number of acres of floor space or the millions of cost than in the artist and the vision which has beautified the community.[54]

Confirmation of the accomplishment of Hoffmann and the others came in a book published in 1929, *Californian Architecture in Santa Barbara*, by H. Philip Staats, an architect from New York. Osborne and Mary Craig's work was featured prominently, his by El Paseo and the Hoffmann House; hers by Logan's Garage (by then identified as Beard's Automobile Co.), the first Slater House, and Mary's own house on Buena Vista. The introduction by Charles H. Cheney was the first to define "Californian Architecture,"

ings Cheney concluded, "Great art is always rare," but he found "... inspiration far beyond the ordinary in a number of Santa Barbara buildings ... the essential quality of beauty, and of charm, which may be said to indicate the soul of a structure." He commented on Mary Craig's "... Beard Motor Company on Carrillo Street, with its generous arches and piers [that were] permitted by the city to project out over the sidewalk because [they] would not interfere with the effective street space needed for traffic. Yet it contributes greatly to the 'city picture,' that picturesque quality unfortunately so rarely sought after or even understood by American communities."[56]

Bernhard Hoffmann gave a copy of the book to Richard Pitman with the note:

> I hope you will accept this copy as a little reminder of the many mutual and pleasant interests which we have had in common in the matter of architectural development in Santa Barbara.[57]

CHAPTER 6

Shifting Tastes

6.01. Harry Drake House, Toro Canyon, Carpinteria, California

FOLLOWING PAGES
6.02. Harry Drake House, Toro Canyon, Carpinteria, California

The early thirties were not as lean for Mary Craig as they were for most architects. She was sustained by commissions for clients whose lifestyles did not change during the Great Depression: houses built locally and reflecting lingering interest in Spanish or Mediterranean influence for Harry Drake and William Spaulding and another responding to new interest in Colonial American design for Amy du Pont in Wilmington, Delaware. There also was a garden pavilion in Montecito for Alfred W. Dieterich and a house for Mr. and Mrs. Andrew Brown in San Marino. Mary worked at the opposite end of the spectrum as well: several residential commissions were very modest. In tune with the zeitgeist, Mary moved away from the Spanish Colonial aesthetic and worked in numerous styles, not unlike many of her contemporaries.

Harry Drake House
Toro Canyon, Carpinteria

With its plaster walls, red tile roof and balcony, the house for Harry Drake is an amalgam of Hispanic influences with a nod to buildings in Monterey so admired by Osborne Craig (Fig. 6.01). There is also playfulness with the roof lines, recalling nothing so much as the garage and gardener's cottage for Mrs. Theodore Sheldon designed by Osborne ten years earlier (Fig. 6.02).

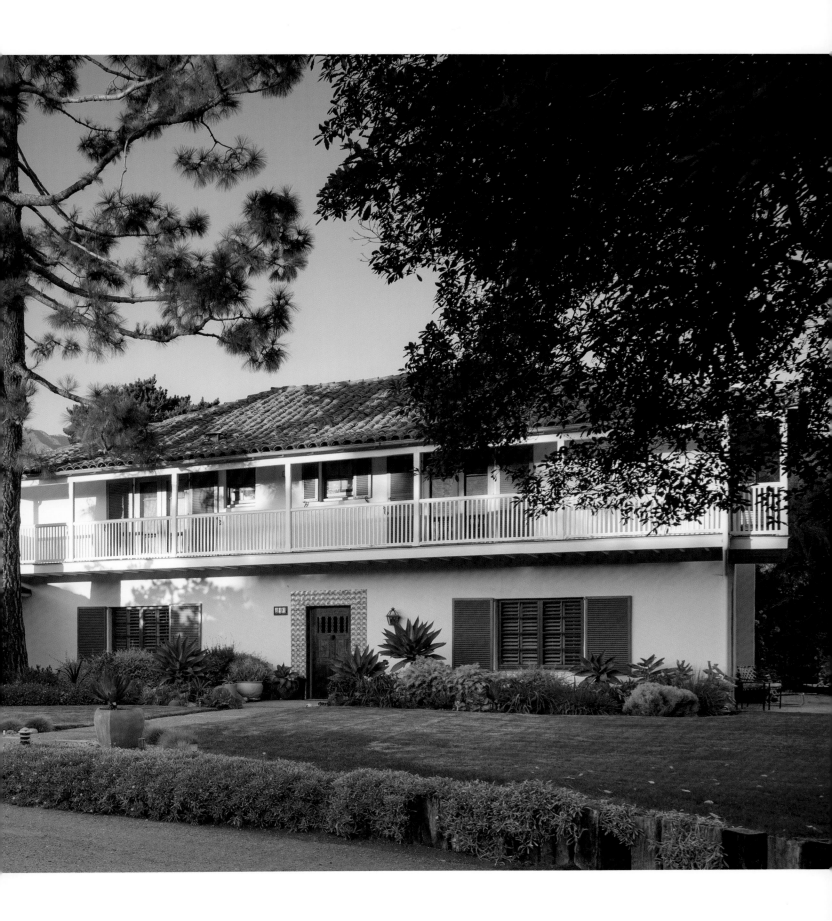

6.05. *Spaulding House, Las Lilas, Montecito, garden*

6.03. *Spaulding House, Las Lilas, Montecito, stair hall*

6.04. *Spaulding House, Las Lilas, Montecito, living room*

William S. Spaulding House, Las Lilas
Montecito, 1930–1931

The Spaulding House belongs with the group of flat-fronted, vaguely Mediterranean, two-story villas that began with the Cramer project in 1924 and continued in later work for E. J. Miley and Ellen Slater. But instead of the axially symmetrical compo-sitions used before, the Spaulding House is entered right of center (*see* pp. 4–5). Though similar in scale to the second Slater House, it has not so interesting a plan: with its grand entrance hall and stair, it seems faintly Georgian in inspiration (Fig. 6.03). The interior spaces are large and relatively neutral (Fig. 6.04). The garden today is the most elaborate of any associated with Mary's work (Figs. 6.05, 6.06).

*6.06. Spaulding House,
Las Lilas, Montecito, garden*

*6.07. Spaulding House,
Las Lilas, Montecito, garden*

Elizabeth and Andrew Brown House
San Marino, 1931

The Brown House was the third Mary Craig designed for the Urmston family. It was commissioned in 1931 as a replacement for a house in Pasadena Mary built for Elizabeth Urmston and enlarged after Miss Urmston married Andrew Brown. The site was comprised of three city lots: two smaller ones side-by-side facing the street and a larger one to the rear on which the house was built, creating a 150-foot setback. Stylistically the house refers neither to a Mediterranean villa nor a Spanish farmhouse but to a type of dwelling built by the grandees of early Califor-

6.08. Dieterich Pavilion,
Montecito

6.09. Dieterich Pavilion,
Montecito

nia, represented by Casa de la Guerra in Santa Barbara and, more pointedly, Casa de las Estudillos in San Diego. Like the prototypes, the Brown House is comprised of three wings, each essentially one room deep, laid out in a U-shaped configuration enclosing a garden overlooked by a porch. But it was not a literal translation: circulation is primarily indoors in contrast to the Early California haciendas in which the porch provided access to all rooms.

Alfred E. Dieterich North Pavilion
Montecito, 1931–1933

The Dieterich Pavilion has a unique pedigree: it is on the grounds of the only house in Santa Barbara—and one of three not on the eastern seaboard—designed by Addison Mizner, the fabled Palm Beach architect. Alfred Dieterich had an ear-

lier house by Mizner in Dutchess County, New York, designed in 1912; the Santa Barbara project dates from 1928. And what a house it is: although they couldn't be more different, along with David Adler's 1916 house for David Jones, it is among the most compelling ever built in Montecito. Mizner's biographer, Donald W. Curl, skirts stylistic description, perhaps a wise decision. It is a theatrically Mediterranean composition with smooth plaster walls embellished with carved Venetian gothic stone door and window surrounds. Inside there are Medievalising groin vaults and carved and deeply coffered ceilings.

Mary's opportunity to work for Dieterich came a few years later. Between 1931 and 1933, she prepared two schemes for a garden pavilion to be placed at the head of a cascade designed by Mizner (Figs. 6.08, 6.09). Instead of responding directly to

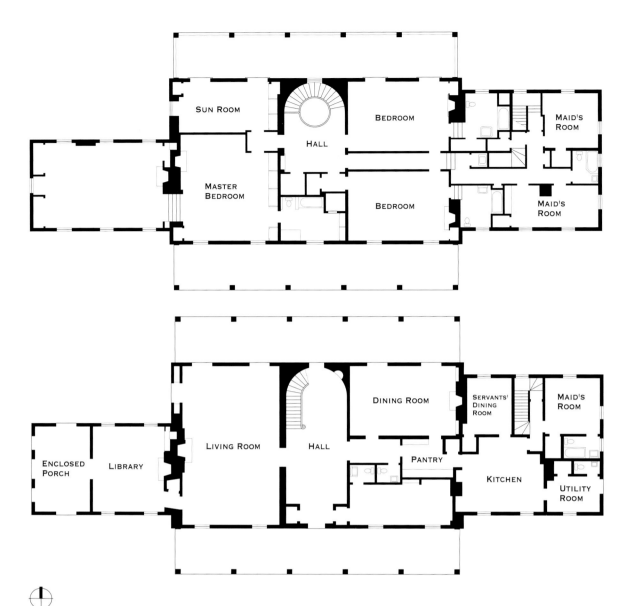

6.13. *Amy du Pont House, Wilmington, Delaware, second floor plan*

6.12. *Amy du Pont House, Wilmington, Delaware, first floor plands*

6.10. *Amy du Pont House, Dauneport, Wilmington, Delaware*

Mizner's design, she turned to Italian Renaissance prototypes for inspiration. Phoebe Cutler has traced the cascade with its double water chains to the Villa d'Este at Cernobbio and the pavilion to twin summer houses at Villa Lante north of Rome.[1] The pavilion serves as a terminus to an axis that extends through the house and central courtyard.

Amy du Pont House
Wilmington, Delaware, 1932–1933

Amy du Pont (1875–1962), a member of the illustrious Delaware clan, began making pilgrimages to Montecito in 1918. Two years later she and her companion, Mrs. W. Mercer Shoemaker, purchased an existing house designed in 1916 by Reginald Johnson and located across Buena Vista from Mary Craig's own house.[2] Seemingly unaffected by the economic turndown, in the early thirties Miss Amy, as she was known familiarly, commissioned her neighbor to design a house for the family nest in and around Wilmington.

The house, ostensibly modeled on Mount Vernon, was a significant stylistic departure for Mary Craig though it was very much in the spirit of the times and the decision to refer to a Colonial Georgian source for inspiration was the client's, not the designer's. Late in life, Mary's daughter recalled that, in preparation, her mother spent a week at Mount Vernon to become familiar with the buildings. She also had several books on Colonial American architecture in her library.

Interest in the Colonial Revival—defined as a largely idealized creation of a national identity and traced by Betty C. Monkman to the 1876 Philadelphia Centennial Exhibition—extended to the highest levels of American society. The most visible early demonstration was the 1902 repair and refurbishment of the White House by McKim, Mead & White under the patronage of Theodore and Edith Roosevelt. Discredited late nineteenth-century exuberance was swept away in favor of the spirit of simplicity and although Charles McKim, who was in charge of the work, described it as a "restoration," there was no attempt to replicate the

original interiors completed by James Hoban in 1800.[3]

The fervor for Colonial design was further fueled by the Rockefeller restoration of Williamsburg that began in 1927. The same year, Eleanor Roosevelt began building adaptations of Early American furniture at Val-Kill, her retreat on her husband's compound at Hyde Park. After a fire in the West Wing of the White House in 1929, Lou Henry Hoover authorized furnishing the rebuilt structure with reproduction American furniture produced in Grand Rapids. The first lady followed up in 1930, commissioning copies of furniture owned by James Monroe for a sitting room at the White House.[4] Perhaps most to the point, the design and construction of Miss Amy's house roughly coincided with her second cousin H. F. du Pont's expansion of his house, Winterthur, nearby as a repository for his preeminent collection of American decorative arts.

The du Pont house conveys the essence—in a Neoclassical sense—not the reality of Mount Vernon. Differences outweigh similarities. Most significantly, Mount Vernon as we know it today is the result of remodeling and enlarging a much smaller house. It grew incrementally over many years and was nearly trebled in size. The du Pont House had not so a site as Mount Vernon (Fig. 6.10). At 8,500 square feet, it is roughly twenty percent larger than the prototype. The most visible similarity is the porch at the rear of the du Pont house that clearly was modeled after the one at Mount Vernon (Fig. 6.11). By contrast, the front elevations of the houses could hardly be more different. Mount Vernon has a flat facade with a central pediment but no porch; du Pont has a porch extending the length of the building. The fenestration of Mount Vernon is irregular, "a product of the accidents of thirty years' growth," to paraphrase Hugh Morrison; the voids of the du Pont house are rigidly symmetrical and in this aspect it more faithfully adheres to Georgian norms.[5] Both houses have appendages to the sides: those at Mount Vernon are connected by covered arcades extending radially from the ends of the building—a Palladian device adopted in the colonies—while the ones at du Pont are simple rectangular volumes with pitched roofs attached

6.11. *Amy du Pont House,*
Dauneport, Wilmington,
Delaware

6.14. *Amy du Pont House,*
Dauneport, Wilmington,
Delaware

6.15. *Jesse Lasky House, Los Angeles*

6.16. *Wetmore Hodges Ranch House, Tucson. Drawing by Richard Pitman.*

directly to the house (Figs. 6.12, 6.13). The only similarity in the plans is the central hall axially bisecting each building (Fig. 6.14). Otherwise, Mount Vernon is laid out mainly as a series of small chambers—the state banquet room, added after 1773, is the only space of any pretention—in contrast with the grander public rooms of the du Pont house. Woodwork inside the house is beautifully detailed in the spirit of Colonial America.

Jesse Lasky House
Los Angeles, 1937

Ted Paramore, Mary Craig's cousin, ostensibly was the catalyst for this project. Moving from New York to Hollywood in 1929, he reinvented himself as a motion picture script writer, working first under Jesse Lasky. He was responsible for the dialogue for four films produced by the Famous Lasky Corp. in 1929–30.[6]

The Lasky House, while gesturing to the contemporary interest in Colonial Revival design, in fact was a response to a specific request from the clients who were enamored of a larger though stylistically similar house on Mapleton Drive in Holmby Hills that the Laskys had rented earlier.[7] The symmetricality of the facade originally was reinforced by an axial entrance from the street defined by gate posts (Fig. 6.15).

Wetmore Hodges Ranch House
Tucson, 1938–39 (project)

A house for Wetmore Hodges (1887–1957) near Tucson, had it been built, would have been Mary's masterpiece. It was designed for a forty-acre ranch on an elevated site five miles north of the city. With mountains as a backdrop, the ranch overlooked

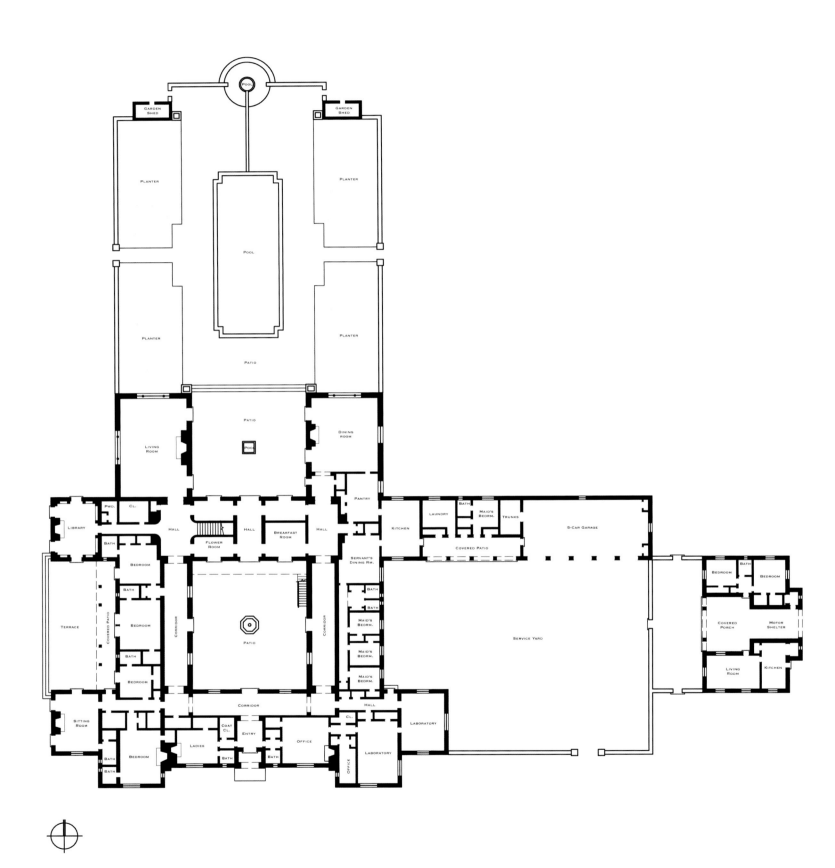

the entire Tucson valley from above and another mountain range in the distance to the south.

Working with Richard Pitman, Mary envisioned a palace for the Southwest. She prepared preliminary plans in 1938; they were reduced in scale the following year though the overall design strategy did not change. There were Spanish Colonial and adobe references and also suggestion of the influence of early modern architecture in California. The central two-story pavilion with its arcaded ground floor and balcony recall the work of Osborne Craig. The appendages suggest analogy with buildings by Irving Gill, particularly his 1914–16 Dodge House with its blocky, unadorned masses (Fig. 6.16). The plan itself with its enclosed central courtyard and second story bridge tying the composition together seems indebted to Frank Lloyd Wright's 1917 Hollyhock House for Aline Barnsdall (Figs. 6.17, 6.18).[8]

The scale of this project, even in its reduced form, was commensurate with the prominence and wealth of the client. Wetmore Hodges had several careers as an industrialist and educator; he also served in the Department of Commerce during the Roosevelt Administration. He is best remembered for his work with Clarence Birdseye in the development of the frozen food business. In 1929, shortly before the economic downturn, he sold his business and the Birdseye process for a staggering $22,000,000.[9]

Though Hodges clearly had the means to do something fine, he ultimately developed qualms of conscience about the financial outlay required to build the house. The project was abandoned.

6.17. Wetmore Hodges Ranch House, Tucson (project), first floor plan

6.18. Wetmore Hodges Ranch House, Tucson (project), second floor plan

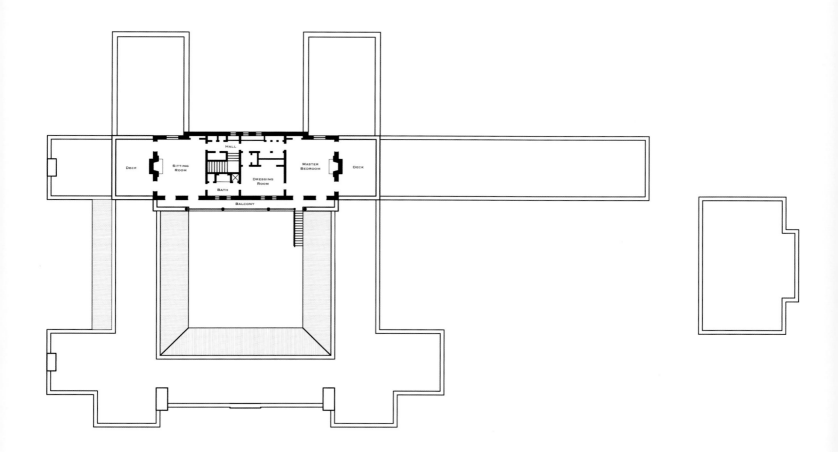

CHAPTER 7

Winding Down

Mrs. James Hayes House
Montecito, 1953–55

Mary Craig faced a special challenge when Belle Hayes (1884–1974) asked her to convert an existing garden pavilion in Montecito into a house. The pavilion originally was designed by Francis Underhill and built for George Owen Knapp on his Arcady compound in 1928. The famous garden was laid out by Charles Gibbs Adams.[1] After Knapp's death, the property was divided; Hayes acquired the structure in 1953.

Formally the pavilion had much in common with the 1902 house designed for James Gillespie, El Fureidis, by Cram, Goodhue & Ferguson; Underhill adapted the style as his own. Client and designer agreed that any alterations should remain within the footprint of the existing structure but that a second story would be added (Fig. 7.01). The formal Greco-roman exterior of the original building would be retained and continued in the addition; the interior was to be "French."[2] Ralph Armitage prepared three distinct schemes for presentation to Mrs. Hayes, though none of these seem to exist today.

Belle Hayes had considerable financial resources at her disposal. Mary's interest was piqued: "It is such a beautiful location and such a challenge to do something very unusual…." Hayes also was a largely absentee client. Drawings were sent to her in Westport, Connecticut, her principal place of residence, and discussed in correspondence and by telephone. There was concern about the "long, narrow living room"; Mary countered that it was "so typically French." She followed up: "After again restudying the big room, the sweep of those windows all the way

around is its great beauty, and I know the furniture will easily fill it. Cutting it up to me destroys the great drama of the house."[3]

There was discussion of the gardens as well. The desire to integrate them into the new work was challenging: they were long neglected. The goal, as in the house itself, was to focus on the incomparable mountain views and the "beautiful sunsets from certain points in the garden" (Fig. 7.02) After much discussion, Mary finally suggested a large lawn that would "… give the place such a clean, well-ordered look, so restful and easy to care for."

There is an aside here on Montecito lifestyle. During the many years she owned the property, Belle Hayes's habit was to travel between New York and Santa Barbara by train; her chauffeur would drive her car across country and meet her. Mrs. George Fox Steedman and Amy du Pont followed a similar routine. Both were interested in horseracing; they went together to Santa Anita from time to time. One of their chauffeurs would drive them to the Santa Barbara airport for the flight to Los Angeles; the other chauffeur would meet and take them to the track.

Mr. and Mrs. David Park Guesthouse
Montecito, 1956

Mary Craig's final work was a guesthouse for Mr. and Mrs. David Park. It was built behind the second Slater House on East Valley Road, which the Parks then owned. The drawings for the project indicate Jean Paul Wolff as an associate. Little information on Wolff has come to light but he surely was the "… excellent new draftsman who was trained at the

Ecole de Beaus Art" [sic] Mary mentioned in a letter to Belle Hayes.

Vaguely Mediterranean, with its flat facade and axial entry, the guesthouse harks back thirty years to Mary's projects for Grace Meeker Cramer and the first Miley House though the scale is more modest. The acreage available provided the opportunity for ample setback from the street and a driveway approach worthy of a much grander building.

The truly notable feature here is Chinese wallpaper in the living room (Fig. 7.03). Hand painted, it depicts folk art images from the Sung Dynasty (960–1279) and probably dates from 1900 to 1920. Production of this wallpaper was highly organized in a manner not dissimilar to tapestry weaving. It was

worked on by a number of specialized assistants who were responsible for specific tasks: one would do the sky; another, the water; and the most skilled artists would depict the people.

Though its provenance is unknown, the paper, mounted on canvas, was installed at the time the building was completed. Mary Craig visited China in 1934 and possibly purchased it then. Typically, owners personalized the paper with painted images of themselves. Likenesses of Mary Craig and Ralph Armitage sitting together can be seen today in the Park wallpaper (Figs. 7.04, 7.05).[4] Stylistically the portraits recall the work of Channing Peake, who Mary Craig knew, but this attribution cannot be confirmed.[5]

7.04. David Park Guesthouse, Montecito, wallpaper detail

7.05. 7.04 David Park Guesthouse, Montecito, wallpaper detail

7.03. David Park Guesthouse, Montecito, living room

ARCHITECTURE

AND SOCIETY

Pamela Skewes-Cox

CHAPTER 8

The Enigmatic Mary Craig

Gender equality in American architecture was rarely, if ever, discussed when Mary McLaughlin Craig became a designer in 1922. Harvard did not allow women to receive degrees in architecture until 1942.[1] Though neither feminist nor activist, Mary Craig unintentionally became one of the first women to break the gender barrier in architecture. While living, she received little public recognition beyond the confines of Santa Barbara. Her self-effacement as a designer, combined with her outgoing nature and love of people, contributed to some extent to her isolation as a professional; most of her friends, many who became her clients, did not have to work. Occasionally seeking out professional advice from architect Lutah Riggs, within architectural circles in Southern California, her only close friends were landscape architects Florence Yoch and Lucile Council.

Mary's success as an architectural designer did not originate with early aspirations or natural drawing talent. She worked without a license, and she had no formal training in architecture or engineering. One hasty sketch demonstrates the simplest of methods she used to work out her ideas with her longtime partner, architect Ralph Armitage, a quiet, often unseen and reserved man who left the talking to Mary. His ability to interpret and transform her ideas into reality rarely let clients down. Nevill Cramer said of the partnership between Mary Craig and Ralph Armitage: "Neither one would have prospered without the other."[2]

Beginning her career at the age of thirty-two, it was a seemingly unexpected decision, there being nothing to indicate such aspirations while married to Osborne. Resolute, she carried on in earnest; referring to her impressive output in a thirty-four year span, one admirer commented "Mary was an engine."[3]

Many years after her death, included with her husband's letters to her, a note was found in her handwriting. It read: "To serve well, and faithfully, some one or some idea, is a great privilege in life."

Mary Craig became an accomplished designer through her natural good taste, sense of beauty, and understanding of the need for practicality in day-to-day living. Space in her houses was rarely trivialized; there was a reason for everything. In the end, surely her inspiration to become a designer was rooted in her six-year relationship with James Osborne Craig, whose artistry and talent she absorbed and understood well. Following his death she wasted no time in crafting what she considered that "privilege"; her most successful houses represent the best of his vision and ideals.

Mary Craig was an enigma, whose outer appearance and mannerisms suggesting a meek Montecito socialite mingling with the rich cloaked a life of richness and intellect. She was social, but she was not a "socialite" in the conventional sense. Highly disciplined in her creative life as a designer, she was unpretentious regardless of whose company she was in. Alone much of her life, but spiritually fulfilled through her strong faith, she lived courageously, especially at times of crisis. She drew unabashedly on and enjoyed sharing her modest beginnings in Deadwood, Dakota Territory, named by the earliest prospectors for the burned timber above the gulch and situated amidst a striking western landscape. Deadwood's unique standing in the American West and its entry into the twentieth century left an indelible mark on the life of Mary Craig. One colleague

characterized her western experience as "the source of her original brave spirit and fine appreciation of humor, which was so strong and vivid." It was also her moral compass, a way to differentiate herself; to her friends it was a likeable trait.[4]

Though Deadwood boasted handsome Victorian houses, two in which Mary lived, overall it was not a pretty town. But it was colorful; its cast of characters, with names the likes of Swill Barrel Jimmy, Deadwood Dick, Cold Deck Johnny, Slippery Sam,

8.03. Miley House I, Montecito, chimney

and Mineral Jack, conjured up the essence of a western mining town. They offered a unique counterpoint to the many memorable people who crossed her path later, including Leopold Stokowski, Greta Garbo, Hollywood's Jesse and Bessie Lasky, and writer Edmund Wilson.

Mary grew up to become naturally outgoing and, by necessity, frugal and industrious. Family photographs and journals reveal the origins of her sociability: summer picnics; dances; evening rides by horseback; camping and day trips to Buffalo Gap and White Rocks for swimming and tennis and, in the winter, sleigh rides; theatrical productions; and dinner and costume parties. It was a rare camaraderie born of circumstance, and one which shaped her adult life.

Her Deadwood journals indicate a gregarious spirit. She could hitch up a horse-drawn buggy and drive it as well as any man, and she had great stamina for long rides into the mountains on her horse Judd. More often than not she was accompanied by an assortment of family friends, young and old. Whether camping, climbing the dramatic rock formations at Sylvan Lake, or falling off her horse into an icy stream, little held her back. Such backbone, acquired from an early age and an anchor during times of unrest, remained with her all her life.

Mary's father and grandfather, both lawyers and highly articulate and principled men, made significant contributions to Deadwood's development. Through their example Mary had time to learn from and absorb this life of grit and gain. She was fiercely proud of these years; when her childhood friend, Grace Jones Hart, came to live in Santa Barbara in the 1950s she expressed to Mary her great discomfort being surrounded by such affluence. Sensing her insecurity, Mary responded with a gentle reminder, "Now Grace, you must always remember we come from the top drawer of Deadwood."[5]

She did indeed love to drop names, but the names Golden Reward, Montezuma, Whizzer, Wasp, Grizzly Gulch, and Big Nellie—the names of the load claims in the vicinity of the great Homestake Mine of Deadwood she had known since childhood—had as much cachet for her (provided she was in the proper company) as any person of title or fame. In social settings, she was a skilled conversationalist but, modest by nature, she rarely spoke of her own accomplishments. She could hold her own in any discussion about geology, the technicalities of the extraction of gold, and the intricacies of mineral and water rights. Names of mining claims also had far more appeal to her than the names of Montecito's large properties, even though she designed houses for many of their affluent owners. Mira Flores, La Parra Grande and Casa Aleli evoked romance and wealth. Yet Mary modestly named her own property One Acre, even after transforming her small board-and-batten cottage into a house of comfortable elegance and handsome simplicity.

Her daughter described her as fully embracing everything that interested her; "whether in architecture or her mining interests, the greater the challenge, the more appeal it had."[6] When Mary first arrived in Southern California at the age of twenty-four, her upbringing, fine education and pride for her Deadwood roots made her a confident young woman possessing modest poise and a rare gentility. Pretty and impressionable, she may have been the momentarily swept away socialite in the days before meeting Osborne Craig, but by the time of his death, her priorities had shifted.

Her early connections to Santa Barbara society did in fact result in many important commissions, but they did not define her friendships, which were genuine, and far from shallow. She lived through a remarkable and transformative period in American history, witnessed by two world wars, the rise of Hollywood, the Great

Depression, the shift to modern art and architecture, political unrest, a literary renaissance, and the evolution of the American city and the modern age. People's lives, almost by necessity rather than choice, took on a particular richness of experience, which through friendship, Mary Craig had the good fortune to share.

Many in Mary's circle were "born retired"; the sons and daughters of gifted and resourceful individuals who defined the entrepreneurial spirit of America at the turn of the last century.[7] Others were writers, artists, diplomats, expatriates, political activists, exiles, and actors. Discerning, but never elitist, she loved the company of interesting people.

There was Hollywood's fun, kind and unpretentious Walter Pidgeon, who on his visits to Montecito to see friends, often stopped in for a cocktail. Mary came to know and deeply respect brothers Zourab and Nicholas Tchkotoua, Georgian princes who were forced to flee their homeland in 1921 and begin life over as exiles. Arriving in California in the 1940s, Zourab, an artist, married San Francisco's Virginia Hobart Baldwin, who, with her late husband Charles A. Baldwin, built Claremont, the grand house in Colorado Springs designed by Osborne Craig's early employer, Thomas MacLaren. While living in Santa Barbara, writer Nicky Tchkotoua published his internationally acclaimed novel *Timeless*, which Mary did her utmost to promote. Then there were her friends the Count and Countess Pecci-Blunt, whose avant-garde lives in Paris in the 1930s with Man Ray and Salvador Dali, and later years in Santa Barbara, were as intriguing as the origin of their names. Known for her special talent in instinctively understanding the chemistry of a successful dinner party, Mary enjoyed the mingling of such friends whose provocative conversations offered up both humor and serious reflection.

She broadened her life with music, the arts, literature, and travel made possible through the generosity of an aunt and several close friends. But she knew herself well enough to be her own person and never forget her humanity. Conversations with writer Austin Strong and his mother Isobel Field, step-grandson and step-daughter of Robert Louis Stevenson (whom Osborne Craig held in high regard), or with her plumber, with whom she would listen to and discuss opera when he came to the house, intrigued her equally.

While growing up in Deadwood, among her greatest pleasures, shared with her father, were trips by horseback to the rudimentary family cabin in Spearfish Canyon, where conveniences were few, and roughing it came easily (Fig. 8.02). Harking back to that experience where one could be content with very little, Mary purchased property in the Santa Ynez Valley in the 1930s, and built a simple cottage on property overlooking the Cyril Lamb ranch. Nevill Cramer wrote of it, "The only house I've thought of which combines charm with extreme economy of construction is a house Mary Craig built in Santa Ynez in the thirties, which I've always loved. It's … farm-like and … livable."[8] It was her Deadwood background, which in leaving its mark

gave her that ability to be practical, basic and economical. Yet in designing for others, she could make a space come alive with attractive antiques, patios and courtyards with articulated walls, pleasing roof lines, gates, arched entranceways and fanciful chimneys, all melding into one overall effect of good taste through simplicity (Figs. 5.83–8.05).

Mary's father insisted on an education equal to, if not better than, his, which she received at the progressive Convent of the Visitation in Washington,

8.04. Miley House I, Montecito, garage

D.C., between the ages of fourteen and twenty. William McLaughlin wanted his older daughter to become a lawyer, which may have come to be had he not died at the age of forty-nine, soon after Mary graduated from the convent. From the time she was very small, captivated by and particularly attentive to her father's business dealings, his teachings in all aspects of life were at the heart of Mary's skills as a shrewd business woman. Her geologist friend Robert Livermore, wishing he had Mary's "knack" for making money, wrote to her in 1937: "You have both talent and imagination and put them to good use, hence deserve your rewards. I ought to add you have persistence amounting to genius, which perhaps is the strongest weapon!"[9]

Though her academic goals in her six years at the convent were ambitious and earned her the highest and most coveted award offered by the school, the Loretto Medal, in later years she tried and failed to get an architectural license.[10] Receiving honors in both algebra and physics while at school, Mary's quick mind was more than capable of absorbing and recollecting the information she needed in the areas of engineering. But according to her daughter, it was the one area of study she felt she could not or wished not to master.

For a woman who had not been raised with servants and by necessity learned to be very capable on the home front, Mary's trepidation by 1920, and throughout her adult life, over basic home skills is curious. Osborne's letters written soon after the birth of their child in 1921 show a man who was the more experienced and comfortable in matters to do with babies and general domestic life. Accepting Mary's shortcomings, he patiently offered advice about household linens, how to pack vegetables for a trip, and schedules for breast-feeding.

While a student in Washington, D.C., and in her twenties, Mary was smitten by fashion, but later throwing off all interest in feminine fineries, she was happiest rummaging around the junkyards of Santa Barbara and Los Angeles searching for corbels, marble mantels and old doors. She laid her own brick path leading to the entranceway of her house and designed a patio for the second Slater House paved in the Spanish manner with stones laid vertically, placing her initials MC at one edge (*see* Fig. 5.81).

Following Osborne's death, Mary knew she had to support herself. Though friends urged her to find employment in a dress shop, she made the decision to carry on with her husband's legacy; no one could persuade her otherwise. She had an innate sense of beauty, yet there was little of it in hardscrabble Deadwood. And when one considers that her exposure to architecture was so brief, it is remarkable to think that she had the confidence to launch this career so soon.

Mary Craig's credibility was perceived straight away, by both men and women. In her first major project, the Campbell Ranch House, she found herself partnered with one of the country's most colorful and publicly acknowledged male chauvinists, financier Joseph Leiter, brother of Nancy Leiter Campbell and son of Levi Zeigler Leiter, co-founder of Chicago's retail empire Marshall Field and Company. Mary had known Joe Leiter since 1908, when he married her school friend Juliette Williams. Mrs. Campbell left all matters of the house construction in his hands; correspondence between Craig and Leiter shows a relationship of mutual respect and total absence of the usual Leiter condescension.

Driven by genuine curiosity from an early age, Mary did indeed have a fondness for meeting people of reputation. Describing earlier times in Deadwood and the Hearsts' involvement with Homestake, she wrote:

> For many years about 51 percent of the stock was held by the Hearst family. After the death of Mr. George

Hearst, his widow, Mrs. Phoebe Hearst, personally became extremely interested, not only in the mine but in the miners and their welfare. Long ago before it was fashionable or the law insisted, in Lead, where the mine is located, she herself built kindergartens for the miners' children and recreation rooms for the miners, a hospital, a general store where the miners and their families could trade with economy. She often came to the Black Hills. I still remember her lovely, gentle face, her charming manner.[11]

But Mrs. George Hearst's visits to Deadwood were as intriguing to Mary as meeting up with the disheveled prospector Panner Joe while on horseback in her beloved Black Hills; she forgot neither one.

Her intent when she dropped names was not to inflate her own ego, of which she had little, but to give her an advantage when she needed it. In the 1930s when traveling by train between Santa Barbara and the East Coast, if a stateroom was not available Mary Craig would call on her friend and onetime railroad president Charlie Perkins to pull some strings, most times successfully. In giving a court deposition in 1938 in regard to her lawsuit against the Homestake Mine and wishing to impart her connections to important people, her testimony made mention of "Lady du Pont." Amy du Pont, her down-to-earth neighbor and friend, a renegade du Pont who cared nothing for pretension, spent many a late night with Mary in the game of canasta. Mary's cousin Ted Paramore and Amy shared a mutual affection for the telling of naughty stories (which Amy kept in a file and ordered to be destroyed upon her death).[12] Amy du Pont would have been the first to take umbrage with anyone calling her Lady du Pont. Yet she would have applauded Mary for using the title under such circumstances.

Mary Craig's one published writing on architecture which appeared soon after Osborne's death is informed and confident, yet over her lifetime she left little else behind in print about the subject.[13] This void was filled with a lifetime of passionate interest, knowledge and writing concerning what had been central to her life growing up in Deadwood, the great Homestake Mine, for over one hundred years the largest gold mine in North America. From the time of her father's death in 1911 she managed her family's mining claims, and bought and sold new ones for speculation. In crafting her syndicates she almost always turned to friends and acquaintances.

Mining historian Robert Sorgenfrei considered Craig a skilled communicator, not only amongst academics and corporate leaders, but amongst mine workers with no power and little education. Two such men, the Stankovitch brothers, spending a lifetime in the mines, turned to Craig following their retirement for help in selling their mining interests. Mary was well aware it would be their only source of income in their last years and she worked hard and successfully on their behalf. She spared nothing to find the country's leading mining lawyers and geologists to advise her. Being both personal and business in nature, Mary's Homestake letters span many years and most notably attest to the qualities of her character.[14]

Homestake president Edward H. Clark remained Mary's friend for years, even after she sued his powerful company for four-and-a-half million dollars in 1938 for breach of trusteeship. Mary's stockholder friends said later that they were "surprised and elated to think that anyone would have the courage to take exception with the great Homestake." Mary lost the case, but Clark, humbled by her intellect, courage and principles, said to her later in his life, "I wish I had known you earlier and had had you in my organization!" Over time Mary's syndicates paid small gains, but she was never able to secure the "great bundle of gold bricks" she wrote of having someday. As her mining papers attest, it was not from lack of trying.[15]

After Osborne's death, Mary Craig received two proposals of marriage, one from Charles Perkins, the other from William Slater, Jr. Both men, whose charm and affluence would have made her financially secure and in all likelihood very happy, were divorced. Deeply conflicted, she was left with two choices: to decline based on the rigid doctrines of the Catholic Church which forbid a woman to marry a divorced man, or to reject her faith for longed-for companionship and financial security. Mary's faith, unwavering since her conversion to Catholicism at the age of sixteen, prevailed. Both Charles Perkins and Will Slater remained close friends, and Mary remained a Catholic, but not a pious one; she questioned religious doctrine for the rest of her life. She was known to say: "Religions are like languages, and I prefer the language of Catholicism."[16]

Though she never remarried, Mary had a long reach in her friendships with men, even late in life. Several held her more serious attentions, including Boston's James Lawrence Sr., whom she had met at Dark Harbor, Maine, in the late 1930s, and Santa Barbara author Cameron Rogers. Her long and comfortable friendship with conductor Leopold Stokowski was notable.

Living with an aunt in the East in the 1930s, Mary met Stokowski while he was conductor of the Philadelphia Orchestra. He attended parties at her aunt's Paoli house, which saw frequent gatherings of Philadelphia notables, artists and musicians. While working in Hollywood, Stokowski's greatest joy was to retreat to his Montecito ranch house, not far from Mary's and built into the rugged terrain of Toro Canyon. He often wrote to her of his impending visits to his "camp"—known as The Monastery—and his wish to see her. During these times, just the two of them would spend the day in the Santa Ynez Valley house, taking particular pleasure in what he referred to as their "bummeln." In 1940, while organizing the "Cruise of the All American Youth Orchestra to South America," he wrote to her: "It is our wish to have as passengers a few of the most interesting personalities from each community in the United States—representatives of intelligent Americans who will give a favorable impression in the various ports where we stop. Would you be willing … to receive a representative from the American Express, and to give him a little advice as to who might be the most appropriate persons from Santa Barbara who might have the wish, the means, and the leisure to go on the Cruise?"[17] Though she had neither the time nor the money to go herself, Mary had no trouble finding those who did. Respecting her acuity, Stokowski was also fond of her ability to be discreet with his indiscretions; sometimes calling on her at her house in the company of Greta Garbo and later, Gloria Vanderbilt. Instructions had been given to invite no one else.

In the early 1950s, after her daughter's marriage to Bennet Skewes-Cox and the arrival of three granddaughters, Mary's attentions turned to family.[18] Then in her mid-sixties, her architectural work had tapered off, yet she was still very much engaged with life. Ever since a bad car accident in 1937 left her in the hospital for two weeks, driving made her nervous. Most Sundays she walked to mass at Mt. Carmel Church, and often made the longer walk to the Miramar Hotel to meet friends for lunch. Having taken up again significant speculations in the Homestake Mine, she sent letters off to presidents Eisenhower and Kennedy urging them to raise the price of gold. Mary Craig was able to live by much the same principle she had set for herself years earlier: "I am happiest when I am busy."[19]

8.05. Miley House II, Montecito, passageway through service wing

Found with her papers after she died was an essay about the last days of the Spanish-born philosopher, George Santayana (1863–1952). As was her habit for preserving what gave meaning to her life, she typed it out. Santayana's words, "I practice the sort of wisdom I have always thought important: taking everything good-humoredly but with a grain of salt," echoed Mary's approach to her own life. In a letter of condolence after her death, Beth Gates wrote, "She was really quite the 'grande dame' in many of her ways—yet always able to laugh with you and sometimes at herself in a most delightful way."[20]

Mary never amassed great wealth. Certainly she was comfortable, and by tastefully making the most of what she did have, she presented an aura of wealth. In her adult life she lived by the dictum of her friend Stokowski: "The greatest art of all is the art of living."[21] After Osborne's death, energetically, hopeful, and without pretense, she did in fact define her life, not by wealth, but by artful living and friendship. Though the luxuries and opportunities that she and her daughter found at certain times were made possible by the generosity of others, Mary Craig found a secure lifestyle by her own wits and hard work. As a single woman she had to face many challenges on her own: a male-dominated profession, periods of debilitating depression, deaths of young friends, the failure to get her architectural license, and unsatisfied hopes for

8.06. *Miley House II, Montecito, second-floor hall*

8.07. *Miley House II, Montecito, corbel detail*

8.08. *Miley House II, Montecito, fireplace in office*

8.09. *Miley House II, Montecito, second floor stair hall*

financial gain. But indomitable, she knew how to get on with life.

At the end of her life she still relied on frugality, though she let her guard down a bit when a few years before she died she uncharacteristically purchased from her friend and neighbor Captain Ernest Crawford May a black Jaguar with red leather seats and mahogany pull-down tables. Her Filipino housekeeper, Benito Abeñis, donning a tattered chauffeur's cap, drove her to the Little Town Club or the Coral Casino to have lunch with friends. Mary, a mere five feet tall, sitting in the back seat, and Benito, whose head barely reached the top of the steering wheel, created the impression of a moving automobile without any occupants in it at all. Mary herself would

have been the first to admit that she took great pleasure in this illusion of wealth, which, she would acknowledge without the slightest bitterness, had escaped her grasp all her life.

After their marriage, Osborne wrote to Mary, "I am not feeling very fit due to too much labour with the whims of the very rich—I'm glad I'm poor—in some ways and on some days." Osborne Craig unquestionably was the catalyst which released Mary from earlier superficial aspirations, including wealth. After his death she worked diligently to increase her coffers, but it never consumed her. She wrote to a good friend in 1935: "Money is ephemeral, but friendship and loyalties are real; without them life has no quality."[22]

CHAPTER 9

Mary McLaughlin's Deadwood *1889–1913*

Mary McLaughlin's life began in the late nineteenth-century gold mining town of Deadwood, Dakota Territory. Established in 1876, the primitive mining camp soon became the heart of the Black Hills gold rush. Main Street ran the length of a long, narrow valley defined by steep cliffs, and was lined with hastily constructed wooden commercial buildings. Like all frontier towns, Deadwood's streets were unpaved and lined with wooden sidewalks. Even after the arrival of the automobile, horse-drawn carriages remained a major form of transportation. The town's rough-and-tumble history is kept alive today by the names of Calamity Jane and Wild Bill Hickok, the notorious lawman, gunslinger and gambler.

This Deadwood that lives in infamy—indeed makes it a mecca for tourists—is not the town Mary knew. After burning in 1879, its rebuilding coincided with a transition from gold rush to steady mining under the shadow of the great Homestake Mine. The imposing new buildings in brick and stone, some with fine Victorian flourishes, reflected the recent wealth of the community. As in many such frontier outposts, there was a small professional class to which Mary's family belonged. Her grandfather, Daniel McLaughlin, having earlier roamed the western states as a lawyer, arrived in Deadwood from Cheyenne with his wife and children in 1877. Deadwood's first elected mayor, he was appointed to the state's Supreme Court in 1889.

Mary's father, William Law McLaughlin, was fourteen when he left for Washington, D. C., to pursue his academic career at Georgetown Preparatory, followed by Georgetown College where he received his law degree in 1884. Returning to Deadwood, he entered his father's law office as a defense attorney and mining consultant for Homestake.[1] Soon after marrying Sarah Patterson Clary, a native of Monroeville, Ohio, the McLaughlins had two children: Mary was born on May 28, 1889 in the house of her grandparents on Williams Street (Fig. 9.01). Her sister Helen was born in 1891.[2] At the age of ten, Mary's family moved into a new house several doors down. Many years later Mary Craig recalled the birth of her father in the back of a covered wagon along the Snake River in 1862:

> It is a long time ago that my grandmother [Ellen McLaughlin] told me about crossing the plains in a covered wagon—their destination California. They traveled in a train of fifty wagons—There was constant fear of Indians in those days. The train ahead of them was massacred by Indians: the people of my grandmother's & grandfather's train had to stop and bury their bodies. It was primeval country, beautiful beyond description. My father was born on that trip—her first child.[3]

Mary and her family lived in Forest Hill, an area terraced out of a cliff overlooking the town. The music of the dance and gambling halls below was within easy earshot. William McLaughlin, a devout Catholic, was pensive, tall and broad in stature and an affectionate and sensitive father. Not hesitant to express his emotions in letters to family, he was prone to periods of deep melancholy. Sarah McLaughlin, principled and reflective like her husband, read a great deal and played the piano two or three hours each day. Taking a dim view of the local priests who turned a blind eye to the drinking, gambling and prostitution amongst many of Deadwood's residents, Sarah would not allow her children to be

9.02. *May Martin Tillinghast, 1907, with her only child, Mary Morgan, who died of pneumonia at the age of seven.*

raised Catholic. Writing of "the calmness with which she viewed the world" and "her invariably sympathetic and cheerful attitude," her grandson George Martin recalled that "she thought the state of the nation grave whenever Republicans were in power. She occasionally smoked a cigarette, mainly to be sociable, but with such repugnance that her outspoken nephew, Ted Paramore, once told her she was holding it as if it were a rattlesnake."[4]

The Homestake Mine was Deadwood's raison d'être. As a young girl, Mary recalled the "constant excitement" of the early days:

> I spent many happy hours riding that beautiful country with my father from mine to mine. Then came the big strike—The Western Federation of Miners demanded they be the only union in the Black Hills. The miners said they would have only a local union. All the mines and mills were shut down and then ensued a fight that lasted over two years, all the operators combined in the fight. I often went with my father in a sleigh to these treacherous mining camps, our pair of black ponies scarcely able to get over the all but impassible roads those bitter cold nights. My father again and again exhorted his men to return to work and leave the Federation of Miners. They were a treacherous lot and ... Homestake had a hundred Pinkerton detectives on guard day and night. At length, the strike was ended, but it broke my father's heart. He never regained his health after this strain.

Absorbing her father's professional acumen, mining captivated and challenged Mary for the rest of

her life. She called it "a fascinating game ... bred in my bones."[5]

In the years leading up to 1913, when Mary moved to Pasadena, Deadwood evolved from a rugged and inhospitable town of "horse thieves, claim jumpers, road agents, painted ladies, and slick ... gamblers to a middle class railroad town." It was bustling and noisy with the usual contrast of the more and less affluent. In one part of town there were the handsome houses of the mining managers and professionals. On the other side were the workers' shacks and Chinese encampments along stream beds and gullies filled with waste products and tailings of the mines. In the 1890s Mary had glimpses of the legendary Calamity Jane whose earlier adventures were well known to her parents and her grandparents. Years later Mary took great pleasure in recalling those stories to her Montecito friends.[6]

Mary's childhood was carefree, and photographs show a happy and confident child, always in the company of friends. From the time they were very young, William McLaughlin mentored and instilled in his daughters an appreciation for writing, literature and the arts. Mary's education at the local elementary school was supplemented with tutoring in French and piano.

In the fall of 1903, then fourteen, Mary entered the Georgetown Visitation Convent in Washington, D. C., adjacent to and professionally aligned with her father's alma mater, Georgetown College. Founded in 1799, the convent had the distinction of being one of the oldest schools for young girls and women in the country.[7] Its rigorous and diverse liberal arts curriculum with an emphasis on music (Mary became proficient as a harpist) provided ballast for the rest of her life. Students were from all faiths, and the school's ecumenical approach engrained in Mary a lifelong interest in theology. Influenced by her father and a close relationship with convent teacher Sister Claude Agnes Keedy, at age fifteen she converted to Catholicism.

The Philadelphia Years, 1903–1909

Mary's six years at the convent were the equivalent of a progressive college education, which, combined with her western values, imparted valuable lessons in tolerance, gracious competitiveness, and modesty. Her close friendships with young women from all parts of the country opened her eyes to affluence and society. At the same time the formative influence of her mother's first cousin, Philadelphian May Martin Tillinghast cannot be overstated. Many of the old Philadelphia families were in Aunt May's orbit, and while on her school holidays, the petite and vivacious young girl from Deadwood was more than eager to fit in and embrace the privileged lifestyle. (May's second marriage in 1912 to Edward Roberts III, an affluent bachelor and lawyer, later afforded Mary Craig many opportunities she would otherwise not have had.) Cultivating many good friendships during this time, for the rest of Mary's life Deadwood remained not only a backdrop, but an anchor, in all of her relationships.

Deadwood, The Last Years, 1909–1913

After graduation with honors in June 1909—she was not only valedictorian, but played her harp for guest Cardinal James Gibbons—Mary returned to Deadwood. She was twenty years old. With frequent trips to the family cabin in Spearfish Canyon, a deep, narrow gorge thirty miles on horseback from Deadwood, Mary's skill at fishing and cutting wood came easily to her. Nearby were the cabins of close friends, the Masons, Martins and Adams, providing ample opportunity for social gatherings. Billy McLaughlin had always found the canyon restorative; weakened by diabetes, he spent his last days at the cabin in the summer of 1911. After slipping into unconsciousness, he was taken back to Deadwood where he died at home on July 28th. He was forty-nine years old. Considered "one of the most talented and successful legal practitioners of the West," McLaughlin was "recognized … as a lawyer of profound learning, possessed of a trained and orderly mind and brilliantly accomplished in the qualities that bring distinction" to the practice of law. Seth Bullock was one of many noted citizens to serve as honorary pallbearer at his funeral.[8]

Among letters of condolence was an especially comforting one from Mary's friend Harry Snead:

I know Mary dear just how it all looks to you—how uncertain the future seems and how dreary the place which has been the scene of most of your good times, but later on it will clear up and the place and associations will bring just sweet memories of one who most surely left you the greatest of legacies, an honored name. In a few months the sorrow will be replaced by your pride in what he did for others and a gratitude for what he did for you.[9]

The void left by her father's death was filled soon enough by attentive letters from various young men, including Harry Gantz of Deadwood and beaus Mary had met in the east through her cousin Jim Paramore.

In the fall of 1912 Mary took a job teaching kindergarten in nearby Trojan, a steep six-mile wagon ride from Deadwood and famous for its Gold Mountain Mine. She stayed until January 1913. Sarah McLaughlin, wishing to escape the bitter cold of the Black Hills, opted to spend the winter with her daughters and mother-in-law in Pasadena. Many years later Mary wrote: "We left in January. It took two engines to pull us out of snow drifts and when we reached Pasadena my mother decided never to return to live in South Dakota." After her exposure to East Coast urbanity and Pasadena's sophistication, Deadwood has to have seemed a backwater. Yet Mary never really turned her back on those "gay, glamorous days in the Black Hills," or the close friends she knew there, keeping them always a counterpoint to her life in California.[10]

9.03. *Mary McLaughlin and friend with the family dog, Buster, Deadwood, ca. 1908*

Santa Barbara

The Anacapa Illusion

Santa Barbara ... lacked substance and reality ... an anacapa illusion of mountains, seashore and channel; of Andalusian architecture, polo fields, tennis courts, golf courses, hotels, costumed festivals, and ceremonial pageants.... Santa Barbara stood in danger of having themed itself into irreality ... a formula for idle days ... an easy agenda of dilettantism, sunbathing, dinner parties, drinking and sexual intrigue while somewhere out there in the rest of America a Depression rages.[1]

Mary McLaughlin, her mother Sarah, grandmother, and sister Helen settled in a house at 1190 South Pasadena Avenue.[2] At the time, Pasadena, the "Crown City," and Santa Barbara were the social meccas of Southern California. Mary and Helen entered Pasadena society almost immediately as noted in newspaper society columns. For Mary, the acquaintance of the very socially prominent Mrs. James Nelson Burnes and her extended family was of critical importance. However the siren call was not Pasadena but Santa Barbara, one hundred miles to the north; some four hours by train and a little more by motor.[3] Since 1912 the permanent home of her relatives, the affluent and colorful Paramore family, Mary visited often between 1913 and 1918. Santa Barbara soon became her de facto home.

Mrs. Edward E. Paramore (Mary Tuttle Clary) was the twin sister of Mary's mother. Expatriates from St. Louis, the Paramores and sons Jim and Ted, Jr., exerted a decisive influence on Mary, assuring her swift entry into Santa Barbara society. Edward Everett Paramore (1861–1928) inherited his money from his father who became rich after the Civil War conceiving and managing the Cotton Belt Railroad that linked St. Louis and Texas. After working briefly for his father following his graduation from Yale, Paramore sought out a life of greater contrast and roamed the country, investing his money and his labor in mining, rice mills in Louisiana, and land development in the Red River area of Arkansas. He lived for weeks at a time on the Louisiana bayou in his riverboat, the *Oie Sauvage* and, as a skilled yachtsman, sailed the world in boats of his own design.

Mrs. Paramore embraced Mary like a daughter, yet she and Mary's mother were dissimilar in all ways. Sarah lived sparingly in the rugged culture of Deadwood. Her sister, by contrast, basked in the limelight of St. Louis society into which her husband had been born. Mrs. Paramore is remembered as very feminine, a prima donna with bountiful red hair who lived for bridge, teas, parties, trips to Europe and her two sons. Opinionated about social matters, vain and politically conservative, she lived in her own self-centered world of morality, fine clothes and social standing. While she tempted her niece with superficial aspirations, Uncle Ed taught Mary McLaughlin what it meant to be human.

Mary's cousins offered up similar differences. Jim's conservative world was guided by all that accompanied upper class values: polo, travel to Europe and endless entertaining. Sharing his bachelor life with Mary while they were both in Santa Barbara, or in long narrative letters written to her from afar, he took on the role of older brother and encouraged her in the pursuit of his privileged Yale and Harvard friends.

The appeal of her younger cousin Ted led Mary down a less predictable path. Creative, impulsive and versatile, Ted called Santa Barbara his "valley of happiness." Later he liked to say it was "a sunny place for shady people."[4] In fact, though he returned to Santa Barbara often, he lived and worked most of his adult life first in New York as a freelance writer, playwright, and theater and book critic, and later in Hollywood, where he moved in 1929 and reinvented himself as a motion picture scriptwriter. For the next eighteen years he was affiliated with Hollywood's

10.02. *Paramore House, Montecito, 1924*

major producers.[5] It would be Ted who secured Mary's commision for a house for his one-time boss, producer Jesse Lasky, and for a smaller project for Hollywood author and screenwriter Ernest Pascal.

The observations of writer, social critic, and journalist Edmund Wilson (1895–1972) offer insight into the Paramore family circle and Santa Barbara society. Wilson and Ted Paramore were two years apart at the Hill School and becoming fast friends, lived together after college in New York. As a guest of the Paramores in 1924, often accompanied by Mary Craig, Ted and their friend Margaret Canby, Wilson recalled the Spanish-style house that "had been full of gaiety, highballs and sunlight," and the upstairs sun porch where he, Ted and Mr. Paramore often gathered (Fig. 10.02). Wilson particularly admired E. E. Paramore, who in a tribute after his death characterized him as "a personality of singular interest and charm," a "raconteur" and "citizen of the world."[6]

Like everyone in the family, Wilson was privy to Uncle Ed's masterful storytelling with his "most extraordinary gift of mimicking the way people talked," imparting "the local accents and dialects of every part of the United States." He saw people's lives carrying, in Wilson's words, a "kind of beauty"

which, without the slightest bit of malice, he could impart effortlessly and richly.[7] Naturally outgoing, and without prejudice or airs, Paramore was equally at home with the farmer, the cook, the stagecoach driver, and the hobo, all of whom fed his deep curiosity for the human experience. He lived long enough for Mary to absorb and respect his uncommon view of the world.

By 1914 Mary's routine was established: she spent several months at a time in Santa Barbara with the Paramores; returned intermittently to Pasadena; and travelled occasionally to visit Aunt May in the township of Paoli, on Philadelphia's Main Line. Mary also enrolled in art and music classes at the State Normal School of Manual Arts and Home Economics, predecessor of the University of California, Santa Barbara, and assisted in teaching at the kindergarten level.[8]

With her Paramore cousins her social anchor, Mary soon found herself affiliated with the "younger set" who, noted prominently in the local paper, took their places in the usual round of society luncheons, dinner dances at the country club, volunteer activity and help with charitable events. Her participation was nowhere better illustrated than by her role in the most dazzling event of the 1915 season, the opening of the

10.03. *Montecito, 1915. Left to right: Mary Paramore, Mary McLaughlin, Ed Paramore, Sarah McLaughlin. Seated: Jim and Ted Paramore*

10.04. *Mary McLaughlin, Pasadena, 1914*

Country Playhouse in Montecito. Mary was among "… society girls in dainty costumes of tulle" ushering guests to their boxes or seats. The *Los Angeles Times* described the opening as a "… blaze of brilliance …" in which "the top of the social set took part.…"[9]

By 1916 Mary McLaughlin's matrimonial intentions took on greater urgency. With serious beaus in California, New York and St. Louis, her decision to spend most of the year in the east may have been based on a need for clarity. After assessing several romantic interests, she was back in Santa Barbara by the fall, finding ample distractions in World War I–era charitable activities. She joined the St. Cecilia Club—formed in 1891 and, then as now, the oldest charitable organization in Santa Barbara—and in October 1916 she and Margaret Waterman assisted Mrs. Edgar Park with "Pencil Day." This was followed in November by announcement of the formation of "… a little sewing group …" of "… Santa Barbara and Montecito girls and young matrons … under the chairmanship of Miss Mary McLaughlin …" who were "… ever ready to assist those less fortunate than themselves." Now twenty-eight years old and restless, Mary's future was uncertain. Several months later, she would meet James Osborne Craig.[10]

CHAPTER 11

James Osborne Craig
From Scotland to America, 1888–1916

I can recall very clearly that April morning in 1905 when I went down to Greenock to see him off on his voyage to America. He was only a boy then. — William Craig to Mary Craig, December 9, 1946

James Osborne Craig was sixteen when he left his native Scotland for America. But for a few photos of him as a child, and mention of him in an Osborne family journal written in 1919, the life of the "boy" growing up in Scotland and the young adult in America and abroad, remain largely conjecture. Mary Craig would have been privy to many details, but she shared little during her lifetime. She did save Osborne's letters to her, and a few photographs, making a partial reconstruction of his life possible. Any diaries or sketch books appear to be lost, leaving little in the way of understanding Craig's own architectural sentiments and development. Yet the work itself, represented by what is extant, and his cogent and inimitable drawings, transcend speculation. They offer us Craig's unwitting gift of an enduring architecture, and what his patron Bernhard Hoffmann sensed soon after meeting him: Craig's ability to transform mere building into art.

Glasgow

Born and educated a Scot, Craig had ample time to observe his maternal family's respected position in Scottish society in and near Glasgow. Then considered a prosperous and sophisticated industrial center, Glasgow, "a city which never slept," was regarded as the "workshop of the world." It was thought by many to be "the most American city in Europe."[1] The dialogue of Craig as an architect in America begins with Glasgow, where the large Osborne family had a firm hold on the intellectual and business life of the place at the turn of the last century. Leaving, never to return, Osborne Craig would take with him his family's values of literacy, social responsibility, moral purpose and innovation, all qualities which the Scot brought to America.

The second child of Archibald and Margaret Osborne Craig (the first was stillborn), James Osborne Craig was born on November 2, 1888, in Barrhead, at Dunterlie Villas, a modest semi-detached brick dwelling at 43 Carlibar Road (Fig. 11.03).[2] Baptized into the Church of Scotland, at nearby Abbey Parish, he would be called Osborne. Barrhead, nine miles southwest of Glasgow and a largely agricultural area lying along the River Levern, became a center for cotton mills and textile production. At the time of Osborne's birth, his father was making his living in the textile business.[3] Four more sons were born to Maggie Craig, but by the time Osborne was eleven, three of his siblings had died; two in infancy and eight-year-old Archibald in a fall from a pony.

Information from Scottish census records indicates a peripatetic and unstable existence for the Craig family. The greatest insight into Osborne's young life comes from the journal written in 1919 by Osborne Craig's uncle, John Cochrane Osborne, his mother's older brother.[4] Going back to Osborne Craig's great-grandfather Robert Osborne (1787–1870), blacksmith of Braehead, and later of Newton Mearns, the journal begins with the lives of his twelve children and ends in 1919. It would be from this very large and well-educated family that Craig found his anchor as a boy.

11.03. James Osborne Craig birthplace, 43 Carlibar Road (left), Barrhead, Scotland.

Osborne's mother, Margaret Osborne Craig (1862–1927) was educated at the village and parish schools in Newton Mearns. Continuing her studies at the Collegiate School in Crossmyloof, she was called back to the farm to help care for her invalid mother when she was fifteen. Osborne's father Archibald Craig (1861–1902) was described by John Osborne as "a man of more than ordinary capacity, a good business man, mayhap rather sanguine. Well principled and with a great capacity for detail, he might in other surroundings have made much of life but he had the misfortune to be placed as the heritor of a declining business and without the means of getting out of it."[5] John Osborne wrote:

> Business with the Craigs was not quite successful in Barrhead and caused many worries. After some years, for the sake of the children, they went to live in Ayr for a time but came back to Glasgow after a few years. Another business venture was tried in Glasgow which for a few years promised well but was eventually given up. The strain and worry of business told on Archie's and Maggie's health but her robust constitution carried her through, when her husband gave way. As a last resort, when he was seriously ill, they went out to Killearn, in the hope that a change of air in that bracing locality might do good but it was evidently too late.

He died there in 1902 when Osborne was thirteen years old.

The one constant in Osborne's young life was Faulds Farm in Newton Mearns (where his mother and her many siblings had been born and raised), and the large house close by called the villa at Rys-land. Designed in 1874 by the Scottish architect Alexander "Greek" Thomson, Osborne's grandfather James Osborne and step-grandmother, Alice Todd Osborne, retired here (Figs. 11.04, 11.05). (The first Mrs. James Osborne, Christina Cochrane, died in 1877.) The farm and Rysland became destinations for "many happy family gatherings."[6]

James Osborne (1819–1903) was a rich man by the time Osborne was born. Not only had he become one of Glasgow's most successful grain and flour importers, he also owned the cartage firm, James Osborne and Sons. Alice Todd Osborne's life work involved the establishment of numerous Soldiers' Homes in Glasgow, Cairo, and Alexandria. Traveling also to Gibraltar and Spain, Mrs. Osborne, whose contentment in life came from caring for others, took young Osborne with her on these missionary trips. Robust and commanding, with "rare discrimination" and "a passion for soul-winning," she was also known for her work among the Spanish Roman Catholics in the town of La Linea, in Andalucia, Spain, just across the isthmus from Gibraltar.[7] In 1928, the press noted that "... as a child ..." Craig "... used to spend the winter in Malaga in the south of Spain and there he first learned to love the beauty of the low white-washed buildings which were the inspiration of his work in Santa Barbara."[8]

Mrs. Osborne was greatly loved by her family as well as the many soldiers she served and "rescued from lives of sin and degradation." The money she raised for her stately and architecturally significant soldiers' homes "came from all parts of the world." Establishing "The Todd Osborne House" in

11.04. Osborne Craig's grandfather, James Osborne (standing), with three of his eleven siblings, Jane, Alexander, and John Osborne. Newton Mearns, Scotland, ca. 1900

11.05. Alice Todd Osborne, Scotland, ca.1906.

Jerusalem at the age of eighty-three, she died a year later in Cairo in 1926. Given military honors she was buried in the Cairo Cemetery.[9] Osborne Craig received unique exposure to the spirit and the exceptional business acuity of his grandmother but, more importantly, her destinations, ripe with their Spanish and Moorish imagery, set the foundation for his later sensibilities, as Mary Craig so often mentioned to colleagues.

School records of Osborne's education up to the age of fifteen have not been found. Nonetheless, Scotland's educational system at the end of the nineteenth century was universally accepted as one of the most advanced in Europe. In 1904, living with relatives in Glasgow, Craig began his studies as a student of architecture at the Glasgow and West of Scotland Technical College. Here he crossed paths with the school's newly hired French architect Eugène Bourdon who was considered a "brilliant" and "inspiring" teacher who "commanded great loyalty and affection among his students."[10]

In early 1905, listing his address as "Crossmyloof," a hamlet near Glasgow, Craig made the decision to leave Scotland. The school log noted him absent for the final exam, thus denying him a qualification award. Robert Osborne's journal confirms that Osborne Craig left for health reasons, writing that he was "early a victim of asthma and in hope of betterment, he left home…and went to America. Here he has studied as an architect and is able to carry on in fair health, although not as robust as he would like to be." Osborne's surviving brother Ernest died at the age of eight soon after Osborne arrived in America. Margaret Craig, left

in reduced circumstances after her husband's death, died in 1927.

Christina and James Strang, Osborne Craig's aunt and uncle, had been in America since 1886, when they joined Osborne's uncle Thomas Osborne in a farming venture in Colona, Colorado. With one hundred dollars and his late father's brother, William Craig, seeing him off, Osborne left from the port of Greenock, on the Firth of Clyde, on April 8th. After an eight-day voyage, he arrived in New York on April 16, 1905.[11]

Listing his final destination Colona, Craig made his way from Ellis Island by ferry to Jersey City, where he boarded the train for his trip west. Much of the country he saw was still a vast frontier, punctuated by the rail line cities of Pittsburgh, Chicago, Burlington, Council Bluffs, Kansas City, St Louis, Omaha, and Grand Junction. Coming from the intellectual energy of Glasgow, Craig would have found Colona isolating. Though he certainly knew agrarian life from his time at Faulds Farm, the Strang farm would be a far cry from the genteel farming of his family. Montrose, some twelve miles away with a population of "1,200, rapidly increasing," boasted two weekly papers, one bank, two hotels and numerous dry goods stores.[12] Neither Colona nor Montrose would be a place of permanency for him.

11.06. Osborne Craig, Redstone, Colorado, ca. 1910

Colorado Springs 1907–1910

America would have been a poor show had it not been for the Scots. — Andrew Carnegie

The skills, discipline, intellect and ambition which Scots brought to America in the early 1900s were unique. Author and historian Bernard Aspinwall refers to the Scottish "state of mind" that accompanied the great exodus: "Scotland went with them wherever they went."[13] Craig was no exception. His Scottish origins, sensibilities and education allowed him easy entry into American society. Aspinwall's premise of the Scots' contribution to America's sense of identity can be substantiated by the many that arrived between 1820 and 1920 and made significant contributions to its prosperity. This vanguard of imported talent included such men as John Muir, Cyrus McCormick, Thomas Mellon, Daniel Webster, Andrew Carnegie, Alexander Graham Bell, and architects James Renwick and Alexander McComb. When Craig found himself employed in America as a young draftsman, it would be with Scottish-born and trained architects.

Craig's decision to live and work in Colorado Springs is not surprising. Since the 1880s, the town's

11.07. Osborne Craig, right, golfing with Tim Riordan, center, Milton (now Flagstaff), ca. 1915

reputation as a health resort with well-established sanitariums was well known. Sitting over a mile above sea level on the eastern edge of the southern Rocky Mountains, it had been a prosperous and popular destination from the time of the gold rush. When Osborne arrived in 1907, it was a sophisticated metropolitan area with wide streets, grand houses and hotels. Colorado College, founded in 1874, was well served by the town's abundance of clubs, churches, hospitals, libraries and opera house. Between 1895 and 1915, there were some twenty-five local architectural firms.[14]

With Pikes Peak and the famous "Garden of the Gods" dominating the landscape, the city was considered "one of the most attractive resorts in America, with … cultured people, drawn from all sections of the world."[15] Photographs of Osborne in the environs of Colorado Springs, and camping and riding in the areas of Glenwood Springs and Redstone, indicate an able-bodied young man. No matter how isolated or rugged the terrain, he is dressed in a three-piece suit and tie.

Redstone, the little town called "the Ruby of the Rockies," was of special interest. Here the legendary James Cleveland Osgood of the Colorado Fuel and Iron Company built his large English Tudor manor, Cleveholm, in 1902 and nearby the progressively conceived housing complex for his coal workers. Its reputation as a model, self-sustaining town would have peaked the interest of any young architect.[16] With the closing of the coal mines in 1909, Redstone was largely vacated by the time of Craig's visit. He is shown there atop a spirited horse with striking markings (Fig. 11.06). He wrote on the back of the photo: "This is a bully good polo pony. I have a heavy saddle on him here, but when I put a light one on

and he is feeling fit it takes me all my time to sit him."

Colorado Springs was host to a large Scottish community. Renting a room in a house at 132 North Weber Street, Craig's first-known American apprenticeship began in the office of Scottish-born architect George M. Bryson.[17] Though he gave Craig entrée into the professional arena and the chance to work, Bryson was nevertheless a minor player in the architectural legacy of Colorado Springs. In 1909 Craig was hired by the better-known Thomas MacLaren, his senior by twenty-five years and whose partner at the time was American-born architect Charles Thomas. As Scots, Bryson and MacLaren were active members of the Caledonian Society and offered Craig easy access to the city's social life. In January 1910 Craig was noted for his participation in the society's Thirteenth Annual Festival, held in honor of the 151st Robert Burns Anniversary.[18]

With Mr. Thomas abroad for much of 1909, MacLaren would have been the more significant mentor to Craig. Born in the county of Perthshire in central Scotland, he spent his youth on a farm near the village of Thornhill. At the age of sixteen, like Craig, MacLaren set out on his own, moving to London where as a student he lived with his older brother, architect James Marjoribanks MacLaren. Thomas MacLaren's commissions in England and Scotland are well documented. After contracting tuberculosis and spending two years in Switzerland, MacLaren moved to Colorado Springs in 1894. Here, under the care of the famous progressive English physician Dr. Edwin Solly, he was cured. Choosing MacLaren to design his facilities, Solly's innovations made Colorado Springs one of the most famous centers for tubercular care in the country.[19]

MacLaren was particularly loyal and attentive to

those of Scottish descent and partial to any young apprentice who could draw; Craig's tutelage under MacLaren was significant.[20] The sophisticated community encouraged a diverse and progressive approach to architecture and city planning. MacLaren was one of the city's most outspoken proponents for a careful aesthetic and high architectural

standards and Craig would have been attentive. Further, Craig's mature drawings replicate the qualities that defined MacLaren's artistry: "interpretation" versus "dramatization," and a talent that became "instinctive."[21] Leaving Colorado Springs sometime after April 1910, Osborne Craig's ideals, set by MacLaren's example, were just beginning to coalesce.

Craig's whereabouts from April 1910, when the census confirmed him still working for MacLaren, to his known arrival in Flagstaff in 1914 are unknown. However, information from his obituaries and later tributes indicate he left America to travel and pursue studies abroad in Spain, France, Italy, and Vienna. His decision to return to America reportedly "after leaving business in London because of ill health" coincided with the outbreak of war in Europe in July 1914.[22]

Flagstaff

11.08. Osborne Craig with R.H.H. Blome, Flagstaff, ca. 1915

> In all the world there is no bluer sky, than that which arches Arizona; in all the world there is no brighter sun, no softer moonlight, no more brilliant setting of stars than there. Indeed, the richness of her heavens has come to be known among astronomers by the distinctive name of "Arizona blue." But there are other things in Arizona and New Mexico beside skies and stars and moonlight.[23]

Arriving in Arizona to begin his independent career, Craig was exposed to the area's geographic wonders and the riches of its native architecture. He also quickly integrated with Flagstaff's most prominent citizens.

The Riordan brothers, Denis Mathew (Matt), Timothy Allan and Michael, arriving in Flagstaff from Chicago in the late 1800s, developed the Arizona Lumber and Timber Company which became central to the economic prosperity of the town. By 1915, in combination with the five entrepreneurial Babbitt brothers, the Riordans dominated and supported the civic, educational and commercial ventures of the town. Though photographs show Craig and Tim Riordan playing golf together on the small three-hole links course on the Riordan property, and Osborne in the company of Tim's daughter Mary, Michael's friendship with Osborne Craig is more readily understood. Their letters, exchanged from 1915 to 1917 and accompanied by articles pertaining to issues of history, politics, war and religion indicate the men were well matched in intellect.[24]

A semi-desert mountain town at the base of the San Francisco Peaks, Flagstaff's high elevation and dry air were ideal for people with lung ailments. But unlike Colorado Springs, with its abundance of sanitariums, "Flagstaff offered 'nothing 'official,' no specialist doctors, no clinics. Most people who went there hoped that the dry, pure air would do the job." Photographs from this time indicate Craig was healthy, whether with professional contacts or riding in the company of friends. They also show him

11.09. Osborne Craig,
Flagstaff, ca. 1915

smoking what may well have been belladonna, a favored homeopathic treatment for asthma that had been used for decades. Both belladonna and stramonium, natural sources of atropine, were easily obtained in cigarette form or for pipe smoking. When used in moderation they were effective and fast acting as an antispasmodic and reducer of lung inflammation. Doctors prescribed them routinely. At the turn of the last century, Marcel Proust, a severe asthmatic who was widely known for his use of anti-asthma cigarettes, contributed greatly to the practice's popularity, "particularly amongst radical intellectuals."[25]

Flagstaff, in many ways isolated, was curiously connected to the rest of the country, both physically and intellectually. Located along the Santa Fe rail line, it was considered a major stop for anyone with an interest in the attractions of the Southwest: the Grand Canyon, mission and archeological sites, and the Hopi and Navajo communities. While Craig lived there, Ford Harvey was not only busy expanding his famous father's southwest railroad hotels and eating houses through the efforts of architect Mary Jane Colter, but his plans for further development in the Grand Canyon and lobbying efforts for national park status were taking shape.[26] Ford and his daughter Katherine were keenly interested in Native American culture and were frequent visitors to Arizona. Seasonal visitors to Santa Barbara, Katherine Harvey eventually lived there year-round, later commissioning Mary Craig to design her beach cottage.

American landscape painter Fernand Lungren (1859–1932), a Santa Barbara resident since 1906, had in earlier years been intimately connected with the Southwest. Hired by the Santa Fe Railroad in 1892 to paint Arizona scenes along the routes, the western desert and canyon landscapes would from then on be his greatest inspiration. On his numerous trips through the Southwest, Lungren (originally encouraged by Matt Riordan to come west permanently in 1903) visited the Riordans, and often based his desert painting expeditions from Flagstaff. As the founder of the Santa Barbara School of Arts in 1920, Lungren, with Craig and others, was among its first group of teachers.[27]

Architects Bertram Goodhue, Santa Barbara's Francis Wilson, and Mary Jane Colter had all made their mark on the landscape of the Southwest in the years Craig was in Flagstaff.[28] Whether Craig visited any of their novel projects merging the Mission, Spanish, Moorish and Pueblo prototypes or whether he travelled south into Mexico with its rich architectural legacy, is left to conjecture. The missions of the Southwest, with their older and purer Spanish vernacular were within easy reach of Flagstaff; they would have almost certainly been a catalyst for Craig's interest in the California missions, all but two of which he visited.[29] Flagstaff had been his time to put into practice fundamental but unimaginative elements of construction. Its environment, perhaps more significantly, offered up the notion that the integration of climate, culture, history and architecture needed to be understood.

Regardless of the reasons for Craig's departure from Flagstaff in 1916, his arrival in Santa Barbara was auspicious. Here, he and George Washington Smith (who had himself passed through Flagstaff on his return from Europe in October 1915) established the local Spanish Colonial vernacular; Craig's El Paseo, the greatest monument to the style, and the Hoffmann House, sealed his legacy.[30]

Santa Barbara

1917–1922

Osborne Craig and Mary McLaughlin

While getting to know Osborne Craig in early 1917, Mary already held the particular attentions of several men. In Pasadena beaus included Roy Bascom Hull, and, in Santa Barbara, Prynce Hopkins (Fig. 12.01). Roy Bascom Hull was the son of a rich merchant from Cleveland, E. H. Hull who in 1899 sold his company to David May who renamed it the May Company. Prynce Hopkins, later becoming a noted socialist, pacifist, psychologist and author, was scion to the Singer Sewing Machine fortune. Like the Paramore boys, he attended the Hill School and Yale. Ted and Prynce, allies in political and social ideology, were close acquaintances. Mary's interest in Hopkins, presumably initiated by Ted, coincided with the creation of Hopkins' progressive new school, Boyland. Listing her occupation as "agriculturist" in the voting record, Mary was noted in the *Morning Press* "cadetting" at Boyland and described as an "assistant gardener, aiding in the task of laying out the gardens and teaching the children this interesting feature of their lessons."[1]

America's entry into World War I on April 6, 1917, presented special circumstances for everyone. Though Montecito would be largely insulated, it was not unaffected. Osborne filled out his draft registration card in June, listing himself as an "alien" and a "self-employed" architect working in Santa Barbara. Due to his health, active duty would not have been an option. Mary did her part by cultivating a vegetable garden, reported in the press as "… her bit in the preparedness campaign in which the Garden Club … is engaging."[2] With conscription pending, the Paramore boys took a less conventional path. Ted was determined to be a pacifist, and with Jim as chaperone, they left for Russia in the late summer of 1917 to become couriers under Ambassador Francis at the American Embassy in Petrograd. Ted would also be a correspondent for *Collier's*. Safely back in California by July 1918, they enlisted in the Navy, though they never saw active duty. The story of their return to America via Asia, prompted by Russia's impending revolution, became famous when it was learned they had transported over one hundred American refugees from Petrograd to safety through Siberia on a stolen train.[3]

While Mary's relationships with Hull and Hopkins ultimately cooled, the one with Osborne Craig slowly evolved. His letters to her, beginning in late July, already display indisputable affection; by November 1917 he was in love with her.

Osborne sat well outside of Mary's circle of former admirers. Though he was ready to marry her in 1918, she remained indecisive for months. From the Paramores there was strong resistance to the relationship. Writing to Mary that the Paramores considered him a "waster" and were "working against our happiness…." he explained:

> [The Paramores] declared their attitude from the first and never have hesitated to air their feelings to others … there is no reason on earth why you should not see them as much as you wish to, but merely arrange it so that I may be freed from going there…. Really sweetheart you are very different when away from influences such as you had this morning: people who live merely for their own selfish ends, especially when these indulgences are of an idle useless nature.

References to delays, indecision and broken promises concerning their marriage are threaded throughout their correspondence in the fall of 1919. While Osborne may have been correct that she was unduly influenced by her family, particularly Mrs. Paramore, Mary clearly had to find resolution on her own terms. She finally sought refuge with Aunt May, spending eight weeks in the East. Following her departure in late September, Osborne wrote to her:

PREVIOUS PAGES
*12.04. Mary McLaughlin
with Osborne Craig (third
from left), and friends,
Santa Ynez Valley, ca. 1918*

It has been far from my mind to be in any way unkind in what I have said in my last two letters, but I am so keenly conscious dear, perhaps that realization is the print of sad experience, that we only are measured out from life's store in proportion as we give, and I am so anxious Mary that we build substantially and perhaps for many reasons I can look ahead a little better than you, and it is only to avoid objectionable obstacles that I am so insistent upon certain matters.

It's damned lonely needless to say, a few more days such as this and I would take to Scotch with a vengeance; I thank God more fervently than ever for my work, but a life without love, no matter what degree of success among men be attained, would be my conception of the nether regions. I am longing for the morning for I hope it will bring a letter from you: where are you tonight I wonder, on your way to Paoli or to a Chicago party, in either event California is far distant, but I know you hear always the call of return, in which I vie with the mountains which meet the sea in giving.

With plans to be married at Mission Santa Inés in Solvang, Craig wrote hopefully:

Two years ago today ... I realized I was in love with you, last year we were arranging to go the Santa Inez [sic], which we did a year ago next Monday; I hope dear we will be there again in love, wandering along the old mission road and breathing from those broken cloisters the grace and beauty of the land of their inception.

Several weeks later, seriously ill, Craig wrote again:

From the dear old Cottage Hospital I write you, I am fighting to keep up belief that all things happen for the best, there are moments when I find this very very difficult almost impossible, but I think of Cowper, of his trials and how he beautifully wrote "God moves in a mysterious way his wonders to perform," and black as the clouds of the moment may seem perhaps the coming sunlight will be all the brighter. For a few days I am in bed properly, not allowed to put a foot out, but it is a hell of a job to kill a Scot and the new week will find me consorting with the skylarks, not the ethereal kind however, much as I admire Mr. Shelley's variety.[4]

Osborne, recovering from pneumonia, finally received from Mary the words he had been waiting for: "I'm on my way to Boston to stay for a few days ... then home, dear heart to you—and never again to leave without you." Osborne and Mary were wed on November 19, 1919, not at the mission, but at the Paramore's house in Montecito. On this most important day of days, he was not freed from going there. They would spend their honeymoon at the small house in Montecito Mary had purchased in 1918.[5]

As Osborne and Mary made the usual adjustments to married life, Mary's social activity continued unabated. In February 1920 she manned the ice cream table at the St. Cecilia Club's twenty-eighth annual bazaar held at the Arlington Hotel. In March she attended a luncheon at Carrillo Adobe in honor

of the upcoming wedding of Miss Nina Jones, daughter of Mr. and Mrs. Milo Milton Potter (of the Potter Hotel). Mary followed up a short time later with a tea for Miss Jones at One Acre. In April, she attended a bridge-tea given by Mrs. Alfred Erskine Brush and a luncheon at the Santa Barbara Country Club as the guest of Alice McCormick. Mary's attendance at other social events was noted in the society columns throughout the year.[6]

Osborne, perhaps co-opted, joined Mary on several occasions. He accompanied her to Nina Jones's wedding in March. In April they attended "Quite the merriest dinner-dance of the season," at the Santa Barbara Country Club, where the guests "... assembled in ginghams and overalls and spent the evening barn-dancing." This was followed in May by a dinner at the country club; Mr. and Mrs. Osbourn [sic] Craig were on the guest list. In July they went to two large swimming parties: one at the Plaza del Mar bath house; the other, followed by a clam bake, given by Miss Natalie More at Las Positas in Hope Ranch.[7]

These social gatherings were attended by a cross section of Santa Barbara society and included members of Mary's immediate circle, including the James Canbys and the Harry Gantzes. Mary's beau from earlier times, Harry married her Santa Barbara friend Beatrice Miller in 1915. While Craig's love for Mary was beyond question, he was outspoken in his distaste for the world of upwardly mobile, and often superficial, society she craved. A month before their wedding, he commented, "... affectation is the cardinal sin of most of the women here ... with women I think pretentions are more innate than with men."[8] Osborne's protestations aside, Mary's contacts proved invaluable in securing his earliest clients.

In the winter of 1920 Mary wrote to her mother from One Acre:

It has been several days, I know since I have written to you, but the past ten days have been very trying ones for me: Osborne was in bed for nearly two weeks, and ... having no one to help me until yesterday; as you well know I am not adept at housekeeping and I had a rather trying time, particularly with the cooking.[9]

Evidence of Craig's ill health was corroborated by Geoffry Lawford, a young office assistant who worked for Craig in 1920. Lawford wrote of the experience many years later:

I was sixteen or seventeen working part time after school on obviously the simplest of assignments. The quality of his work grew on me in the years that followed and as my own interest in architecture developed. I remember him as ... a man who suffered continuously from asthma.[10]

Despite his poor health, Craig's work went on uninterrupted through much of the year. Mrs. James Nelson Burnes, widow of a well-known banker and philanthropist from Missouri, and whose children were among Mary's earliest acquaintances in Pasadena, became one of his most important contemporary clients. The cottage Craig designed for her

12.05. Osborne and Mary Craig, Santa Barbara, ca. 1921

at Fernald Point was recalled many years later by her granddaughter as "…so very right…it was a small house, but the spaces were ideal for a family of four with staff to help. It absorbed well the usual activities, but it never felt crowded. It was superbly proportioned for a typical family of that era. It was total magic."[11]

In the fall of 1920 Osborne's respiratory attacks were becoming more frequent. He left for Palm Springs in late November, hoping its dry air and rest at the well-known Desert Inn and Sanitarium would bring relief. Soon after arriving he met architect Harold Bryant Cody, who had been stricken with tuberculosis some years earlier.[12] Craig wrote to Mary:

> I made rather an interesting discovery, I found here a chap called Cody and Mrs. Cody; he is one of the cleverest young Architects who ever came West, and he draws and paints with great skill—poor devil he is in bad shape with TB's, started about four years ago just after he had opened an office in Los Angeles and was on a sure road of success; his plucky wife has a string of horses which she rents out and so supports them … now why should such conditions exist, what possible good, (and look at the suffering) can be brought about either to them or to others, as far as I can see there is nothing but loss, sad, hopeless, heartbreaking loss.[13]

Craig's many letters to Mary during this time were hopeful concerning his health. He was also honest with her concerning what he believed to be her excessive preoccupation with and love of society. Though it fueled to a large degree his client base, at the same time he resented her desire to keep it so central in their married life. From Palm Springs, expressing his wish to come home, but only under certain conditions, he candidly wrote: "I am sorry dear that your many social activities prevent you from sending a short note to your distant husband each day…." He continued, "God knows I would rather get home …," then explaining that he could:

> … not [go] out at night, one dinner and the attending late hours, is quite enough to upset me and I am not going to do it under any consideration, so please do not let us even discuss the matter but simply tell people that I never go out; my state of health has now got to a point where I cannot play with it as I used to be able to do, and if it is to be ruined entirely, it will be through some cause more worthy than idle cavorting in Montecito.[14]

Relapsing upon returning to Santa Barbara in December, Craig was too ill to stay long. Back in Palm Springs, he not only missed Christmas with Mary, but the birth of his child, Mary Osborne Craig, on January 28, 1921. Renting a house, Mary and the baby joined him in early March. Just before their arrival, Craig wrote to her:

> Have Diehl [the Santa Barbara grocer] pack up either the night before or the morning you leave and have Pit-

man get the box and bring it to the train, lettuce, beets, carrots, sweet butter from the creamery packed with the wet leaves of the vegetables, about two each of the vegetables and have them put in a cardboard box ... oh yes—and have a dozen bananas put in, it is impossible to get them here.... I suggest you nourish the child at half past one and then about five, otherwise she would be too much upset.[15]

Despite his gaunt appearance in photographs, Craig was remarkably productive. Many drawings for Hoffmann were done during this time, as well as plans for resident doctor J. J. Kocher for his Sunshine Court in Palm Springs, one of the first motor courts in the country. The tedious process of preliminary sketches, schemes, and directives, followed by working drawings, went back and forth by mail between Craig and his draftsman Richard H. Pitman. Missouri-born Pitman had attended Washington University in St. Louis. Moving to San Jose, he studied architectural engineering at Oakland's Polytechnic College of Engineering. A serious and shy man, Pitman never received an architectural license due to his fear of failing the examinations.[16]

Craig's letters to Pitman are exacting and dense with technical information. His sequential sketches for the Hoffmann House are more fluid than ever, revealing a process where the physical act of drawing seemed to inform his mind first, before the ideas came. Architect Addison Mizner once referred to this process when speaking of architects whose ideas "run out of their pencils." Pitman's ability to transform the hurried concepts into working drawings went on uninterrupted from late 1920 to April 1921 when the Craigs returned to Santa Barbara. It was an unusually rigorous time for the ailing Craig and it was equally demanding on Pitman, a man who seemed to take the long distance working relationship with exceptional equilibrium and loyalty.[17]

In a letter to Mary, Osborne wrote soon after the birth of their daughter:

The fireside is a poor place without you, but when I think of the days to come with both you and little Mary there, I am cheered no end, in fact having a daughter is not only bucking me up but making me awfully conceited, she will be a well occupied young lady in living up to what I have planned for her career, doubtless she will offer a voice of her own in the matter, and without doubt more than offer it if she has much of either of our temperament within her, but bless her dear little soul, she is going to be a wonderful help to us Mary, "for of such is the kingdom of Heaven" and I feel that that is what I need more of in my life and how often do you see the little hand of a child leading where nothing else could.[18]

In the fall of 1921, renting the O. W. Robertson House in the warmer climate of Ojai, Craig had reason for confidence; he was building and he was making money. He also had the support of licensed architect Carleton Monroe Winslow who acted as his supervising architect.

The origins of the professional relationship between Osborne Craig and Carleton Winslow have never been determined, but as an unlicensed architect, Craig valued Winslow as his collaborating architect. Twelve years his senior, Winslow gave the younger Craig the opportunity to work on his own commissions without risk of legal liability. Though allied in their architectural ideals, including preservation of California's missions, they were vastly different in temperament and politics.

From a modest upbringing in Damariscotta, Maine, Winslow had a natural talent for drawing and during high school indicated his interest in architecture. Schooled in Brunswick, Maine, he later wrote of the experience:

I was well acquainted with a number of the members of the faculty of Bowdoin College. I was interested in buildings and "superintended" the erection of everything being built in the neighbourhood, the great cotton mills, the lovely Walker Art Gallery at Bowdoin, and Dr. Wilson's fine residence on our street.

Completing high school in Portland at the age of sixteen, and committed to a career in architecture, he left Maine for Chicago, where he found work as a "cub-draughtsman and office boy." After working for several Chicago firms, he found employment in New York, later travelling through Europe for a year and a half, all the while pursuing independent studies in languages, drawing, history and mathematics. Finding work on his return in the Boston office of Cram, Goodhue and Ferguson, Winslow wrote of the experience: "Here I entered into a lifelong friendship with Bertram Goodhue to whom I owe obligations which I shall never be able to repay."[19]

Goodhue sent Winslow to San Diego in 1911 to superintend the buildings of the Panama California International Exposition. By 1918, he had opened offices in Los Angeles and Santa Barbara, where in all probability he met Osborne Craig.

From church architecture, the California missions, politics, religion and spirituality, to his disdain of liberals, Winslow wrote on a wide range of subjects. Confident and with a bold and distinct viewpoint, he loved to expound:

Most of the Liberals I have ever known are intolerant of anything but Liberalism, furthermore they are usually intolerant of any variety of Liberalism but their own ... I am tired of Liberalism and Liberals, I am not liberal myself and am not ashamed to say so.

In notes for a lecture on "The necessity of thorough training of all artists in the allied and sister arts," he wrote:

The Architect particularly must know about

a painting
b sculpture
c metal work
d wood craftsmanship
e ceramics
f stained glass
g plastering.[20]

Described as "ebullient," "energetic" and always "beaming," Carleton Winslow was a "round little man, with round glasses and short." Self-assured, ambitious, and with a cheerful and optimistic disposition, he was known as the "original Renaissance man" who prided himself on his knowledge of many topics of the day. Illustrating several books, including Julia Sloane's *The Smiling Hilltop*, Winslow was far more partial to sketching than doing formal drawings for his projects, which he often left to his office staff. When his charismatic and close friend Neal Dodd ended up in Hollywood as an Episcopalian minister who attracted many of the Anglican film star notables, Winslow was afforded numerous commissions from the upper tier of Hollywood. These included the development of Laughlin Park (backed by Cecil B. DeMille) and, with the support of Alphonzo Bell, the development of Bel-Air. Winslow relished the limelight of these connections through Dodd.

In a brief autobiographical sketch he wrote:

Personally, I am an Episcopalian and a Republican … I am interested in Mediaeval Latin, gardening, ecclesiastical ornaments and going places in an automobile. I have spent considerable time in connection with the restoration of the California missions. I enjoy bridge and watching circus parades. I never ride in an aeroplane if I can help it. I am partial to good Scotch and am conceited enough to think I can mix a fair Tom Collins.[21]

Winslow's legacy is not only tied to his prolific output of buildings but to his role in completing Osborne Craig's El Paseo. A man whose ego was unabashedly present throughout his life, Winslow graciously supervised its construction, making few revisions. Until he moved his office to 114 De la Guerra Street in 1925, he worked alongside Mary Craig, Richard Pitman and Ralph Armitage while the Hoffmann House and El Paseo were completed. In 1928, Winslow's addition to El Paseo of the Anacapa Annex artfully merged his sensibilities with the late Mr. Craig's. In his substantial writings, no references to Osborne Craig have been found. Winslow died in Southern California at the age of seventy, leaving behind a prodigious and well documented body of work.

Craig's visible success in 1921 seems to have led to rapprochement with the Paramores: he prepared two schemes for a new house for them. From Ojai he made several trips back to Santa Barbara to meet with Pitman, and with Hoffmann and church officials about plans for St. Anthony's Seminary. Through the Community Arts Association under the leadership of Hoffmann and Pearl Chase, Craig and George Washington Smith were collaborating on ideas for the restoration of the Old Opera House, later to be replaced by the Lobero Theatre.[22]

By the end of the year, though working on an extraordinary number of commissions, it was clear that Osborne's health was of concern to Mary's family. After spending Christmas dinner with the Paramores in Montecito, Jim Paramore wrote to his brother Ted, "… poor Osborne was noticeably suffering with his asthma and coughing continuously." Back in Ojai, Craig came down with the flu in early March. It quickly developed into bronchopneumonia. On March 9, Ojai doctor B. L. Saeger was called to the house. Numerous calls to immediate family and several doctors between March 9 and March 13 indicate that Mary knew with some certainty that Osborne was dying. A nurse, Miss Carstens, came in to care for him. With the baby and her nurse Florence Hall at the house, Mary, nurse Carstens and

Dr. Saeger were with Osborne when he died late on the evening of March 15. Outwitting death so many times, the thirty-three-year-old Craig was unable to hold off what he had earlier referred to as "the Grim Reaper, and the call of the Chancellor of the Exchequer."[23]

Bernhard Hoffmann and Carleton Winslow, driving to Ojai the next day to be with Mary, stayed to attend the small service at the Robertson House Saturday morning. Osborne was buried Sunday at Santa Barbara Cemetery on a site overlooking the Pacific Ocean. Soon after, Mary purchased a wrought iron cross from Cannell & Chaffin in Los Angeles and had it set into a small stone to mark the site (Fig. 12.06).[24]

12.06. James Osborne Craig grave marker (replication of original), Santa Barbara Cemetery

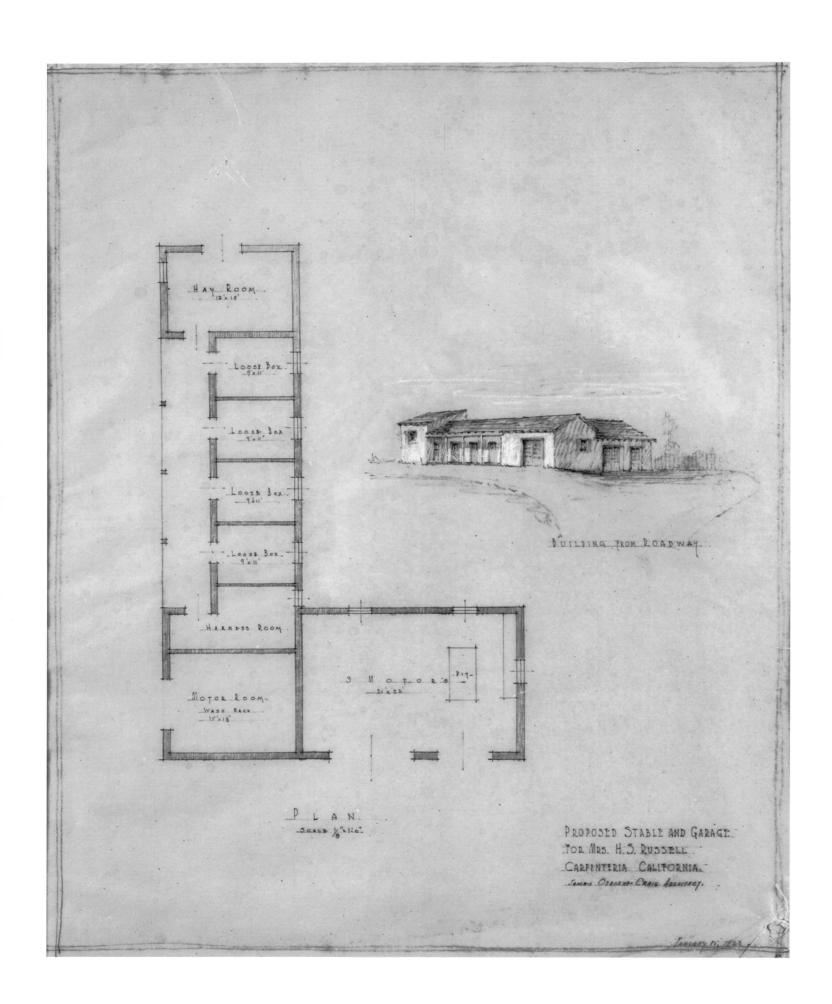

HAY ROOM.
12'x18'

LOOSE BOX
9'x11'

LOOSE BOX
9'x11'

LOOSE BOX
9'x11'

LOOSE BOX
9'x11'

HARNESS ROOM

MOTOR ROOM.
WASH RACK.
15'x18'

3 MOTOR'S PIT
21'x22'

BUILDING FROM ROADWAY.

PLAN.
SCALE ⅛"=1'0"

PROPOSED STABLE AND GARAGE
FOR MRS. H.S. RUSSELL.
CARPENTERIA CALIFORNIA.
JAMES OSBORNE CRAIG ARCHITECT.

January 15, 1922

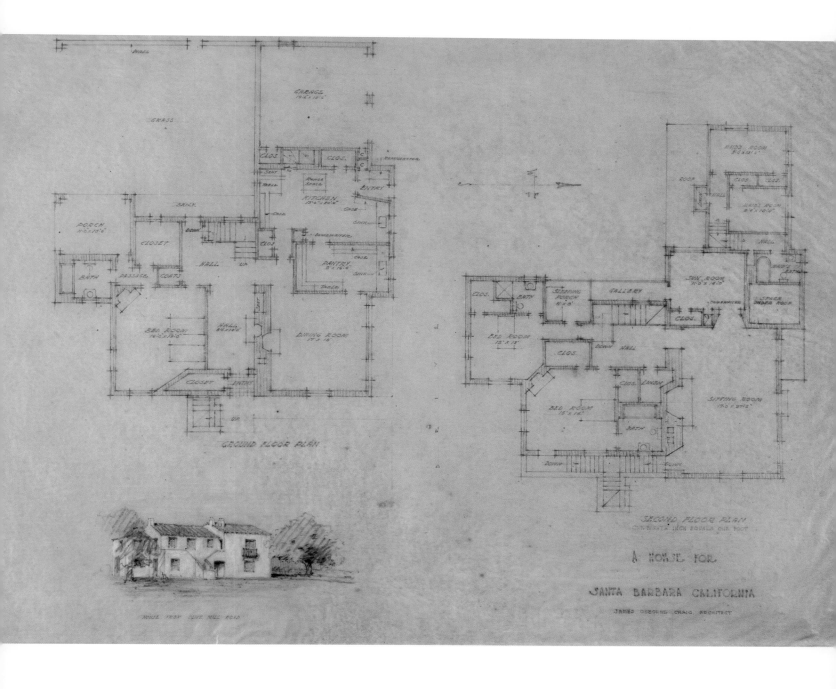

GROUND FLOOR PLAN

SECOND FLOOR PLAN

A HOUSE FOR

SANTA BARBARA CALIFORNIA

JAMES OSBORNE CRAIG, ARCHITECT

Margaret Craig, informed of Osborne's death by cable, had not seen her son since he left Scotland in 1905. In response to Mary's sending her a sketch of Osborne in 1924, Margaret replied:

I'm pleased to have it, though he does seem changed and seems to have a rather sad look. Was that quite like what he was before he died? I think too he looks rather delicate. I have a photo he sent me about ten years ago, the only good photo I have of him. He looks much stronger looking in it.

Expressions of condolence to Mary and to Hoffmann were numerous. Architect Irving F. Morrow wrote to Hoffmann that his friend, architect David Allison, knew Craig and "admired him greatly." Pearl Chase, in a telegram to Mary, wrote: "We feel a personal loss and great regret that so splendid and faithful a disciple of the beautiful in art and life should have gone from us. That remembrance of his courage

and soul strength will help you now is the hope of [the] Community Arts Association."

Hoffmann himself, referring to the recent "Hispanicization of Santa Barbara," wrote of Craig: "I feel so strongly that his imagination fired us to the splendid results that are coming along now...."[25]

Craig's finest work held the essence of what architect C. Sumner Greene referred to as the architect's "imperishable ideal." Described after his death as a man with "the imagination of a poet and soul of an artist" Craig was memorialized in 1928 as "Santa Barbara's dean of architects." From his quick, deft sketches, to the masterful finesse of his formal drawings, Craig's hand had been his voice. His work, posthumously acclaimed in the August 1922 issue of *Architect and Engineer*, was described as "unpretentious," "intimate," "atmospheric," and "unacademic." His "subtle" and "naively beautiful" houses, once built, fulfilled their "prime function—to be lived in."[26]

12.07. Osborne Craig, Russell Stable and Garage, Carpinteria

12.08. James Osborne Craig, Paramore House, scheme 1, Montecito (project)

CHAPTER 13

Mary Craig, Designer

1922–1939

13.01. Mary Craig and daughter, Montecito, 1925

13.02. Edward Borein with Mary Osborne Craig, Santa Barbara, 1926

Relying on her extended family and close friends Bob and Grace McGann, the Daniel Nugents, and the Colin Campbells for support, Mary was nevertheless unusually single-minded in the weeks following Osborne's death. She took a number of photographs at the Hoffmann building site, showing the first rows of hollow concrete blocks and draft horses removing large boulders. Before the summer was out, she listed her name in the city directory with an office at 400 Constance Street; the address of the small building belonging to the Hoffmanns at the bottom of the drive.[1] Despite her interest, it seems Hoffmann used the expertise of Carleton Winslow and Richard Pitman to complete both El Paseo and his house.

Hiring licensed architect Ralph Armitage in 1923, Mary worked from Osborne's office on the second floor of the Oreña adobe. Accessed by a darkened steep stairway, a narrow door at the top opened into a modest space with little natural light and low ceilings. Mary's friendship with artist Edward Borein, working in the nearby Oreña studio, began at this time.

Ralph Armitage, son of San Francisco architect William Henry Armitage, began his training at the age of eighteen as an office apprentice and night student at Van Der Nailens' School of Engineering in San Francisco. He entered Columbia University in the summer of 1908 but returned home in the fall "due to family trouble." He never returned to academia. Working without interruption as an apprentice and draftsman in the San Francisco Bay Area, including three years at the firm Salfield and Kohlberg, he received his license in February, 1915. When asked for "collegiate and office training" on his 1929 appli-

cation to become a member of the American Institute of Architects, he wrote only "25 years office training." Armitage made Santa Barbara his home in 1915 and, with draftsmen Albert Larsen and Richard Pitman, worked in the office of Francis Underhill until 1919. He married Charlotte Hund in 1918, and their only child John Edward Armitage was born in 1919.

After working several years on his own, Armitage joined the office of Carleton Winslow in 1923, where he came to know Mary Craig and began working for her as well as for Winslow. Armitage left Winslow's employment in 1926 to work exclusively for Craig. At various times in his career he supplemented his income by working as Santa Barbara's Chief Building Inspector. During the war, from 1941 to 1946, Armitage left Mary Craig's employment entirely to work for the Navy as an architectural engineer at the U.S. Marine Corps Air Station in Goleta. Predeceased by his son in 1953, Armitage died in Santa Barbara on January 29, 1966.

Armitage's drafting, construction, and engineering skills were sophisticated; his experience and his drawings convinced Mary's clients that their houses would be exceptionally well built. When Armitage received the "Meritorious Civilian Service Award" for his war effort in 1945, he was praised for his "outstanding ability in all phases of architectural work," and "his ability to grasp and transfer onto paper the ideas of others presenting their needs to him." It was this rare quality that was at the heart of the successful collaboration with Mary Craig. Mutually dependent on one another, it was a unique relationship. Armitage designed a few minor buildings during his career, including his own house in Santa Barbara, but the significance of his legacy lies in his talent as a draftsman

and long affiliation with Mary Craig.[2]

Setting her own goals, Mary Craig was ready to establish her singular reputation through a masterful combination of persuasion, talent and trust and, frequently, friendship. Such was her commission for Nancy Leiter Campbell.

Discussions between Mary and Nancy Campbell and the initial concept of the main house ostensibly began just before or just after the sudden death of Colonel Campbell in May 1923. Travelling abroad in 1924, Nancy made provisions to have her brother

13.03. Dovecote, Campbell
Ranch, Goleta

Joe Leiter, by then managing all of her financial affairs, oversee the project with Mary. Leiter became a mentor at a critical time in Mary's development as a designer and businesswoman.

Demonstrating a solid grasp of construction principles, Leiter's multi-layered business and personal life did not prevent him from focusing on the details of his sister's house. The commission became a testing ground for almost everything Mary would have to grasp later about client and contractor relationships, construction, building costs, materials, and livability. Through telegrams and letters, the Chicago-based Leiter and Craig discussed the timing of the ordering and delivery of building materials, and the importance of well-dried adobe bricks.

Keeping her correspondence with Joe Leiter both formal and light hearted, Mary began one letter:

My dear Mr. Leiter, According to your instructions we are proceeding with all speed on the Campbell house. I hope it will please you to know that all the adobe brick will be laid in ten days, and the framing of the roof will be completed by the first of July. I can see no reason why Mrs. Campbell should not step into a completed house when she comes back from China. Your little speech to Mr. Snook was just like Aladdin rubbing his lamp….

Asking for weekly progress reports, Leiter pushed Mary hard to have the house completed by the time his sister returned. Despite the extraordinary speed with which the contractors Snook & Kenyon worked, the integrity of the house almost ninety years later attests to the quality of the undertaking. Even the 1925 earthquake could not budge it. Leiter wrote to Mary in July:

It will be a large advertisement for you if you have it done, as most of the people who build houses in your part of the world want to approve the plans and have a house to live in when they return … the glory will be so much the more … so fly at it and win your spurs … For your own sake, as well as for Nan's, I want this building operation to be a great success and also because I have contributed my mite [sic]. I hate to see a lack of efficiency in anything I have to do with.

Mary thanked Leiter for his mastery in dealing with the contractor:

When I went out to the Campbell house this morning I found plumbers, and plasterers, and painters, and bricklayers, and masons, and millmen, and carpenters, and cement workers, and floor layers—a crowd worthy of the setting up of the Tower of Babel…. I like the house a lot, and must add what a tremendous help, and how corking you have been about the whole thing. I think I should have wavered on many an occasion if I had not had you to lean upon.[3]

Mary's photographs, sent to Leiter, show the scale of the project, from the long, wavy rows of adobe bricks drying in the sun, the massive adzed timbers used for trusses and beams, piles of red clay roof tiles made on site by the master craftsmen of the Angulo family, the complex wood scaffolding system, and the thick adobe walls before they received the final stucco coating. A circular dovecote, combining the traditional Scottish design with a tile roof, is also attributed to Mary Craig.[4]

In 1925 Mary sought Leiter's advice in career matters. Responding with two pages of constructive remarks relating to clients, contractors, commissions and record keeping, he wrote: "Work undertaken except with a profit resulting from its doing, is for fools who either don't know what their costs are or who let their desire to get the work blind them into the belief that the more work they take at a loss, the more they will make." He ended his letter with cautionary advice:

I am writing you these suggestions as I am much interested in seeing you make a success and feel that you can refer to a writing when your memory might not serve you as well. Finally, remember that being a woman, you have to do your business better than any man as there is a prejudice against a woman in business which you have to overcome.[5]

Clearly, in Joseph Leiter's mind, Mary Craig had won her "spurs."

When a massive earthquake struck Santa Barbara on June 29, 1925, Gertrude Hoffmann wrote:

> I was visiting at the Bernhard Hoffmanns on upper Garden Street, and was sound asleep.... Suddenly I was awake ... there could be no doubt as to what was happening ... I was not actually frightened. I had seen this massive house in the building, and had said then: "If an earthquake ever strikes Santa Barbara, I hope I will be in this house." Here was the earthquake; here was I ... How the house itself had stood without one crack or even a broken pane of glass was a marvel....[6]

The destructive earthquake was in the words of Charles Lummis "a blessing in disguise," a "catastrophe giving to Santa Barbara 'the Chance of its Life' artistically."[7] El Paseo and other newer buildings constructed along Spanish lines sustained little damage. The Spanish style, which Mary Craig intuitively understood, began its promising climb in popularity.

From 1925 to 1930 Mary Craig's work was plentiful. Her patron Margaret Andrews, holding to a strong aesthetic and the belief that the town should adhere to low building heights and its Spanish heritage, offered Mary Craig important opportunities, among them Plaza Rubio.[8] Other clients during these years had ample means to build large noteworthy houses, which included Craig's 1927 and 1929 houses for the William Slater family. Mrs. William A. (Ellen) Slater's late philanthropic husband was the son of one of the richest men in New England, and the grandnephew of Samuel Slater, founder of the first machine cotton factory in America. Ellen did not care for excess, and wrote to Mary that the proposed house (for herself and her son Will, then thirty-six) was too big. Explaining to Mary that she was making "too important a house" and that "Willie's people don't care much for manual labor," she asked her to decrease the number of servants' spaces. Wishing for a smaller version of the same plan, she ended her letter, "Your own house is sweet and why complicate life."[9]

Many of Mary Craig's commissions can be traced, like the projects for J. Percival Jefferson and Nancy Campbell, to early acquaintance. Such was her work designing cottages and making improvements to the ranch house for Charles Perkins, Jr., and his sister, Mary Russell Perkins, at their Alisal ranch in 1927. Mary remembered her excitement as a young girl in Deadwood when their father, Charles Elliott Perkins of Burlington, Iowa, then president of the Chicago, Burlington and Quincy Railroad, arrived in his private railroad car, the Black Hawk, to see her father on business. Since the 1800s, Santa Barbara's environs had been familiar ground to the Perkins and their Cunningham and Forbes relatives, many of whom Mary came to know in the years before her marriage to Osborne.

Success of the Alisal, forty miles to the northwest of Santa Barbara, as a watering hole for blue-ribbon personalities from all parts of the country was immediate: guests included Edward Borein, Alice Roosevelt Longworth, David Niven, Julia Child, architects Mary Colter and Ambrose Cramer, and a who's who of Santa

13.04. Alisal guest book, 1927

Barbara and Hollywood society. Ogden Nash, visiting in 1937, wrote in the guestbook of his gratitude to his hosts: "Physically saturated and a mental pauper, I thank you, dear Mr. and Mrs. Perkins, for this magnificent Sunday afternoon torpor."[10] The guestbook began with an illustration by Edward Borein and a poem by Robert Forbes Perkins (Fig. 13.04).

Aunt May Roberts, widowed in 1926, came to play an ever more influential role in Mary Craig's life, making possible opportunities that would have been financially out of reach otherwise. Always including little Mary, a 1927 summer trip abroad was the first of several she arranged.[11] Sailing from New York on the *Berengaria*, she brought her car, chauffeur, per-

sonal maid and a nurse. Thirty-eight-year-old Mary Craig had never traveled outside the United States. Leaving little Mary and her nurse in the care of the chauffeur's family in Switzerland, Aunt May and Mary Craig were driven to Spain. Mary's daughter remembered that, after arriving home, over a dozen large packing crates were unloaded in the courtyard at One Acre, filled with Spanish doors, tiles, glass and iron lanterns, large ceramic urns and jars, wrought iron stands, and wooden corbels (Figs. 13.05, 13.06).

In the fall of 1928 Mary began to suffer from fatigue and depression. Her uncle E. E. Paramore, after exhausting his inheritance, had died in May. Mary's decision to decline two marriage proposals generated some regret, and the Mileys' misfortune left one of her most important commissions unfinished. More significant may have been what her daughter remembers as the great disappointment in 1928 when she failed the engineering portion of an exam she took after completing courses in architecture. Earlier, in the fall of 1925, appearing before the state architectural licensing board, she was told she had to take courses in construction and engineering before re-applying. It was now three years later, and her chances to attain a license were dimming.[12]

In 1929, following a road trip to the Grand Canyon with Ellen Slater, Mary moved her office to a small cottage she built on her property. Mr. Armitage, assistant Thomas Lawford Lingham, and other hired draftsmen worked at various times here until her retirement. French-born Henry Mario Barone, AIA, worked for Mary during the years she was designing the Miley houses. He received his training at Columbia University (1924) and the University of Pennsylvania (1925). While working for Craig, he was also employed by George Washington Smith. In 1937 Mary hired Los Angeles draftsman Peter Obninsky to work on the plans and oversee the Lasky project. Russian-born Obninsky, of Austrian aristocratic heritage, immigrated to New York in 1920. Living there until 1931, he received his architectural training at Columbia University's School of Architecture (1926) followed by five years working for McKim, Mead & White and Charles Adams Platt. Platt, a gifted artist before he made his mark as an architect, had a strong influence on the talented young exile.[13]

For many years Mary contended privately with the duality of her desire to succeed as a designer and to be important through that medium, and her equally strong wish to escape responsibility. It left her at times feeling as if she had been "dragged through a knothole," a term she often used when speaking of life's complexities. Her daughter recalled, "My mother's determination to carry on with my father's legacy often carried a certain burden of responsibility. At times it overcame her ability to work productively. But even with all the pressures, she always won that battle."[14] In April 1929 Mary went east to spend two weeks under the care of Dr. Austen Riggs and his colleagues at The Austen Riggs Foundation in Stockbridge, Massachusetts. Craig deeply admired Riggs,

a man who prepared his patients for "intelligent living," and to understand that "without fear there is no real courage."[15]

With her health restored by late 1929, and wishing to promote her work, Mary turned to the well-known New York photographer Jessie Tarbox Beals to photograph her own newly renovated house and the Slater houses. Arriving in the summer of 1928, Beals established herself briefly in Santa Barbara. Her photographs of El Paseo and numerous other houses

and gardens commissioned by Pearl Chase appeared in H. Philip Staats' 1929 *Californian Architecture in Santa Barbara*. Moving on quickly, Beals decamped for Hollywood in late 1929.[16]

Like all architects, Mary's work in the 1930s moved away from the once-popular Spanish themes. Always focused on pleasing her clients (a quality which explains in large part why she had an almost flawless history of positive business relationships), Mary usually gave them what they asked for, which meant new styles, new materials, and extensive research. Feeling confident she could pass the oral examination and with more work behind her, she appeared again before the licensing board in late

13.05. Slater House II, Montecito

13.06. Slater House I, Montecito

1930. With new rulings requiring a written examination and fearing failure again, Mary decided to end her pursuit of a license.[17]

In early 1931 before she left to begin work on the du Pont house in Wilmington, Delaware, Amy du Pont invited Mary on a trip to Mexico where they traveled privately by rail in a leased Pullman for several weeks. By late winter Mary was in the east. With occasional trips back to California, she lived at Aunt May's home Carnarvon, in Paoli, for the next two years. Ralph. Armitage remained in Santa Barbara and worked with Mary by telephone and mail. Some assistance came from New York architectural designer and draftsman Alain de Bouthillier, about whom little biographical information has been found. Surrounded by the enchantments of her temporary home, little Mary attended school in Villanova. From Paoli, Mary wrote to her mother, "There is no news, just work and a simple quiet life when I am here."[18]

With the du Pont house nearing completion, and back in Santa Barbara in March 1933, Mary received a letter from Pasadena architect Reginald Johnson suggesting a partnership:

> My dear Mrs. Craig,
>
> Since our two conferences the early part of this week, I have been giving considerable amount of thought to the matter of our possible association on certain pieces of work, and it seems to me that it might be advisable for me to jot down in an informal manner some of my conclusions, to which you in turn could be giving consideration before our next meeting.[19]

The idea of an association seems to have been Johnson's; Mary gave it serious consideration but in the end turned it down. She was still very busy and after so many years of working successfully on her own, a partnership with Johnson may have presented too many complications. She had recently completed plans for a large formal house for Mr. and Mrs. Louis Soles in Montecito, assuring at least another year of work (Fig. 13.07). Alice Soles' father, Colonel Lewis Walker, a lawyer whose curiosity and efforts in 1913 launched the first zipper factory known as the Hookless Fastener Company, Inc., in Pennsylvania, afforded Alice a sizeable income. The commission abruptly ended in early 1935 when the Soles purchased a house at Fernald Point.[20]

With her daughter in the east at school, Mary spent much of 1935 and 1936 traveling between Deadwood, Paoli, Montana (where friends the Wetmore Hodges lived), and Washington, D.C. After visiting her daughter, en route back to Santa Barbara in February 1937 Mary wrote to her:

> You are an understanding person— no longer a child— I cannot tell you what it means to have you place so much confidence and trust in me. Life will not always be gay and merry, but faith and trust and loyalty and love are the things that carry one along. Though my judgment may seem a bit at variance with your plans, I am thinking of building for future spiritual qualities rather than for the ephemeral ones of momentary pleasure.[21]

Throughout 1938 Mary worked on plans for a house on the Arizona ranch of Dorothy and Wetmore Hodges. The Hodges lived a peripatetic life of both pleasure and accomplishment, moving between Washington, D.C., Santa Barbara, their Jumping Horse Ranch in Montana, and the Southwest. Wetmore was a man of extraordinary energy and focus, whose early success allowed him to live a life of broad interests and great generosity. Dorothy Chapman Hodges, as fascinating as her ancestor, "pirate" Joseph Chapman of California mission fame, was an accomplished rider, angler and wildlife advocate. Both trained in archeological excavation, the Hodges funded several important Smithsonian archeological surveys in Arizona and Mexico, working alongside some of the best known archeologists of the last century. While visiting Tucson, Mary Craig, along with the Hodges's friend Anna Roosevelt Boettiger, participated in one of their digs.[22]

In 1939 the first stage of the Hodges's construction began with the onsite production of the adobe bricks. Following Germany's invasion of Poland in early September, Mary spent several weeks with the family at the Montana ranch. Describing it as "a small principality," she wrote to Aunt May: "This is the most beautiful place. It seems like heaven—so far removed from all the turmoil and upset of these horrible times. The mental pictures drift in over the radio, but rather vaguely. It is surrounded by so much beauty and infinite space, that one's spirit achieves a certain equanimity. I shall be sorry to leave it." While there, the Hodges informed Mary they could not go ahead with the project; Wetmore felt that building such an expensive house went counter to the deprivations of so many others during troubling times. Though the Hodges covered all of Mary's costs associated with the plans and her travels to Tucson, the decision not to build was a great disappointment and cause of some financial worry. She ended her letter to Aunt May: "The Hodges are not going on with their house at this time…. These are times when one must count every move if one is to survive spiritually as well as financially."[23]

The Hodges's son Bill later wrote of the proposed Tucson house (see Fig. 6.16):

> I'm sure Mother and Dad brought their love of Mexico's rancho living to bear on the ideas represented in the architecture of the design your grandmother developed for them…. I recall that over four thousand adobe bricks, approx. 4' thick by 18" square would be required. Over half of these were made and stacked on location when the job was stopped…. They made quite a big pile when I saw them and the outline of the design was staked out so one could see it was plenty big enough for all of us.

In the spring of 1948, Bill Hodges remembered seeing "the huge pile of adobes, slowly melting under the elements. The site was almost hidden among the big Mesquite trees that must have been 100-plus years old. I remember how grand it would have been. Anyway, the dreams and aspirations of most of us were changed by the war."[24]

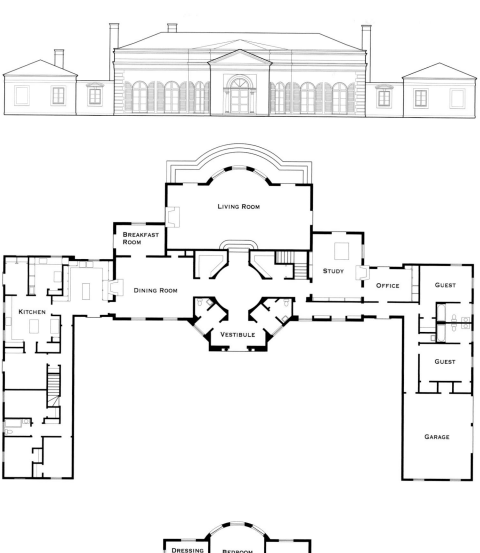

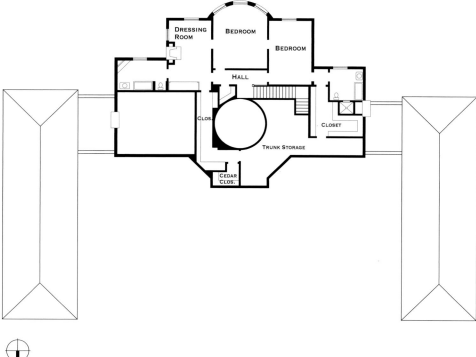

13.07. Soles House, Montecito (project), top to bottom: north elevation, first-floor plan, second-floor plan

CHAPTER 14

Winding Down

1940–1964

The economic slowdown during World War II affected the professional lives of many; new building virtually stopped. Throughout the 1940s Mary received only three commissions: houses for artist Isabel Adams, Ruth Peabody Fleming and Mrs. Charles Perkins. She supplemented her income with smaller interior jobs for friends, sold some of her shares in the Buena Vista Water Company, and managed to bring in a small steady income from her cottage rentals and mining interests. The losses of the Hodges commission and her 1940 Homestake lawsuit were compounded by the death of Aunt May Roberts in August 1942. For reasons unknown, the vast majority of her aunt's estate was returned to the Roberts family. The realization that she could count only on her own efforts to see her through her remaining years was greatly on her mind when she returned to Santa Barbara from the east in late 1942.

As the country settled into postwar prosperity, Mary found herself invigorated by the August 1946 marriage of her daughter to San Franciscan Bennet Skewes-Cox. His grandfather, Benito Forbes Smith, was a first cousin to Edith Forbes Perkins, whose family Mary had known since her first days in Santa Barbara. The marriage took place at the mission, followed by a large gathering of family and friends at One Acre. Having sent wedding invitations to several Osborne and Craig family relatives in Scotland, Mary received a letter from Osborne's uncle William Craig that December:

> Hearing of this happy event has naturally cast my mind back to the far-off days of long ago when Osborne was a small child. I was thinking of those days recently when his birthday came round on the 2nd of Novem-

ber. I can hardly realize that had he lived he would now be 58 years of age … it is rather difficult for me to visualize him in his young manhood. His untimely death was a great grief to us all and must have been particularly so to you, his wife. We have at any rate the consolation and satisfaction of knowing that he made the most of his short life. I often wonder how he would have fared had he lived to more mature years. I have no doubt that his early successes would have been repeated in later years and that he would have won for himself an honoured place in the roll of America's famous architects.[1]

In 1950 Mary Craig was sixty years old.[2] A diary, found with her papers and recording the years 1950 and 1951, offers just a hint into Mary's inner life. Mention is made of visits with family and friends, reading quietly at home, listening to newly purchased recordings of Gregorian chant, a "quiet morning sitting in the sun" or staying up "until 2 AM listening to beautiful music." The brief notations account for a life lived calmly, purposefully and often alone. On November 19, 1950, she wrote: "My wedding anniversary," the only known reference to her short life with Osborne Craig.

Before ending her career Mary Craig took on five more commissions, all of them influenced to some degree by the modernist movement that had swept the country. She kept up with the shift in the teaching of architecture in major academic institutions, even if she did not fully accept the tenets of modernism. Though her last commissions indicate her traditional tastes, she nonetheless was instinctively curious about the work of younger architects. While on a trip to the East Coast, she visited the well-publicized prefabricated house designed by Carl Koch for physicist Fran-

cis Bitter. Her response in her diary: "hideous, I thought." More charitable about Philip Johnson's glass house in New Canaan, she noted: "beautiful day and beautiful place, but house impractical."[3]

Mary's most accessible source for the contemporary architectural climate was architect Adrian Malone. Grandson of Mrs. William Slater, Malone met Mary in the 1930s while attending the Cate School in Carpinteria. But the connection grew even closer after her daughter's marriage to Bennet Skewes-Cox whose sister Joan was married to Malone. Making frequent trips to northern California to see her daughter, Mary often crossed paths with Adrian at family gatherings. A 1941 graduate of the Harvard Graduate School of Design, Malone was there during the distinguished era led by Walter Gropius and Marcel Breuer that included Eliot Noyes, Philip Johnson, I. M. Pei and Paul Rudolph among its alumni. He and Mary often exchanged ideas about the state of building, styles and the modernist post-war movement. His wife, often part of the discussions, described Mary as a person of "great character" with "plenty of courage and a bit of gall."[4]

In the fall of 1951 Mary entered the Silver Hill Foundation, a clinic in New Canaan which she found conducive for rest, good company and introspection. Staying in one of the campus rooms at River House, where her doctor William B. Terhune also lived, Mary made suggestions for improvements to the imposing Gothic structure built in 1913–14 for artist Daniel Putnam Brinley. Returning to Silver Hill in 1956, she saw that most of her recommendations had been carried out. She took umbrage at one that had not:

> But one of the main things I thought I had emphasized and which you had not done but which is disturbing to my aesthetic sense was to remove the quite ugly Gothic lamps and chisel off the heraldry around the front entrance.

In exchange for her suggestions, Mary requested a reduction in her bill. She explained, "I did not supervise the work of remodeling your house, but I did give you all the ideas…. Of course in work of this kind it is the ideas that cost."[5]

The years 1953 to 1955 when Mary designed a house for Belle Hayes were some of her happiest. Intrigued by the idea of planning such a grand house over the original Knapp pavilion, Mary wrote to Belle that it was so solidly built "it could hold the Empire State building on top of it." Voluminous correspondence between architect and client makes clear the issues at hand and how decisions were made. In one letter Mary wrote: "I have thought of using the wide eclectic molding of fine cement, and marble-izing them as we did in Mrs. Slater's house with great effect and economy, making them exactly alike. It is often done in a French house…. The time element, we assure you, will be taken care of, and if you will instruct us to go ahead at once, we can promise you the house in the minimum amount of time, for both Mr. Armitage and I will give it our undivided attention. Nothing else will seem important to me, and our best energies and time will be given to it."[6]

In April 1955 Mary received a letter from Ralph Armitage indicating that he no longer wished to work for her "in any capacity." Issues with the Hayes House had caused some sort of rift, their first in a long relationship. Accustomed to addressing him as Mr. Armitage, Mary dispensed with the formal salutation and responded:

> Dear Ralph,
> …. After thirty years of work together it is quite baffling. We have had so many problems to meet together year in and year out.
> Of course you know your construction better than anyone in town and are such a perfect draftsman…. I am and always have been your loyal and devoted friend as I think I have proved many, many times. Come what may, you and Charlotte will always have my very deep affection. If you no longer wish to work for me … that is your decision.
>
> Always sincerely, Mary Craig.

Armitage's work on the Hayes House was his last project with Mary Craig. At the end of November

1955, she wrote to Belle: "Armitage and I are friends again, he was here the other day but says he is too old to do any more building and he did look old and tired. It makes me sad after so many years of work together...."[7]

Mary's rental cottages at One Acre embellished her social life. One of them was occupied over ten years by Percy Alexander Blair, whom she had met in Madrid in 1927. A member of the family that for more than a century owned Blair House in Washington, D.C., he was indefatigable in his efforts to persuade Roosevelt and the Federal Government to take over the house as the country's official diplomatic guest house. Distinguishing himself in the Foreign Service, Blair later served as first curator of the very grand Larz Anderson House on Dupont Circle after it was given to the Society of the Cincinnati in 1938. He, along with Ted and Anna Paramore, who rented one of Mary's cottages in the early 1950s were frequent dinner guests at Mary's parties. So too was James (Jimmy) Henderson Douglas, III, grandson of Bob McGann, who remembered Mary as "lively and quick mentally" but "unmotivated to exercise or move." When Stokowski appeared, Douglas recalled Mary teasing her friend and imploring "Oh Stoki, do strike a tune!" Stokowski dutifully obliged, playing the piano well into the night.[8]

With diminishing health in the late 1950s and finding it difficult to stand for long periods of time, Mary found she could be more productive reclining on her bed after dressing in the morning. It was in this manner, surrounded by papers, books and her telephone, that she conducted much of her business and often saw friends. Most took the situation in stride, including stonemason Oswald Da Ros who met regularly there while working on the Park House.[9] Meeting Mary in "her office," as David Park used to say, they frequently reviewed the plans for his new house in her bedroom.

Eugene Louie, son of Mary's retired housekeeper William Wah Thuen Louie, visited Mary Craig with his father in the 1950s and described the scene: "I recall Mary Craig met with us in her bedroom, which was filled with books stacked on the floor ... I had never seen so many books outside of a public library."[10]

Mary took her last trip abroad in early 1962, departing San Francisco aboard the RMS Caronia for a six-week cruise to the Far East via Honolulu. In October 1963, she made plans to spend the year-end holidays with her daughter's family, then living in Georgetown, Washington, D.C. With her doctors in Santa Barbara unable to determine why she was having great difficulty with movement, she went first to Boston for a medical evaluation. She was diagnosed with advanced myositis, a condition causing acute muscle inflammation. Prescribed a routine of new drugs, she arrived in Washington just before Thanksgiving and in good spirits spent the next few weeks seeing old friends and shopping. After Christmas she came down with the flu. Instead of recovering as her doctor expected, the myositis attacked her respiratory muscles and she slipped into unconsciousness. She died several days later, on February 2, in her room at the Fairfax Hotel. She was seventy-four years old. A requiem high mass was held at the Roman Catholic Church of the Epiphany in Georgetown on February 4. She was buried alongside her husband at the Santa Barbara Cemetery on March 28, 1964.

The accolades to Mary Craig in the months following her death were both a reminder of her talent as an architectural designer and her loyalty as a friend. In a letter to a business acquaintance she expressed the sentiment she came to understand fully while married to Osborne Craig, and which guided her for the rest of her life:

> I should like to consider you also a friend. As one grows older these relationships are the most important things—money is secondary. My father often quoted to me: If thou art rich, thou art poor; / For, like the ass whose back with ingots bows, / Thou carriest thy heavy riches but a journey, / And death unloads thee.[11]

Mary Craig–A Remembrance

by Joan Skewes-Cox Malone

It must have taken considerable courage for Mary Craig to take over her husband's architectural office when he died at the age of only thirty-three. She had her little girl to bring up and she got to work.

She was fortunate … in having inherited a functioning architectural office, and the sense to engage one of the area's finest licensed architects, Ralph Armitage. She also inherited her husband's excellent reputation as a California Spanish designer, a style he was largely responsible for establishing. He had left behind a respectable body of work.

Mary had the connections, and she got the jobs. She dealt with the clients, something no one else in the office had an appetite for. She had great taste, and she understood how her clients (mostly well-off transplants from the East and the Midwest) wanted to live in this gentle southern California land, with its Spanish history.

"She worked with the clients"—a simple statement that in no way reflects the endless meetings, the explanations, the expositions, that must occur before a plan is accepted by the future owners. Eventually the dream of a house turns into reality—a lot of work in between.

She built many appealing houses and she developed a reputation of her own. Hearing about this accomplishment, you might imagine an executive, energetic commanding woman, tall and brisk. Nothing could be further from the truth. She was small,

intensely feminine, and a little on the plump side as she grew older. Her style of makeup came from the twenties; a daub of pink lipstick on a rosebud mouth (Fig. 14.01). She was given to small fluttering gestures with her hand. "No matter!" she would say gaily, dismissively. She hardly ever raised her voice, and had a tinkling laugh.

To meet her she gave the impression of vagueness—and she *was* vague about many things, but not her work or her feelings about architecture. From time to time she would decide to depart from social life and repair to a very up-scale clinic, "Silver Hill," in Connecticut, which sounded more like a spa to the rest of us.

She would return…all brisked up, doing a bit of name dropping—a well-known socialite here and a prominent philanthropist there (fellow residents). She had very few prejudices and this is the only overt snobbery I remember.

At the time that Mary Craig was practicing architecture there were very few women in the field. It was a real challenge to step into the role usually played by a man; I believe that she might actually not have achieved her very real success had she not been exactly what she was: non-threatening, accommodating, "savvy" about what might appeal to her clients, determined (but not advertising it) and SMART (without advertising it). She did a man's job as only a woman of her time could do it."[1]

A 01. James Osborne
Craig, Hoffmann House,
Santa Barbara, dining
room

A 02. James Osborne
Craig, Hoffmann House,
Santa Barbara, corridor

A 03. James Osborne
Craig, Hoffmann House,
Santa Barbara, stair hall

Santa Barbara emerged as a small city of international importance in the teens and twenties. Heretofore it had been difficult of access: the transformation from sleepy outpost to destination for extremely affluent seasonal visitors began with the arrival of railroad service in 1887. Aside from geographic and climatic blessings, the town offered a strong and appealing Hispanic heritage that ultimately defined its identity.

Osborne and Mary Craig were critical to the transformation. He left two buildings of such potency—even precocity, given his age—completed posthumously, that one suspects he would have given George Washington Smith ample competition if not for his premature death. One was Casa Santa Cruz, the house for Irene and Bernhard Hoffmann. The other was El Paseo, which set the standard for Santa Barbara's architectural rebirth in the twenties and continues to be a reference today as the city cultivates Hispanic imagery. Craig was a master illusionist, an essential component of Spanish Colonial Revival architecture. Until recently, El Paseo provided the indispensable backdrop for Fiesta pageantry: revelers in full costume, many on horseback, transported the twentieth century back to a time and place that never were. The quality of the place was not lost on Hollywood: Scenes from Joy Street, a late silent movie produced by Fox Film

Corporation and released in 1929, were shot here. Many of Craig's sketches for domestic interiors are similarly evocative, conveying at once a mastery of space and a sense of mystery, a critical component of architectural composition.

One wonders how Osborne Craig's career would have developed and is left to speculate that his reputation may be stronger because he did not have the opportunity.

Mary Craig is indelibly linked with Plaza Rubio. Completed with Margaret Andrews, it represents a remarkable synergism of strong women in the 1920s and coincides with gradually shifting ethos in a profession historically dominated by males. Here lies Mary's true legacy. Though lacking formal training, she needs to be recognized with a group that includes, most famously, Julia Morgan but also Lillian Rice in Rancho Santa Fe; Mary Colter, best remembered for her work for the Fred Harvey Company; and Lutah Maria Riggs, who began with George Washington Smith and went on to establish her independent career in Santa Barbara.

No ingénue she, Mary's work was published regularly and she received accolades throughout her career. Unlike Osborne, she bridged the transition when the fervor for things Spanish ended around 1930 but she did not embrace the European Mod-

ernism that had been developing since 1922 and was famously introduced in the *Modern Architecture* exhibition at the Museum of Modern Art in 1932. She opted for a traditional path, providing her clients with a level of intellectual and physical comfort antithetical to the modernists' vision. Her work was never formulaic but one senses an intuitive drift toward the "good taste" of designers such as David Adler in North Shore Chicago and William Lawrence Bottomley in Richmond. In her commissions that nod to the Mediterranean and the Southwest, analogy with Reginald Johnson seems fair. Though in the wrong timeframe, one imagines that Mary would have felt kinship with Betty Sherrill who, as longtime doyenne of McMillen Inc., interior designers to the quiet, established rich, was a latter-day Frances Elkins.[1]

Today, the Craigs' buildings stand in varying states of repair and alteration. The most satisfying rescue is the Hoffmann House; it was brought back from the brink by its current owners. Taste, wit and educated judgment are needed to recapture the spirit of El Paseo, though, admittedly, the economic challenge is staggering. First the bulldozer must be stopped—and this requires a victory of attitude and perception—then, the Campbell House will be ripe for imaginative recycling. Other buildings face an avalanche of issues as diverse as they are compli-

cated but mostly concerning land value and accommodation of a twenty-first-century lifestyle.

The Craigs' legacy—and the premise for this book, architecture and society—was the result of a reciprocal chemistry of talent and enterprise combined with a singular aspect that has long distinguished Santa Barbara from its neighboring communities. Much of the contemporary culture, lingering today, resulted from the extraordinary wealth of its transplanted citizenry. Many of these people came to play, although on their own terms and with astonishing flair. Private clubs abounded. The Montecito Country Club can trace its roots to 1894; the Valley Club was established in 1928. There also were the Santa Barbara Club and Little Town Club, downtown; and La Cumbre Country Club in Hope Ranch. Edgecliffe, on the beach near the Miramar Hotel, flourished for a time as a social mecca and, in the thirties, Coral Casino, designed by Gardner Daily of San Francisco, became a destination. Perhaps the most hedonistic private pleasure palace was Ralph Isham's Islamic natatorium in Carpinteria, designed by George Washington Smith.

Osborne and Mary Craig had access to this world. An astonishing number of their clients figure prominently in the local society columns. This was a time in Santa Barbara when, for a select few, work was a four-letter word.

APPENDIX

Postmarked January 18, 1919, from Santa Barbara to State Street in Pasadena. Written on January 17, 1919:

Friday night

Mary dear:

I am hoping your little house will not be occupied before you come up, it will be very enjoyable to go there and talk over our many affairs. Kamatzu has not wasted his time, and for one day a week the boy has done well, but of course like all vegetation it is need of the rains. I am wondering what you meant by an "indefinite" leave, would it be wise to make it too long? and please be sure to have a lease contract executed which will cover all important points; the last one you know was scarcely worth the paper it was written on. I am busy these days but hope that I will be able to get hold of a good draughtsman who can execute working drawings and so enable me to give my time to further formative work and seeing possible clients. Some multi-multi friends of the Harris's have bought quite a bit of property here and I am hoping that they will be persuaded to retain me as their architect. When you come up we will go and call on the Harris's among other people.

I am anticipating even now my next visit to Monterey, this last time I had to get back as quickly as possible, so there was little opportunity to see much of that quaint old town, in many respects the most interesting in California. I managed to put in about two hours in its confines and as I stood at the little station down near the water's edge waiting for the train I was transported by what I saw to be old world prototypes; truly it was both pleasing and sad to behold, the simple grandeur of the expression of Spain's influence was satisfying, but what a discordant note is struck in the work since American occupation, fortunately it was dusk, and all was a half-tone, a lamp from a window here and there was reflected in curious shapes in the rippling water and against the slowly vanishing light of the western sky were myriad little fishing boats in silhouette, the scene bespoke a benediction which cheered me and gave me strength, for like the good and the beautiful in life, stood at the good and the beautiful in that old Spanish sea port, if one only would but see it.

With lots of love
Osborne.

Postmarked on October 20, 1919 from New London, Ct. to Santa Barbara*

Dearest –

I'm on my way to Boston to stay a few days—then back to Paoli—& then home, dear heart to you—and never again to leave without you—& I hope you'll not be wanting to come for some time—I wish I might tell you of the hoards & mobs in N.Y.—and the fearful prices for everything! How I hate it! Ted & I had a nice time, but he is so unhappy Osborne—& lives in an apartment alone—trying to cook his meals—& is not very well—he is very much on my mind just now—for this is his first hard ordeal! Yet I can only advise one thing—to play his game fairly! I do hope his mother will decide to come to him.

I had dinner with Ruth Maitland on Saturday & Ted & I spent yesterday with the Seligmans—motoring to the country with them—I didn't buy a thing except some spats to warm myself, as it is cold here—but prices are terrific & I wanted to get away before I was tempted! Can I do for you any shopping before my return? Wanamakers English Shop is marvelous—just as good as Brooks—

This country is very beautiful now & the air cold & snappy—but it cannot compare with our mountains & sea & the glory of these autumn colours fades into magnificence compared with our sunsets! How I long to return! Do write you'll meet me at San Bernadino—Keep well & happy & patient, patient with me particularly in all my failings—Sweetheart for I love you—& shall try with all my soul to make you happy & be a good wife.

Mary

*This is one of only two letters to Osborne that Mary saved.

THE COMPLETE WORK OF JAMES OSBORNE CRAIG AND MARY McLAUGHLIN CRAIG

Note: Executed buildings are indicated in boldface type. All of the entries from Mary Craig's ledger book have been included, though in many cases the nature of the work is not indicated. Mary Craig's principal collaborator was Ralph W. Armitage. Others who worked in her office as draftsmen included Robert Barnhart, Henry M. Barone, Thomas Lawford Lingham, Richard H. Pitman and Peter Victor Obninsky.

JAMES OSBORNE CRAIG

1915 Masonic Temple, Flagstaff, Arizona. *See p. 18.*

Girls' Dormitory, Northern Arizona Normal School, Flagstaff. Extant with interior remodeling. *See pp. 18–19.* The building was connected to another dormitory, Morton Hall, in 1931 and the interior was remodeled in 1935 and 1950 but the front elevation remains virtually unaltered.

Boys' Dormitory addition, Northern Arizona Normal School, Flagstaff. Extant with significant remodeling. *See pp. 19–20.* A wing projecting diagonally to the southeast was added in 1935, essentially doubling the size of the building. At the same time the porch was remodeled in the fashionable Colonial Revival style and the building was resurfaced with scored cement plaster over the original brick. Finally, in 1955, the projecting porch was removed and replaced with the simplified entry seen today.

Mohave County Union High School, Kingman, Arizona. *See p. 20.*

Riordan Entrance Gate, Milton, Arizona. Partially extant. *See p. 20.* The tall piers were relocated and the low walls removed when the Riordan houses and property were deeded to Arizona State Parks in 1979. The site is managed by the Arizona Historical Society.

1916 Maryland Hotel Cottages, Pasadena. *See pp. 20–21.*

1916–1917 Michael J. Riordan Belfry, Milton, Arizona. *See p. 21.*

1917 Helen C. Heberton House, Montecito, Schemes 1, 2, 3. *See pp. 24–25, 30.*

1918 Martin Redmayne House, Montecito. *See p. 26.*

James M. Warren Cottage, El Encanto Hotel, Santa Barbara. Construction not confirmed.

Mary McLaughlin Motor House, Montecito. Remodeled and enlarged. *See 1926, 1933.*

Mrs. Theodore Sheldon Garage/Gardener's Cottage, Montecito. Extant. *See pp. 26–29 and* Mrs. M. Russell Perkins, 1926.

Mrs. Theodore Sheldon addition to Garage/ Gardener's Cottage, Montecito. *See pp. 27, 30.*

Mrs. Theodore Sheldon House, Scheme 1, Montecito. *See pp. 27, 31.*

Mrs. Theodore Sheldon House, Montecito, Scheme 2.

Mary Sheldon House, Montecito, Schemes 1, 2.

Mission Santa Inés Restoration, Santa Ynez. *See p. 32–33.*

1919 James Leslie Doulton Apartment House remodeling, Santa Barbara.

Mrs. Charles E. Bigelow House, Carmel Highlands. Extant with additions and remodeling. *See p. 33.*

Edith Chesebrough House, Pebble Beach. *See pp. 34–35.* The drawing for this house subsequently was re-identified: Chesebrough's name was erased and replaced with "A House for Mrs. James Osborne Craig in Montecito."

J. B. Alexander House remodeling, Montecito. Extant with some remodeling. See pp. 36–37.

Alfred E. Brush House, Montecito, Schemes 1, 2. *See pp. 37–38.*

Oreña Adobe restoration, Santa Barbara. Extant. *See pp. 38–41.*

Oreña Studio for Doña Acacia Oreña Rickard, Santa Barbara. Extant. The studio is intact; the courtyard cannot be reconciled with 1920s descriptions but invites imagination. *See pp. 39, 42.*

Rudolph B. Gring House, Montecito. Extant with additions and extensive remodeling. *See pp. 38–39.*

Gantz Gardener's Cottage. Location and construction not confirmed.

John E. C. Kohlsaat House, Serena (now Carpinteria). Most enigmatic is a reference in a newspaper account of the Craigs' wedding in late 1919 that Osborne was "making plans" for an oceanfront house in Serena for the parents of wedding guest Mrs. Learner Blackman Harrison (the former Frances Kohlsaat). One undated drawing by Craig shows a small Spanish-style garage and farmhouse for the Kohlsaats, apparently not built. Records indicate the house was completed by June 1920. Retired Cincinnati lumberman John E. C. Kohlsaat purchased the property from architect Francis Wilson; a more likely scenario is that Wilson himself provided the ideas and then, leaving Santa Barbara for good, gave Craig the job as supervising architect. Extant with some remodeling.

John E. C. Kohlsaat House

1920 Mary Craig Wall, One Acre, Montecito. Extant with modification.

Harry Gantz House, Crossways Cottage, Montecito. Extant with some remodeling. *See* pp. 42–45.

Mrs. James Nelson Burnes cottage, Fernald Point, Montecito. Relocated on original site and reconstructed with changes, 2008. *See* pp. 43, 46.

Mrs. James Nelson Burnes garage, Fernald Point, Montecito. Extant.

Nugent, Chase and Leeds Cottages, Sandyland. Demolished. *See* pp. 47–48.

Robin Y. Hayne House, Montecito.

Bernhard Hoffmann Guest Cottage, Mission Canyon, Santa Barbara. Extant with some remodeling. Chosen as one of the "five most notable examples of small houses," 1924. *See* pp. 66–68.

El Encanto Cottage Number 9 remodeling, Santa Barbara. Extent of work completed unknown. A blueprint drawing dated October 20, 1920, indicates that the cottage was comprised of a living room, three bedrooms and two bathrooms. A building permit issued October 21, 1920, describes the work as a "cottage alteration." Alexander MacKeller was the contractor. Remodeled by Edwards and Plunkett in 1929. Designated one of several historic landmarks in the El Encanto Historic District.

Bernhard Hoffmann, measured drawings of McCalla House, Santa Barbara. *See* p. 53.

Bernhard Hoffmann, McCalla House remodeling, Santa Barbara. *See* p. 53.

Dr. J. J. Kocher, Sunshine Court, Palm Springs. Demolished.

Dr. J. J. Kocher, Sunshine Court

University Club, Santa Barbara. *See* pp. 48–49.

De Witt Parshall House, Montecito. Though the drawing is undated, it was most likely done in 1920. Parshall commissioned both Craig and George Washington Smith to make plans for converting his then Victorian house into one along Spanish lines. Parshall gave the commission to Smith. Another drawing by Craig for a gardener's cottage has the erasure "For Mr. and Mrs. De Witt Parshall." Construction of this cottage has not been confirmed. (*See* P. R. Babcock House by Mary Craig.)

De Witt Parshall House

1921 Bernhard Hoffmann Guest House Garage, Mission Canyon, Santa Barbara. Extant. The earliest drawings for the garage are dated March 11, 1921, and show a simple rectangular structure to accommodate one automobile. Like the house, it had plaster walls and an Angulo Tile roof. The drawings were revised May 5.

William H. Cowles Reservoir, Montecito. Extant. *See* pp. 92–95.

William H. Cowles Reservoir

William H. Cowles Gardener's Cottage, Montecito. Extant.

William H. Cowles Gardener's Cottage

Bernhard Hoffmann Gardener's Cottage, Mission Canyon, Santa Barbara. Remodeled beyond recognition or demolished. *See* p. 68.

Bernhard Hoffmann Office, Mission Canyon, Santa Barbara. Demolished or remodeled beyond recognition. *See* pp. 67–68

Bernhard Hoffmann House, Casa Santa Cruz, Santa Barbara. Extant with extensive restoration. *See* pp. 51–66, 68–69, 225, 228, 242–243

Bernhard Hoffmann House, Casa Santa Cruz

Bernhard Hoffmann Service Building remodeling, Santa Barbara. Extant.

Bernhard Hoffmann additions and alterations to St. Anthony's College, Santa Barbara. *See* p. 70.

E. E. Paramore House, Montecito, Schemes 1, 2. Paramore asked Osborne Craig to propose two schemes for a new house in Montecito. Scheme I was Spanish (*See* Fig. 12.08). Paramore ultimately built a house in the Spanish style (*See* fig. 10.02) but based primarily on his own ideas, rather than Craig's. The exterior of the finished house showed little resemblance to Craig's plan but the interior did adhere to many aspects of the architect's suggestions. Demolished 1950s.

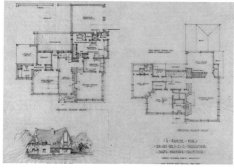

E. E. Paramore House, Scheme 2

Lionel Armstrong House, Scheme 1, Pasadena. *See* p. 92.

Lionel Armstrong House, Scheme 2, Pasadena. Extant with significant remodeling. Armstrong made minor alterations in 1925; the second owner carried out extensive additions and alterations in 1928. *See* p. 92.

1922 **Mrs. H. S. Russell Stable and Garage, Carpinteria.** Extant. *See* fig. 12.07.

Bernhard Hoffmann, El Paseo, Santa Barbara. Extant. *See* pp. 70–91, 100, 138, 169, 217, 225, 231, 233, 242, 243. Also identified in contemporary literature as Street in Spain and de la Guerra Studios. *See* also Mary Craig, Paseo de las Flores, 1924.

Bernhard Hoffmann, de la Guerra Plaza, Santa Barbara. *See* pp. 70–75, 98, 168.

Mrs. William Law McLaughlin House, Pasadena. Extant with extensive remodeling. *See* pp. 92, 97.

Bernhard Hoffmann Fireplace, Lugo Adobe, Santa Barbara. Extant. *See* pp. 97, 99.

Mrs. C. D. Wilcox House, Santa Barbara. Commission given to another architect.

In addition to those listed above, there are two projects by Osborne Craig that require additional research: "Court Group of Houses," with the erasure "Fullerton" (possibly for Harry Gantz who had a ranch in Fullerton); and an undated drawing by Craig, which became the prototype for the Von Waldt-Hausen studio designed by Mary Craig (*see* p. 148).

MARY CRAIG

1922 Dispensory [*sic*] for Associated Nurses, Santa Barbara Commission given to Carleton Winslow.

1923 **Paseo de las Flores for Santa Barbara Seed Company, Santa Barbara.** Demolished. *See* pp. 100–101.

1924 Edward Sajous House, Santa Barbara

James Marwick subdivision, Braemar Ranch, Santa Barbara One undated subdivision drawing shows twenty-nine lots accessed by two new internal roads. Another drawing, dated October 1924, shows thirty lots, each roughly 70' x 100' though dimensions vary.

Campbell Dovecote, Campbell Ranch, Goleta. Extant. *See* p. 230.

Mrs. M. Waterman Canby House, Montecito. Extant. *See* p. 101.

Mrs. Colin Campbell House, Campbell Ranch, Goleta. Extant in ruinous condition. Designated as Santa Barbara County Historical Landmark No. 27 on September 8, 1987. *See* pp. 104–111, 112, 156, 198, 230,243.

Speculative House, Hermosillo Court, Montecito. Extant with remodeling and additions. *See* pp. 102–104.

1924– 1926 **Mrs. J. A. Andrews, Plaza Rubio, Santa Barbara.** Extant with some remodeling. *See* pp. 132–145, 146, 231, 242 and 1926.

1925 **Mrs. Ambrose Cramer House, Montecito.** Extant with some remodeling. *See* pp. 128, 130–132

Elizabeth Urmston House, Pasadena. Extant. No plans for this house have been found. It was constructed of cement plaster walls and had a tile roof. *See* Mrs. Andrew Brown, 1926.

Ott Hardware.

Dr. Singleton.

E. J. Miley House I, Montecito. Extant. *See* pp. 112–113, 196–197, 233.

E. J. Miley House II, El Prado, Montecito. *See* pp. 104, 112, 114–129, 156, 199, 233. The unfinished house was purchased in 1933 by John T. deBlois Wack and completed by Chester Carjola. Now serving as La Casa de Maria Retreat & Conference Center.

Marguerite (Mig) Bayard, Montecito. Work undetermined.

P. R. Babcock House, Montecito. The floor plan and overall design of this house was based on the mirror image of a drawing by Osborne Craig of a "Gardener's Cottage." The drawing is undated and the name of the client is erased. The erasure appears to read "On the Goleta (or Gould) Property of Mr. and Mrs.De Witt Parshall." Extant. *See* also 1927.

P. R. Babcock House

E. J. Miley Guest House. Extant.

E. J. Miley Guest House

E. J. Miley Plastered Service Cottage. Extant.

Mrs. Colin Campbell addition to main residence, Campbell Ranch, Goleta.

Mrs. Colin Campbell Barn, Campbell Ranch, Goleta. Extant.

Mrs. Colin Campbell Barn

Salisbury Field House remodeling, Serena. Demolished.

Mildred A. Crow Store, Jade Tree, Santa Barbara.

Mildred A. Crow Store

Construction status undetermined.

E. J. Miley Gate Lodge, El Prado, Montecito.

Harry L. Day House, Montecito.

M. L. Fitzgerald House, San Luis Obispo.

Clarence Alexander Black alterations to house designed by Winsor Soule and Russell Ray, 1921, Santa Barbara.
Nature of project and construction not confirmed.

Santa Barbara Board of Education Open Air School, Santa Barbara. *See* p. 146.

Mrs. J. A. Andrews, 502 Plaza Rubio, Santa Barbara. Extant with remodeling. The house originally was constructed in 1906 by Mrs. Charles

Austin and used subsequently by her daughter-in-law, Camilla Waterman Austin (sister of Margaret Waterman Canby), as an artist's studio. Mrs. Andrews purchased it in 1925, shortly before the June 29 earthquake. Mary Craig both completed repairs and converted it into the new Spanish style.

State Street Development, Santa Barbara.

Dr. Harold Sidebotham, Campbell Ranch, Goleta. Demolished. Mary Craig oversaw the move of an existing house onto the property.

Mr. and Mrs. Robert Woods Bliss House, Montecito.

Mrs. T. Stewart White House, Santa Barbara.

Californian Hotel, Santa Barbara.

Mrs. J. A. Andrews automobile showroom and garage for W. C. Logan, Santa Barbara. The garage was demolished in 1979. The arcade was replicated during construction of the office building that replaced it. *See* pp. 146–147.

Mrs. Colin Campbell earthquake repairs, Campbell Ranch, Goleta. Nature of repairs unknown.

E. J. Miley stable, Montecito. Extant. *See* pp. 244–245.

Lena M. Gilmore, Santa Barbara.

Ford Harvey house, measured drawings and addition, Montecito.

Mrs. Colin Campbell reception room ceiling, Campbell Ranch, Goleta.

Mrs. Norman T. Mason bedroom and bath addition, South Pasadena. Original house extant; status of Mary Craig's additions unknown.

Mrs. Milo Potter living room addition, Montecito. Extant.

Mrs. J. A. Andrews commercial building, La Hacienda Carrillo, Santa Barbara. Demolished. *See* p. 147.

1926 **Mrs. J. A. Andrews House for Elizabeth Knight, Plaza Rubio, Santa Barbara.** Extant.

Mary Craig House remodeling and addition, One Acre, Montecito. Extant. *See* pp. 149–153.

Mary Craig House

Mary Craig Beach Cottage, Sandyland Cove, Carpinteria. Craig's house was the first to be built on the numerous ocean lots. She added a large addition to the house in 1932. Demolished.

Chandler P. Ward House, San Marino.

E. J. Miley Swimming Pool and Loggia, El Prado, Montecito

Herman Von Waldt-Hausen Studio Buildings, Santa Barbara. *See* p. 148.

Mrs. M. Russell Perkins alterations to Sheldon House, designed by Osborne Craig for Mrs. Theodore Sheldon, Montecito.

W. H. Cowles Garage, Montecito. Demolished. The building can be described from surviving drawings. It included space for five cars; a tool room was attached. The garage had a hipped, tiled roof with varying slopes; the tool room had a shed roof capped by a weathervane and dovecote.

Mrs. Colin Campbell addition to sewing room, Campbell Ranch, Goleta.

J. P. Jefferson Chauffeur's Cottage, Montecito. Extant. *See* p. 154 and fig. 5.64.

Mrs. Andrew Brown addition to Urmston House, Pasadena. Extant.

Gudron Thorne-Thomsen House, Ojai.

Veronica Springs.

Mrs. J. H. Denison House alterations, Montecito. Mary Craig's ledger indicates that blueprints were prepared but provides no additional information.

Montecito Water District administration building, Montecito. *See* pp. 162–164 and 1929.

J. P. Jefferson alterations to two service cottages, Montecito. Extant. *See* pp. 154–155 and figs. 5.65, 5.66.

1927   **Mrs. Alma S. Urmston House, Pebble Beach.** Extant. *See* pp. 154, 156–159.

Charles E. Perkins Ranch House Renovation, Cottage #1, Cottage #2, Alisal Ranch, Solvang. Demolished. *See* p. 231.

E. J. Miley House I alterations, Montecito.

Mrs. William A. Slater and William Slater, Jr., House, Montecito. Extant. *See* pp. 156, 160–162.

La Cumbre Country Club, Santa Barbara. Unspecified work. Original building designed by George Washington Smith.

P. R. Babcock House alterations, Montecito. Extant.

A. E. Borie.

1928   Dwight Faulding House, Santa Barbara.

Colonel G. Watson French Dining Room addition and Garage Building, Montecito. Demolished. *See* also 1930, 1931.

Rachel P. Ogilvy, Santa Barbara.

1929   **Mrs. William A. Slater House, Montecito.** Extant. *See* pp. 164–169.

Mary Craig Office, One Acre, Montecito. Moved to rear of property, 1933. Demolished after 1980.

Montecito County Water District. Administration Building, Montecito. Extant with some remodeling. *See* pp. 162–164.

Harry Drake House, Carpinteria. Extant. *See* pp. 170–173.

1930   **A. E. Dieterich Beach Cottage, Sandyland.** Demolished.

A. E. Dieterich Beach Cottage

Francis V. Lloyd alterations. Francis V. Lloyd was the second husband of Grace Meeker Cramer.

J. Percival Jefferson, Entrance Gate, Mira Flores, Montecito. Designed by Florence Yoch and Lucile Council; construction supervised by Mary Craig.

Colonel G. Watson French Library, Montecito. *See* also 1931. Mary Smith, widow of George Washington Smith, was involved but her role is unclear.

1930–   **William S. Spaulding House, Montecito.**
1931   Extant. *See* pp. 174–177.

Colonel G. Watson French South Garden, Montecito (in collaboration with Florence Yoch).

Buena Vista House #1 (for Robert Livingston Beekman, 1866–1935) at corner of Lilac and Tollis. *See* Swift, 1932.

Malcolm Douglas, Montecito, "grills, etc." *See* also 1933.

Elizabeth and Andrew Brown House, San Marino. Extant.

1931–   **A. E. Dieterich Pavilion, Montecito.** Extant.
1933   *See* pp. 170, 178–180.

1932   **Amy du Pont House, Wilmington, Delaware.** Extant with some alterations. The chimneys have been removed from the wings and a cupola was added. *See* pp. 180–184, 234.

Walter M. Keck Mausoleum, Glen Abbey Cemetery, Bonita, California. Extant. A modest rectangular building with unadorned white plaster walls and a gabled roof clad in green-glazed ceramic tile.

Walter M. Keck Mausoleum

Peter Cooper Bryce Beach Cabana, Hope Ranch. Extant.

Peter Cooper Bryce Beach Cabana

Louis F. Swift Buena Vista House #1, Montecito. Downsized version of house designed for Robert Livingston Beeckman in 1931.

1933   **Mary Craig Guest Cottage Number 1, Montecito.** Extant. Given First Award "For a Distinctive Small House" in 1934 by Santa Barbara's Community Arts Association "Better Homes in America" competition.

Mary Craig remodeling and expansion of Motor House designed by Osborne Craig, One Acre, Montecito. Became Guest Cottage Number 2 Extant.

Mary Craig Three-Car Garage, One Acre, Montecito. Demolished

Amy du Pont Garage, Wilmington, Delaware.

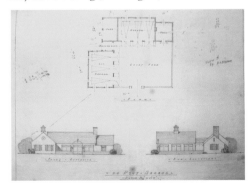

Amy du Pont Garage

Felton Elkins, Montecito.

Dr. Malcolm Douglas Paneled Library, Sycamore Canyon, Montecito. Original house designed by George Washington Smith.

Ronald de L. Kirkbride additions to Spaulding House, Montecito.

William A. Slater Beach Cottage, Serena. Extant; relocated to Montecito and subsequently enlarged.

Katherine Harvey Beach Cottage, Serena. Demolished.

Louis Soles House, Montecito. *See* pp. 234–235.

1934   Cudahy sisters, Clara, Mary and Elizabeth (Mrs. William P. Nelson), Mt. Carmel Church, Montecito. Commission given to Ross Montgomery.

John William Heaney (Dorothy Fithian Heaney) House, Montecito. Addition to original house designed by Reginald Johnson.

Sandyland Cove Association, Caretaker's Cottage. Extant.

1936   **Mary Craig House, Rancho de los Olivos Santa Ynez.** Demolished. Same as plan for Guest Cottage Number 1, One Acre, Montecito.

1937   **House for Academic Head, Foxcroft School, Middleburg Virginia.** Extant. In collaboration with Theodore Dominick, AIA.

House for Academic Head, Foxcroft School

Jesse Lasky House I, Los Angeles. Extant with some remodeling. *See* p. 184.

Ernest Pascal Garage and Guest Room addition, Los Angeles. Extant.

Stephen and Beth Gates House, Solvang. Extant?

Stephen and Beth Gates House

1938   **Wetmore Hodges House, Tucson, Arizona.** *See* pp. 184–187, 234.

1939   **Mary Craig Speculative House, Lilac Drive, Montecito.** Demolished. Received "Special Award In the 5 Room Class" (House at 139 Lilac Drive) in 1941 from the Better Homes in America competition.

Cameron Rogers Pump House, Glendessary, Santa Barbara. Extant.

Mrs. Frederick Garvin Hodson House, Montecito. Extant. Awarded second place, 1941 Small Homes Competition.

1940   **Henry Culley House addition, Montecito.** Extant? Original house by George Washington Smith.

Pauline M. Finley House, Santa Barbara. Extant. Received honorable mention in a "Small Homes Competition," 1941.

1946   **Ernest Crawford May Cottage remodeling, Montecito.** Demolished.

1947   **Isabel (Mrs. Charles E.) Perkins House, Montecito.** Demolished.

Isabel Adams House

Isabel Adams House, Montecito. Extant.

1948   Wetmore Hodges House, additions and alterations, Woodside. Demolished. Extent of work completed by Mary Craig undetermined.

Jesse Lasky House II, Los Angeles. Commission given to another architect.

1949   **Ruth Peabody Fleming House, Montecito.** Altered. The site was originally part of the City of Santa Barbara; blueprints for this house are archived with the city.

1950   **Mary Craig House, Maison du Plaisance, Montecito.** Extant. Mary Craig purchased this property, moved an existing house onto it, renovated the house and lived in it during the 1950s, renting One Acre on Buena Vista. She sold the house to Rhoda Prud'homme, for whom she did an addition. *See* 1958.

Mary Craig Guest Cottage Number 3, One Acre, Montecito. Craig converted her office into a one-story rental cottage. Demolished.

1951   Gladys Van Heukelom alterations to Isham House, Montecito. This substantial house as first constructed was designed by the Chicago firm Childs and Smith for Ralph Isham in 1916–17. It was acquired by Gladys Van Heurkelom in 1951 and she at once commissioned Mary Craig to make several minor alterations, more utilitarian than aesthetic. The house was demolished and reconstructed on the original footprint.

Dr. William Terhune House, alterations, Silver Hill Hospital, New Canaan, Connecticut. Extant. Renovations carried out in 1956 by architect Charles E. O'Hara. *See* pp. 238.

Dr. William Terhune House

1952   **Nevill Cramer House, Santa Barbara.** Extant.

Nevill Cramer House

1953   **Belle (Mrs. James) Hayes House, Montecito.** Extant with extensive remodeling. *See* pp. 188–189.

Belle (Mrs. James) Hayes House

Mary Craig Guest Cottage #4, One Acre, Montecit. Craig converted a large shed into another rental cottage. Demolished.

1956   **Mr. and Mrs. David Park Guest House, Montecito, 1956.** Extant with remodeling and additions. *See* pp. 188, 190–191.

1958   **Rhoda Prud'homme addition to house, Maison du Plaisance, remodeled and enlarged by Mary Craig in 1950, Montecito.** Extant.

———

One additional building should be mentioned to clear the record. In a note deposited at the Montecito History Committee, Lutah Maria Riggs attributed Bellogia, a house built for Emily Martindale in 1932, to Mary Craig. In fact, the house was designed by J. R. Whittemore.

ENDNOTES

Unless noted, all correspondence cited is held by the Craig family. Other material in the possession of the Craig family is identified CFP [Craig Family Papers]. James Osborne Craig is identified as JOC. Mary McLaughlin is identified as MMcL. Mary Craig is identified as MC. Mary Osborne Craig Skewes-Cox [Osborne and Mary Craigs' daughter] is identified as MCSC. Material from the Pearl Chase Collection, Community Development and Conservation Collection, Special Collections, Davidson Library, University of California, Santa Barbara, is identified as Chase Papers. Documents from the Architecture and Design Collection, Art, Design & Architecture Museum, University of California, Santa Barbara, are identified as ADC.

CHAPTER 1: THE TRAIL FROM BARRHEAD

1   Elizabeth King, Research Assistant, Royal Academy of Arts, to author, August 17, 2006. The myth about Craig's attendance at the Royal Academy can be traced to several press notices. "McLaughlin–Craig Wedding Is Nuptial Event of Week," *Morning Press*, November 16, 1919. "Sincuidado Is Scene of Wedding," Jessie Mary Bryant, "The Daily Round of Society," *Morning Press*, November 20, 1919. "James O. Craig Architect, Dies in Ojai Today," *Santa Barbara Daily News*, March 16, 1922. "James O. Craig Architect, Dies," *Morning Press*, March 17, 1922. "Passing of Two Architects," *Architect and Engineer* LXIX, no. 1. (April 1922): 111.

2   The Glasgow and West of Scotland Technical College. Annual Report Adopted at the Eighteenth Annual Meeting of Governors. Held on the 20th September, 1902, 8, 13–14.

3   "Colona," *Montrose Press*, July 21, 1905.

4   A good overview is provided in Geo. Rex Buckman, *Colorado Springs and Its Famous Scenic Environs* (Colorado Springs, Colorado: Geo. Rex Buckman, 1893).

5   "New Library Plans," *Colorado Springs Evening Telegraph*, July 12, 1903. I thank Jocelyne Sansing, Old Colorado City & UTE Pass Libraries, Colorado Springs, for her help. "Working Plans for New Library," *Colorado Springs Gazette*, August 11, 1903. The building currently serves as a branch of the Pikes Peak Library District.

6   Andrew Potter, Royal Academy Library, e-mail message to Pamela Skewes-Cox, February 2, 2012. Tricia Lawton, RIBA Information Centre, e-mail message to Robert Sweeney, March 29, 2012.

7   The 420-acre site of Cragmor Sanatorium is today the campus of the University of Colorado, Colorado Springs; the building serves as Main Hall. Claremont, built for C. A. Baldwin, now houses Colorado Springs School. The Salida Public Library and Masonic Temple, Colorado Springs, are extant.

8   "James O. Craig Architect, Dies," *Morning Press*, March 17, 1922. "Architect of El Paseo Eulogized; Prediction Now Lovely Reality," *Santa Barbara Daily News*, March 23, 1929. Mark Alan Hewitt, F.A.I.A., Kate Lemos and William Morrison generously responded to questions based on their intimate knowledge of the Carrère & Hastings archive, Avery Architectural & Fine Arts Library, Columbia University, New York.

9   "James Osborne Craig," [January 28, 1919]. Minutes, Southern California State Board of Architectural Examiners, 1901–1923, Sacramento, California. Ultimately, Craig never received a license.

10   Babbitt Brothers Trading Company Ledgers, 1914–1916. Cline Library Special Collections, Northern Arizona University, Flagstaff. Ms. 83, series 7, volumes 31–36.

11   "Masons Planning for Splendid Masonic Temple," *Coconino Sun*, April 30, 1915. "Flagstaff to Experience Biggest Boom in History This Spring," *Coconino Sun*, March 10, 1916. Ground finally was broken in 1917 for the temple standing today. "Local Brevities," *Coconino Sun*, July 20, 1917.

12   Rudolph H. H. Blome was president 1909–1918. Platt Cline, "Number of Students, Faculty, and Books by Years," in *Mountain Campus. The Story of Northern Arizona University*. With a Foreword by Bruce Babbitt (Flagstaff, Arizona: Northland Press, 1983), 358–59. R. H. H. Blome to C. O. Case, State Supt. of Public Instruction, December 26, 1914, Arizona State Library, Case Papers, Archives and Public Records, History and Archives Division, Phoenix; hereafter Arizona State Library.

13   1915 Session Laws, 2nd. Legislature, 1st Spec. Session, pp. 4–48. Cited in Melvin T. Hutchinson, *The Making of Northern Arizona University* (Flagstaff: Northern Arizona University, 1972), 43. "The New Buildings at the Northern Arizona Normal School," *Coconino Sun*, October 29, 1915. Contract by and between Board of Education of The Northern Arizona Normal School and James Osborne Craig, Architect, Case Papers, Arizona State Library.

14   Hutchinson, p. 44. "The New Buildings at the N.A.N.S.," *Coconino Sun*, October 8, 1915. "Normal Buildings," *Coconino Sun*, November 19, 1915. "Flagstaff's Splendid Showing for Past Year," *Coconino Sun*, January 7, 1916.

15   Blome to Case, December 30, 1915, Case Papers, Arizona State Library.

16   "Contract Awarded," *Coconino Sun*, June 10, 1905. "The New Buildings at the Northern Arizona Normal School," *Coconino Sun*, October 29, 1915. Hutchinson, p. 43. Blome to Case, December 30, 1915, Case Papers, Arizona State Library.

17   "Local Brevities," *Coconino Sun*, January 21, 1916. The incentive to build Mohave County Union High School can be traced to at least 1904. Craig's project was among many other sets of plans submitted to the Board of Education. The commission was awarded to Norman F. March and V. O. Wallingford on October 16, 1915. [news clipping, source unknown, Mohave Museum, Kingman], April 30, 1904. "Notice," *Mohave County Miner*, May 13, 1916. In the Superior Court of the State of Arizona in and for the County of Mohave, O. D. M. Gaddis vs. O. W. Walker, I. M. George, & W. B. Stephens, constituting the Board of Supervisors of Mohave County, Complaint 1310, 1916.

18   Michael Riordan had a profound interest in the history and culture of the Southwest which he later imparted to Osborne Craig. He was responsible for naming the hotel El Tovar, taking license with Pedro de Tobar, "the first white man to hear of the Grand Canyon." M. J. Riordan to W. G. Barnwell, Atchinson, Topeka & Santa Fe Railway Company, September 30, 1903. A. G. Wells, Atchinson, Topeka & Santa Fe Railway Company, July 15, 1904. Arizona Historical Society, Flagstaff, Riordan Family Collection, 1883–1931; hereafter Riordan Family Collection).

19   [Michael Riordan] to JOC, January 18; March 2, 1917, Riordan Family Collection.

20   "James O. Craig Architect, Dies," *Morning Press*, March 17, 1922. The article states: "Later he came to Los Angeles where he was associated for a time with Myron Hunt, one of the leading architects of that city."

21   The hotel was virtually destroyed by fire in April 1914. It was rebuilt in an extraordinary seven months and opened in November. "Roses Smother Homes under Blossoms," *Pasadena Star News*, April 20, 1916.

22   Riordan to Craig, September 20, 1916, Riordan Family Collection.

23   Riordan to Craig, February 8, 1917, Riordan Family Collection.

CHAPTER 2: SANTA BARBARA

1   "The Impress of a Personality," *Santa Barbara Community Life* (April 1923): 6–7.

2   Riordan to Craig, September 20, 1916, Riordan Family

Collection. Jessie Mary Bryant, "The Daily Round of Society," *Morning Press*, May 18, 1919.

3 "The Merry-Go-Round of Society," *Morning Press*, February 17; January 11, 1917.

4 "The Renaissance in Spain," *Pacific Coast Architect* 7, no. 4 (June 1914): 132.

5 "'El Fureidis' at Montecito, California. The Villa of James Waldron Gillespie, Esq.," *House & Garden* IV, no. 3 (September 1903): 97–103. H. H. Saylor, "The Twelve Best Country Houses in America. 'El Fureidis,' Home of J. Waldron Gillespie, at Montecito, California," *Country Life in America* 28 (October 19 15): 29–31. "'El Fureidis,' Santa Barbara, Cal., 1903," *Architectural Record* 29, no.1 (January 1911): 14–16. Una Nixson Hopkins, "'El Fureidis': The Little Paradise," *Craftsman* 29, no. 1 (October 1915): 33–39. "The Residence of F. F. Peabody, Esq., Montecito, California: Francis T. Underhill, Architect," *Architectural Record* 43, no. 5 (May 1918): 394–403. "United States Post Office, Santa Barbara, Calif.," *Architecture* [New York] 32, no. 1 (July 1915): 178, 180.

6 "Y.M.C.A. Building, Santa Barbara, Cal.," *American Architect* 114, no. 2341 (December 4, 1918): 176–78. "Modern in All Its Appointments Will Be New Institute for Boys and Girls," *Morning Press*, November 25, 1916. "Santa Barbara County Detention Home, Santa Barbara, Calif.," *Architectural Record* 46, no. 1 (July 1919): 86–89. "A Public Garage at Santa Barbara, Cal.," *Building Age* 42 (August 1920): 22–25.

7 Marion Craig Wentworth, "A Civic Center of Real Beauty for the People of Santa Barbara," *Craftsman* XXVII, no. 3 (December 1914): 320–23.

8 J. Corbley Pool to JOC, September 11, 1918. CFP JOC to Bertram Goodhue, November 9, 1918. Avery Architecture and Fine Arts Library, Columbia University, Goodhue, box 6: 1918: 3(c). Hereafter Goodhue Papers, Avery Library.

9 Craig to Goodhue, December 9, 1918. Goodhue Papers, Avery Library.

10 The new building for the Montecito Country Club, designed by Bertram Goodhue, was under construction at the time; the building and the golf course were completed in 1918. See David F. Myrick, Montecito and Santa Barbara, Volume I (Pasadena, California: Pentrex Media Group, LLC, 1988), 157–58.

11 JOC from Highlands Inn, Carmel, to MMcL, [January 10, 1919]. JOC from Santa Barbara to MMcL, [January 17, 1919].

12 "A Lumber Dealer," *The Mexican Herald* (December 8, 1898). "By-paths of the Old Spanish Padres," *Los Angeles Herald* (October 19, 1900). Riordan Family Collection.

13 "Personals," *Riverside Enterprise*, June 12, 1909. "Quietly Wed," *Los Angeles Times*, March 25, 1916.

14 "The Merry-Go-Round of Society," *Morning Press*, April 16, 17, 21, 1918.

15 William Winthrop Kent, "Domestic Architecture of California," Part II, *Architectural Forum*, 32, no. 4 (April 1920): 154.

16 Jessie Mary Bryant, "The Daily Round of Society," *Morning Press*, October 28, 1922; March 8, 1924; October 11, 1924.

17 JOC to MMcL December 16, 1918. "The Merry-Go-Round of Society," *Morning Press*, August 18, 1918. JOC to MMcL, December 29, 1918.

18 Jessie Mary Bryant, "The Daily Round of Society," *Morning Press*, March 8, October 26, 1924. Jessie Mary Bryant, "Daily Round of Society," *Morning Press*, October 24, 1925.

19 Mamie Goulet Abbott, *Santa Ines Hermosa. The Journal of the Padre's Niece* (Montecito, Santa Barbara, California: Sunwise Press, 1951), 3–4, 17, 71, 78-80, 83–84.

20 Ibid., 159–60, 164, 166, 172, 168. Fr. Zephyrin Engelhardt, O. F. M., *Mission Santa Ines. Virgen y Martir and its Ecclesiastical Seminary* (Santa Barbara, Calif.: Mission Santa Barbara, 1932).

21 JOC to Bertram Goodhue, November 9, 1918. Goodhue to Craig, November 18, 1918. Goodhue Papers, Avery Library.

22 There are no drawings for this project. The date is established in JOC to MMcL, December 16, 1918. "Persons and Products of Pen and Palette," *Carmel Pine Cone*, June 8,

1922. Bernhard Hoffmann, "Up the Valley and Down the Coast. A Letter from Carmel-by-the-Sea," *California Southland*, no. 68 (August 1925): 15, 26–27.

23 JOC to Dearest, [January 14, 1919].

24 Irving F. Morrow, "A Step in California's Architecture," *Architect and Engineer* LXX, no. 2 (August 1922): 84–86. Walter Webber, "The Economical House and the Architect," *California Southland*, no. 34 (October 1922): 8-9.

25 JOC to Dearest, October 7, 1919.

26 JOC to [MMcL], September 30, 1919. JOC to [MMcL], October 7, 1919. [Gring house], *News Press*, April 20, 1920. "City's Most Beautiful Homes and Gardens Named by Contest Board," *Santa Barbara Daily News*, February 28, 1924.

27 JOC to MMcL, December 29, 1918. JOC to MMcL, January 14, 1919. "Miss Yeoman" was probably Donna I. Youmans who had a store selling art goods at 1201–1203 State Street; she also was affiliated with Kem Weber as an interior decorator. JOC to MMcL, Sunday [October 12, 1919].

28 "Society," *Morning Press*, July 27, 1920.

29 "Society," *Morning Press*, August 10, 1920.

30 "Architects Chapter Visits Santa Barbara," *Southwest Builder and Contractor*, 58, no. 8 (August 19, 1921): 9, 10. Rexford Newcomb, *The Old Mission Churches and Historic Houses of California* (Philadelphia & London: J. B. Lippincott Company, 1925), 331.

31 "Residences," *Southwest Builder and Contractor*, 55, no. 2 (January 9, 1920): 38.

32 Jessie Mary Bryant, "The Daily Round of Society," *Morning Press*, March 30, July 8, 1920.

33 Robert Sweeney, "Creating Casa del Herrero," in *Casa del Herrero: The Romance of Spanish Colonial* (New York: Rizzoli, in association with The Casa del Herrero Foundation, 2009), 32.

34 "Social and Club Activities of Pasadena," *Pasadena Star-News*, July 31, 1916. Jessie Mary Bryant, "The Daily Round of Society," *Morning Press*, April 25, 1920.

35 Jessie Mary Bryant, "The Daily Round of Society," *Morning Press*, September 14, 1919.

36 Jessie Mary Bryant, "Society," *Morning Press*, September 21, 1920. "Mrs. Burnes Dies in South," *Morning Press*, November 16, 1920.

37 Selden Spaulding, "Sandyland," Noticias, VIII, no. 4 (Winter 1962): 20–23. Stella Haverland Rouse, "Early Development of Sandyland Cove District," *Santa Barbara Daily News*, July 11, 1982.

38 Craig's drawings for the cottages are undated save for the Leeds scheme: May 14, 1920. The building was complete by December. "Society," *Morning Press*, December 1, 1920.

39 Minutes, University Club of Santa Barbara [hereafter: Minutes], April 7; May 2; June 20, 25, 1919.

40 Minutes, December 15, 1919; January 22, February 23, March 15, April 19, 1920; May 26, 1922. The Lacy House originally was contructed around 1879 for J. W. Calkins. It was acquired in 1903 by Thomas J. P. Lacy. Walter A. Tompkins, "University Men Once were Scarce," *Santa Barbara News Press,* April 1, 1962.

41 "Suggestions for the Requirements for the Proposed New Building for the University Club of Santa Barbara, California," [ca. July, 1920]. Minutes, September 20, 1920.

42 Minutes, September 20; November 15, 18, 1920; May 26, 1922.

CHAPTER 3: IRENE AND BERNHARD HOFFMANN

1 Jessie Mary Bryant, "The Daily Round of Society," *Morning Press*, November 16, 1919. Michael J. Phillips, "To Take City Back to the Golden Days of Yore," *Santa Barbara Daily News*, February 6, 1922.

2 Jessie Mary Bryant, "The Daily Round of Society," *Morning Press*, May 18; September 28; November 16, 1919. Michael J. Phillips, "To Take City Back to the Golden Days of Yore," *Santa Barbara Daily News*, February 6, 1922.

3 M. U. Seares, "Building De la Guerra Plaza and Paseo— Santa Barbara," *California Southland*, no. 52 (April 1924): 13.

4 "Jessie Mary Bryant, "The Daily Round of Society," *Morning Press*, May 1; 18, 1920. Deed, Elizabeth Hazard McCalla to Irene B. Hoffmann, October 15, 1920.

5 "City's Most Beautiful Homes and Gardens Named by Contest Board," *Santa Barbara Daily News*, February 28, 1924. "Santa Barbara's Best Examples of Architecture," *Southwest Builder and Contractor* 63, no. 13 (March 28, 1924): 46. Ervanna Bowen Bissell, "Within Garden Gates. The House and Garden of Mr. and Mrs. Bernhard Hoffmann, Santa Barbara," *California Southland* no. 75 (March 1926): 13–14. Bissell is remembered in local history for her book *Glimpses of Santa Barbara and Montecito Gardens* (Santa Barbara: privately published, 1926) that was timed to coincide with the fabled 1926 visit by the Garden Club of America.

6 Tanny Keeler to Pamela Skewes-Cox, April 24, 2006.

7 *House Chronicles of St. Anthony's Seminary*, 1897–1922, December 2, 3, 13, 14. Courtesy of Brother Timothy Arthur, O.F.M., Provincial Archivist. Information on Wewer and the sequence of construction come from *St. Anthony's Seminary Construction and Building Resumé*. The December 2 meeting would have been at the McCalla House.

8 Duncan Aikman, "Santa Barbara Has a Fiesta," *American Mercury* IV, no 13 (January 1925): 50.

9 Preservation Planning Associates and Milford Wayne Donaldson, *Historic Structure Report on The Casa de la Guerra* (Santa Barbara: Santa Barbara Trust for Historic Preservation, 1991), 1. Rexford Newcomb, *The Old Mission Churches and Historic Houses of California* (Philadelphia & London: J. B. Lippincott Company, 1925), 321.

10 "Residences," *Southwest Contractor and Manufacturer* XVIII (September 10, 1910): 12. Preservation Planning Associates and Milford Wayne Donaldson, *Historic Structure Report on The Casa de la Guerra* (Santa Barbara: Santa Barbara Trust for Historic Preservation, 1991), 9.

11 "Historic De La Guerra Mansion to be Restored as Nucleus of Quarter Fashioned after Street in Spain," *Morning Press*, September 22, 1921.

12 "De la Guerra Home Project Is Enlarged," *Morning Press*, December 15, 1921.

13 "Council Asked for New City Hall Election," *Morning Press*, February 5, 1922.

14 "To Take City Back to the Golden Days of Yore," *Santa Barbara Daily News*, February 6, 1922.

15 [Thomas M. Storke], "That Wonderful Thing," *Santa Barbara Daily News*, February 6, 1922.

16 "Council Asked for New City Hall Election," *Morning Press*, February 5, 1922.

17 Ibid.

18 "Ask Community Arts Committee to Draw Sketches of Plaza," *Morning Press*, April 13, 1922.

19 "Construction Started on City's 'Street in Spain,'" *Morning Press*, October 25, 1922.

20 "De la Guerra Studio Apartments … Now Available for Rental" [advertisement], *Morning Press*, July 10, 1923. Jessie Mary Bryant, "The Daily Round of Society," *Morning Press*, October 14, 23, 26, 1923.

21 "New Restaurant to be Spanish," *Morning Press*, September 19, 1923.

22 The numerous alterations are beyond the scope of this book but it may be useful to list some of the more ambitious projects. Unit #5, a freestanding three-story building for the southwest corner of Anacapa and Canon Perdido Streets was designed by Carleton Winslow in 1925 but never constructed. Drawings for a barbecue for the southwest corner of the patio were prepared in 1930. In 1937, Winslow prepared a scheme to convert the patio separating the 1928 dining room and the shops facing Anacapa into a Cocktail Room. The space was to be enclosed with a glass roof; a semicircular bar was to be built in front of the chimney; and a "frieze of rich tropical foliage" was to be added around the room. This project happily was not carried out but another alteration, designed at the same time, was constructed. This was a semicircular bar projecting into the courtyard west of the patio restaurant; it remains today. Drawings for all of these projects are housed in the Winslow Papers, Architecture and Design Collection, Art, Design & Architecture Museum, University of California, Santa Barbara.

23 "Additions (Santa Barbara)," *Southwest Builder and Contractor*, 71, no. 20 (May 18, 1928): 56. The notice indicated that the work was for the California Brookside Trading Co., and that additional space was to be provided for dining room, kitchen, coffee shop, restrooms, three stores, arcades and a court; the cost was $75,000. "El Paseo Is Leased to Diehl Grocery Co., to be Remodeled," *Morning Press*, June 15, 1928.

24 "New Anacapa Street Entrance and Store Being Built for El Paseo," *Morning Press*, September 27, 1928. "New Building Plans Filed," *Morning Press*, November 6, 1928.

25 The drawings are dated November 12, 1924. This space was later called the St. Francis Room.

26 "The Re-Opening of El Paseo Santa Barbara, December 1928. Leaflet in El Paseo file, Gledhill Library, Santa Barbara Historical Museum.

27 John M. Gamble, "El Paseo's Charm Set the City's Pattern for Its Renaissance in Architectural Way," *Morning Press*, April 19, 1929.

28 "Recognition Is Accorded for Special Merit," *Morning Press*, February 21, 1930.

29 "Back to the Days of the Idle Forties," *Santa Barbara Community Life* (December 1922): 18–19. "The Impress of a Personality," *Santa Barbara Community Life* (April 1923): 6–7.

30 "City's Most Beautiful Homes and Gardens Named by Contest Board," *Santa Barbara Daily News*, February 28, 1924.

31 M. U. Seares, "Building De la Guerra Plaza and Paseo— Santa Barbara," *California Southland*, no. 52 (April 1924): 13.

32 Henriette Boeckman, "Street Has Old Spain Air," *Los Angeles Times*, September 21, 1924.

33 Harris Allen, "The 'Street in Spain,' Santa Barbara, California," *Pacific Coast Architect* XXVII, no. 3 (March 1925): cover, 22-23, 25, 27, 29, 31–33, 35, 37, 39.

34 It is easy to speculate that Irene Hoffmann was the catalyst for the visit. She attended the Garden Club's national convention in Richmond in 1924, and became a director in 1925. Jessie Mary Bryant, "The Daily Round of Society," *Morning Press*, April 18, 20, 1924. Jessie Mary Bryant, "The Daily Round of Society," *Morning Press*, April 3, 1925. In a self-published history of the club, the meeting is recalled as "… our first adventure in the Far West [and] shines like a star in Garden Club of America history." *The Garden Club of America. History 1913–1938*, 68–69.

35 "De la Guerra House Glorious Landmark of Early California," *Morning Press*, August 2, 1928.

36 "Series of Shops on Anacapa Street Front," and "Architect of El Paseo Eulogized: Prediction Now Lovely Reality," *Santa Barbara Daily News*, March 29, 1929.

37 G. A. Martin, "Vision of Osborne Craig Is Fulfilled in Newest Addition," *Morning Press*, April 19, 1929.

38 Lannie Haynes Martin, "Santa Barbara's 'Street of Spain,'" *Los Angeles Times*, June 29, 1930.

39 The original Chinatown in Santa Barbara was located on Canon Perdido between State and Anacapa streets. By 1920, however, city directories reveal that the Chinese had begun to infiltrate a Japanese neighborhood in the block bordered by Anacapa, Canon Perdido, De la Guerra and Santa Barbara streets. After the 1925 earthquake destroyed most of the shanties on Canon Perdido, the former Chinese occupants relocated to the Japanese neighborhood. Rebecca Wamsley, "A History of the Chinese in Santa Barbara," Manuscript Division, Department of Special Collections, University of California, Santa Barbara. Linda Bentz, "From Canton to Canon Perdido: Chinese Fisherman of Santa Barbara," *Noticias* XLIV, no. 3 (Autumn 1998): 82.

40 Historic Landmarks Commission, City of Santa Barbara, Staff Report, May 25, 1994, n.p. Subject files, Post Office File, Gledhill Library, Santa Barbara Historical Museum.

41 [Title unknown], *Santa Barbara Daily News*, March 23, 1929.

42 Louis La Beaume and Wm. Booth Papin, *Picturesque Architecture of Mexico* (New York: The Architectural Book Publishing Company, 1915), 14.

43 The building now is known familiarly as Casa de los Once Patios (House of the Eleven Patios). Pátzcuaro, today a town of fewer than 50,000 inhabitants, served as capital of the province of Michoacán until 1580 when Philip II transferred both secular and ecclesiastical authorities to Valladolid, renamed Morelia in 1828. Philip's extraordinary building program, guided by his Laws of the Indies, dictated arcaded buildings fronting the streets and was the source of much planning strategy in Santa Barbara after the 1925 earthquake, although the contrast between Philip's richly detailed baroque stone buildings and the vastly less formal stucco and tile buildings in Santa Barbara could hardly be more emphatic. George Kubler, *Mexican Architecture of the Sixteenth Century* (New Haven: Yale University Press, and London: Geoffrey Cumberlege, Oxford University Press, 1948), 188.

44 Bernhard Hoffmann to Mrs. Vhay, January 15, 1923, Chase Papers. The exhibition of 200 photographs was on display at the Chamber of Commerce building for five days, February 13–17. "Art Association Holds Exhibit of Mexican Pictures," and "Mexican Picture Exhibition May Be Seen At Night," Morning Press, February 14, 15, 1923. According to the 1923 Santa Barbara City Directory, the Chamber of Commerce was located in a building at 14 East Carrillo Street, extant today but remodeled beyond recognition. Michael Redmon, e-mail to Robert Sweeney, January 29, 2015. A. L. Murphy Vhay and David Vhay. *Architectural Byways in New Spain Mexico* (New York: Architectural Book Publishing Co., Inc., 1939), vii.

45 Ada Louise Huxtable, "Singing the Downtown Blues," *New York Times*, April 16, 1967. Bill Mahan, "Listening to El Paseo, A Lesson in Architecture on a Human Scale," *Santa Barbara Independent*, March 22, 2007.

CHAPTER 4: FINAL WORKS

1 David F. Myrick, "William Hutchinson Cowles," in *Montecito and Santa Barbara, Volume II: The Days of the Great Estates* (Glendale, California: Trans-Anglo Books, 1991), 340–42. An architect based in Spokane, Kirtland Cutter (1860–1939) designed many of the city's most prominent early buildings.

2 JOC to Pitman, March 15, 1921. JOC to MC, April 12, 14, 1921. JOC to Pitman, Wednesday. Minutes, Montecito County Water District, March 6, 1923.

3 "Reservoir at 'Eucalyptus Hill,' Montecito, Estate of Mr. and Mrs. William H. Cowles," *Architectural Digest* VIII, no. 1 (1930): 112–13.

4 "Prominent Pair of Crown City, Montecito Wed.," *Los Angeles Times*, August 23, 1921. Jessie Mary Bryant, "The Daily Round of Society," *Morning Press*, September 11; October 26, 1921; November 15, 1922.

5 Irving F. Morrow, "A Step in California's Architecture," *Architect and Engineer* LXX, no. 2 (August 1922): 68. *Picturesque Pasadena* (Pasadena, California: Chamber of Commerce and Civic Association, [1925?]), 32.

6 Although some sources place the date of construction around 1830, John Woodward has speculated that it was built after the original street survey of 1851. He bases his conclusion on the fact that the adobe is aligned parallel with De la Guerra Street and also on stylistic evidence. Woodward to Sweeney, January 13, 2014. Jessie Mary Bryant, "The Daily Round of Society," *Morning Press*, May 23, 1922.

7 [Bernhard Hoffmann] to Mrs. William H. Bliss, April 1 [May 1?], 1922. Chase papers.

8 [Michael Riordan] to Mr. Craig, August 10; 18; September 21, 1917. Riordan Family Collection.

9 JOC to MMcL, December 16; Friday [December 20], 1918.

10 JOC to MMcL, October 5–6; [18–19], 1919.

11 JOC to MC, November 26; Friday [December 3], 1920.

12 "The Daily Round of Society, " *Morning Press*, January 25, 1922. California State Board of Health, County of Ventura, Standard Certificate of Death, March 16, 1922.

13 "Personal and TradeNotes [sic]," *Southwest Builder and Contractor* 59, no. 15 (April 14, 1922): 10.

14. Pearl Chase to _____, n.d. Chase Papers.

15 Community Arts Association Plans and Planting Committee Bulletin (August 25, 1922).

16 Morrow, "A Step in California's Architecture," 46–103; a section of drawings follows, paginated A-H.

17 Mrs. James Osborne Craig, "The Heritage of All California," *California Southland*, no. 33 (September, 1922): 7–9.

CHAPTER 5: MARY CRAIG, ARCHITECT

1 Jessie Mary Bryant, "The Daily Round of Society," *Morning Press*, January 14, 1923.

2 Local lore in Santa Barbara associates Mary Craig with an earlier building, a Dog Hospital on Haley Street, but evidence to substantiate this claim is fraught with contradictions and ultimately inconclusive. Drawings for the project corresponding to the building as it was constructed are housed with her papers at the ADC. They are dated December 25, 1922, but are not signed. Stylistically, the drawings suggest the work of Ralph Armitage; however, he stated later that he began working with Mary in 1923. Surviving records in the Santa Barbara building department are silent concerning the designer. Attribution is further complicated by a notice appearing in *Southwest Builder and Contractor* on November 17, 1922, that "Archt. W. A. Brownell, Montecito, is preparing plans…for Dr. J. H. Moore…."the first occupant. "Hospitals," *Southwest Builder and Contractor* 60, no. 20 (November 17, 1922): 40. Other than a listing in the 1922 city directory, no information on Brownell has come to light. The building was completed in early 1923 at a cost of $5000; Max Fleischmann, of the yeast fortune, was the registered owner.

3 Stella Haverland Rouse, "El Paseo De las Flores," in *Santa Barbara's Spanish Renaissance & Old Spanish Days Fiesta* (Santa Barbara: Schauer Printing Studio, Inc., 1974), 53–54. "City's Most Beautiful Homes and Gardens Named by Contest Board," *Santa Barbara Daily News*, February 28, 1924. Henriette Boeckman, "Street Has Old Spain Air," *Los Angeles Times*, September 21, 1924.

4 "Small Home Plans Exhibit Is Opened," *Morning Press*, May 23, 1924. "Small Home Plans Placed on Exhibit," *Morning Press*, June 3, 1924.

5 The house, originally constructed in the late nineteenth century, was significantly enlarged by Margaret Waterman's father Isaac.

6 On Slater's occupancy see Jessie Mary Bryant, "Daily Round of Society—A Page for Women," *Morning Press*, October 17, 21, 1925; and Audrey Saxby, "Club and Society News," *Morning Press*, March 9, 1928. For Staats, see Audrey Saxby, "Society Page/Woman's News," *Morning Press*, April 7, May 11 and June 7, 1928.

7 "New Court to Go on Market," *Morning Press*, April 4, 1923. "Santa Barbara," *Southwest Builder and Contractor* 61, no. 14 (April 6, 1923): 39. "Hermosillo Court Units Sell Fast," *Morning Press*, April 21, 1923. The tract was primarily laid out on land acquired from Frederick Gould. A very small portion of the development was carved out of the neighboring parcel on which George C. Stewart built his house designed by Frank Lloyd Wright in 1909.

8 Jessie Mary Bryant, "The Daily Round of Society," *Morning Press*, August 14, 1924.

9 "Residences," *Southwest Builder and Contractor* 56, no. 13

(September 24, 1920): 40. "Heart Attack Brings Death to Campbell," *Morning Press*, May 12, 1923.

10 "Heart Attack Brings Death to Campbell," *Morning Press*, May 12, 1923. John Bradley, ed., *Lady Curzon's India: Letters of a Vicereine* (London: Weidenfeld & Nicholson, 1985), 7. Charlotte Cory, "The Delhi Durbar—1903 Revisited," *The Sunday Times* (London), December 29, 2002. Frank A. Randall, *History of the Development of Building Construction in Chicago* (Urbana: The University of Illinois Press, 1949), 13, 60, 88, 89, 124, 159, 172, 174.

11 JOC to MC, December 21, 1920.

12 Nancy Campbell to Mr. Laurence, November 25, 1920. Chicago History Museum, Levi Leiter and Leiter Estate Papers, Box 217, Folder 1; Box 160, Folder 5. Transcription of Nancy Leiter Campbell's handwritten correspondence courtesy of Alison de Frise.

13. The occupants of the bedrooms are identified in Gary B. Coombs and Phyllis J. Olsen, *In the Grand Manor: The Story of Devereux Hall* (Goleta, California: Institute for American Research, 1987), 12.

14 Clive Aslet, *The Edwardian Country House: A Social and Architectural History* (London: Francis Lincoln Limited, 2012), 95–96.

15 Mary continued to work on the house for two years. According to her ledger, an unspecified addition was completed in 1925. A coffered wood ceiling was installed in the reception room and the sewing room was enlarged in 1926. B. Byron Price, Director, Charles M. Russell Center for the Study of Art of the West, e-mail message to Pamela Skewes-Cox, January 17, 2014.

16 Jessie Mary Bryant, "The Daily Round of Society," *Morning Press*, October 4, 1924. "Rare Goods of Curzon Kin Arrive," *Los Angeles Times*, September 7, 1924. *Auction Catalogue. Estate of Colin L. Campbell. Goleta, Santa Barbara, California. In Three Parts. Part I.—Real Estate. Furnishings.* Clennell & Madole, July 9th, 1941. Hugh Clennell, Foreword; front; 11, 25, 29, 41, 47, 51, 53. A copy of this catalogue, including Parts II.-Silverware, and III.-Library, are in the collection of the Gledhill Library, Santa Barbara Historical Museum. I thank Juliet C. Folger for information about the vermeil flatware.

17 Jessie Mary Bryant, "The Daily Round of Society," *Morning Press*, January 25, 1925. "Mrs. Campbell Hostess to Prince and Other Officers; Dinners Honor Mrs. Cramer," *Morning Press*, September 12, 1928. Mrs. Campbell's daughter Audrey recalled that Prince Edward also attended the dinner-dance and that the date was 1926. Coombs and Olsen, *In the Grand Manor*, 21. In fact, Prince Edward was not in the United States in either 1926 or 27. Miss Pamela Clark, The Royal Archives, Windsor Castle, to author, June 18, 2013. "Prince George Is Entertained in Hollywood," *Morning Press*, September 13, 1928. "Prince, Having Seen Stars in Sky, Sees Those in Films," *Morning Press*, September 14, 1928.

18 *Marland Mansion & Estate* (tour brochure).

19 Jessie Mary Bryant, "The Daily Round of Society," *Morning Press*, April 24, 1925.

20 While there are several monographs on David Adler, much work remains to be done on Ambrose Cramer and Frances Elkins. The *AIA Guide to Chicago*, edited by Alice Sinkevitch (Orlando et al: A Harvest Original Harcourt, Inc., 2004), 202, lists Ambrose Cramer's house at 2710 North Lakeview Avenue, 1917, and describes it as one of a "… cohesive block [that] seems straight out of Georgian London…." Frances Elkins was a fixture in the Santa Barbara society columns in the early twentieth century. Her lasting contribution was her acquisition, restoration and furnishing of Casa Amesti in Monterey, still intact and serving today as the Old Capitol Club. "The Daily Round of Society" *Morning Press*, July 6, 1920. I thank Richard Barrett for taking me through the club in February 2013.

21 "Residences," *Southwest Builder and Contractor* 60, no. 19 (November 10, 1922): 35.

22 Alexander MacKellar to Mary Craig, December 2, 1924.

23 [Mary Craig] to Mrs. Andrews, December 4, 1924. Bids came from three contractors: S. Maitland, Alexander MacKellar and E … oe [illegible] Mary Craig file, Prints and Photographs Division, Library of Congress.

24 There is confusion in the source material about this house. A letter from Grace Strong Gee, Architectural Board of Review, to MC, August 14, 1925, giving final design approval, indicates that the house was located at 2046 Emerson. Mary Craig file, Prints and Photographs Division, Library of Congress. The building permit issued August 17, 1925, lists the same address and indicates "repairs". In fact, 2046 Emerson is nonexistent; similarly, contemporary city directories have no listings for this address. The intersection of Emerson and Plaza Rubio is the 2100 block of Emerson.

25 Jessie Mary Bryant, "Daily Round of Society—A Page for Women," *Morning Press*, May 5, 1926.

26 "Santa Barbara Where Beauty and Utility Blend," *Morning Press* Rotogravure Section, January 31, 1926. "In a Beautiful Neighborhood at Santa Barbara," *California Southland* no. 78 (June 1926): 3, 75.

27 Ibid.

28 "Better Homes Board Selects Best in Types," *Morning Press*, May 23, 1927.

29 Michael Redmon, "History 101: Peabody School," *Santa Barbara Independent*, February 2-9, 2006. F. F. Peabody to MC, May 21, 1925, Mary Craig file, Prints and Photographs Division, Library of Congress.

30 Geo. D. Morrison, Survey in Block 190, Request of School Board, October 3, 1925, ADC. "Santa Barbara News," *Southwest Builder and Contractor* 66, no. 12 (September 18, 1925): 57. MC to Frederick Forrest Peabody, September 28, 1925, Mary Craig file, Prints and Photographs Division, Library of Congress.

31 Bernhard Hoffmann to William Templeton Johnson, August 4, 1925, Santa Barbara Trust for Historic Preservation. "Open Air School in Use Here," *Morning Press*, October 13, 1925. Minutes, Regular Meeting Board of Education, November 19, 1925, Mary Craig file, Prints and Photographs Division, Library of Congress. The Franklin Kindergarten, now the Lawrence M. Parma School, is located at 915 East Montecito Street. It was designed by Soule Murphy & Hastings.

32 "Church Sells Logan Block for $73,500," *Morning Press*, January 10, 1924. Eleanor Graham, who wove in and out of the lives of Osborne and Mary in the teens, was the purchaser. "Business Buildings," *Southwest Builder and Contractor* 61, no. 24 (December 14, 1923): 50.

33 Ibid: *Morning Press*. King Phillip II of Spain (and others), The Laws of the Indies, 1573. Translated by Zelia Nuttall, 1921, 1922; revised translation by Axel I. Mundigo and Dora P. Crouch, 1977. "The City Planning Ordinances of the Laws of the Indies Revisited: Part I: Their Philosophy and Implications," *Town Planning Review* 48, no.3 (July 1977): 247–268.

34. "W. C. Logan Co., Dodge Dealer, Housed in New Home on E. Carrillo Street," *Morning Press*, January 17, 1926. "Dodge Building to Open Today," *Morning Press*, February 6, 1926. Community Arts Association certificate, February 1928, Hoffmann House Library. "Judges Award Biltmore Hotel and San Marcos First Prizes," *Santa Barbara Daily News*, March 5, 1928.

35 "Business Buildings," *Southwest Builder and Contractor* 66, no. 7 (August 14, 1925): 58"Residences," *Southwest Builder and Contractor* 66, no. 18 (October 30, 1925): 57 "Santa Barbara Permits," *Southwest Builder and Contractor* 66, no. 19 (November 6, 1925): 61."Permit Issued for Adobe Store" and "Special Permit for Adobe Store," *Morning Press*, October 28; November 1, 1925. Santa Barbara City Directories, 1926–27, 1927, 1936.

36 "Herman von Waldt-Hausen," In Michael James Phillips, *History of Santa Barbara County California*, Volume II (Chicago, San Francisco, Los Angeles: S. J. Clarke Publishing Co., 1927), 355–56.

37 Permit A-3669 (office), January 4, 1928; Permit A3784 (shed), February 15, 1928. "Santa Barbara Permits," *Southwest Builder and Contractor*, 71, no. 20 (May 18, 1928): 70. "Santa Barbara Permits," *Southwest Builder and Contractor* 72, no. 14 (October 5, 1928): 67.

38 "The House in Good Taste," *House Beautiful* LXVII, no. 6 (June 1930): 753–56. According to Beals's appointment book, the photographs were taken in October 1929. Papers of Jessie Tarbox Beals, Schlesinger Library on the History of Women in America, Radcliffe Institute, Harvard University.

39 Information about the chauffeur's cottage comes from H. Philip Staats, *Californian Architecture in Santa Barbara* (New York: Architectural Book Publishing Company, Inc., 1929, 123. Mary lists this building in her ledger between April and December 1926. The other two are listed November 1926–March 1927.

40. "The Daily Round of Society," *Morning Press*, July 6, 1920. Kathryn Masson, "Casa Amesti," in *The California House* (New York, Paris, London, Milan: Rizzoli, 2011), 22–29. Adler's work was completed in 1944. Richard Pratt, *David Adler* (New York: M. Evans and Company, Inc., 1970), 201.

41 MC to Mrs. William A. Slater, May 23, 1927. Marc Appleton, grandson of the Bryces and himself an architect in Santa Barbara, stated that, as far as he knew, his grandparents never willingly allowed their house to be published. Appleton to author, December 20, 2012.

42 MC to Mrs. William Slater, March 31; April 14, 1927.

43 MC to Mrs. William Slater, April 14, 1927.

44 E. S. [Ellen Slater] to Mary, n.d., [MC] to Mrs. William A. Slater, May 5; October 13, 20, 27; November 7, 1927.

45 Minutes, Montecito Water District, May 15, 22; October 31; November 8, 1922.

46 Minutes, Montecito Water District, September 14, 1926.

47 Minutes, Montecito Water District, October 27; November 19; December 26, 1926.

48 Minutes, Montecito Water District, March 12; April 9; July 9, 1929.

49 "Recognition Is Accorded for Special Merit," *Morning Press*, February 21, 1930.

50 Ella Winter, "A Conspiracy for Beauty," *Carmelite* (Carmel-by-the-Sea, California), November 21, 1928. Ella Winter was the wife of Lincoln Steffens, the journalist and muckraker; he also was the nemesis of Pauline Schindler, owner and editor of the paper.

51 Ferdinand Lungren to J. B. Lippincott, July 24, 1925; Hoffmann to Myron Hunt, September 23, 1923; Hoffmann to T. Mitchell Hastings, November 20, 1925, Architectural Advisory Committee, 1925, PCC. Santa Barbara Trust for Historic Preservation.

52 [Minutes], January 27, 28, 1926, Bound minute books, CAA, 1921–1928, Box 499, PCC.

53 Hoffmann to Mrs. F. F. Peabody, December 9, 1927, Box 499, CAA Bound Minute Books 1921–1928; Minutes, January 19, 1928, Box 499; William G. Paul to Hoffmann, January 20, 1928, Series I, CAA Ad Records, 1920s–1930s Box 509, PCC.

54 "Civic Leader of Santa Barbara Is Honored by Southern California Chapter, A.I.A.," *Southwest Builder and Contractor* 73, no. 7 (February 15, 1929): 36. "Declares Architecture the All Pervading Art for Society and the Average Man," *Southwest Builder and Contractor* 73, no. 8 (February 22, 1929): 32–33.

55 Pearl Chase to Robert L. Davis, *Architectural Record*, March 28, 1929, Chase Papers. H. Philip Staats, *Californian Architecture in Santa Barbara*. With a Preface by Charles H. Cheney, A. I. A. (New York: Architectural Book Publishing Company, Inc., 1929), iii, viii.

56 Ibid., v, vi-vii.

57 Bernhard Hoffmann to R. H. Pitman, May 28, 1929. This letter and the copy of the book Hoffmann gave to Pitman were a generous gift from Pitman's daughter-in-law, Mrs. John (Harriet) Pitman, to the author in 2008.

CHAPTER 6: CHANGING TASTES

1 Phoebe Cutler, e-mail message to Pamela Skewes-Cox, September 6, 2012. Cutler is a landscape historian based in San Francisco.

2 The house was designed for Mrs. R. W. Rives. It was published in *The Architect* XV, no. 4 (April 1918): pls. 60–63.

3 Betty C. Monkman, "National Identity and the Colonial Revival, 1900–1950s," in *The White House: Its Historic Furnishings and First Families* (Washington, D. C.: White House Historical Association, and New York, London, and Paris: Abbeville Press, 2000), 186.

4 Monkman, Ibid., 210-12. Emily L. Wright, "Eleanor Roosevelt and the Val-Kill Industries" (master's thesis, State University of New York College at Oneonta, 1982). William Seale, "Irony: Hoover," in *The President's House: A History*. Volume Two (Washington, D. C.: White House Historical Association with the cooperation of the National Geographic Society and New York: Harry N. Abrams, Inc., 1986), 911.

5 Hugh Morrison, "Late Georgian in Virginia," in *Early American Architecture from the First Colonial Settlements to the National Period* (New York: Oxford University Press, 1952), 356.

6 Anna Paramore Brando to Pamela Skewes-Cox, April 28, 2009. The motion pictures were, 1929: *A Dangerous Woman*; *Saturday Night Kid*; and *The Virginian*; and, 1930: *Only the Brave*.

7 Betty Lasky in conversation with Pamela Skewes-Cox, Reggie Sully and Robert Sweeney, Hotel Bel Air, Los Angeles, August 4, 2008.

8 The Dodge and Barnsdall houses would have been available to Mary—and Pitman—through publication, if not first-hand exposure. For Dodge, see "California House of Distinguished Simplicity," *House Beautiful* 49 (February 1921): 94–95. The Barnsdall House was published first in Europe in the twenties, in Holland, Germany and France. It was introduced to American audiences in 1928 in a series of articles by Wright published in *Architectural Record*.

9 "Wetmore Hodges, Industrialist, Dies at 69; Co-developer of Food-Freezing Process," *New York Times*, April 4, 1957.

CHAPTER 7: WINDING DOWN

1 Winifred Dobyns, *California Gardens*. Foreword by Myron Hunt (New York: The MacMillan Company, 1931), pagination ends on page 20.

2 MC to Belle Hayes, August 12, 1953.

3 MC to Belle Hayes, August 17, 1953.

4 Brian Gracie (Gracie Studios, New York) in discussion with Pamela Skewes-Cox, May 1912.

5 James Main, James Main Fine Art, Santa Barbara, to Pamela Skewes-Cox, February 14, 2014.

CHAPTER 8: THE ENIGMATIC MARY CRAIG

1 Gabrielle Esperdy, "The Incredible True Adventure of the Architectress in America," 1, *The Design Observer Group* web site; accessed September 10, 2012.

2 Nevill Cramer in discussion with author, April 22, 2008.

3 Tanny Keeler in discussion with author, October 28, 2009.

4 Adrian Malone to MCSC, March 15, 1964.

5 Anna Paramore Brando in discussion with author, April 3, 2009.

6 MCSC in discussion with author, January 28, 2008.

7 Nathaniel Burt, *The Perennial Philadelphians* (Boston & Toronto: Little, Brown and Company, 1963), 67.

8 Nevill Cramer to Ambrose Cramer, January 7, 1952, Mrs. Nevill Cramer Collection.

9 Livermore to MC, February 24, 1937.

10 The medal was based on the ability to maintain academic excellence during one's entire academic career.

11   Mary Craig, "Gold in the Homestake," 1958, CFP.
12   Brando in discussion with author, April 25, 2009. Ted Paramore and Anna Chernoff Frenke met in 1943 through her father Eugene Frenke, a Russian expatriate working in Hollywood as a producer. After Ted's death, Anna was married for a time to Marlon Brando, Sr. Her memories of Mary Craig were drawn from the two years she and Ted lived at One Acre in the 1950s.
13. Mrs. James Osborne Craig, "The Heritage of All California," *California Southland*, no. 33 (September 1922): 7–9.
14   Robert Sorgenfrei, e-mail message to author, October 25, 2007. Mary Craig's mining papers were donated in 2006 to the Colorado School of Mines Special Collections Library in Golden, Colorado. The collection makes up "arguably one of the most important surviving archives" detailing the development of South Dakota's Homestake Mine. Fred N. Holabird to author, September 20, 2006. Holabird, geologist, author, and appraiser, specializes in mining and its development in the West.
15   Dr. Kenneth MacPherson to MC, April 18, 1939. Mary Craig, "Gold in the Homestake." MC to Patti Wyman, January 20, 1958.
16   Brando in discussion with author, April 28, 2009.
17   In discussing the inspiration for her 2010 erotic fantasy novel *Obsession*, Gloria Vanderbilt wrote of Stokowski's mountain hideaway in Toro Canyon: "I drew on memories of that magical place and called it Acaru." Gloria Vanderbilt, e-mail message to author, January 6, 2011. Elaine Griscom, "Leopold Stokowski's Canyon Hideaway," *Montecito Magazine* IX, no. 1 (Spring 1989): 20–23, 48–51. Michael Redmon, "Leopold Stokowski," *Santa Barbara Independent*, November 3, 2011. Stokowski to MC, January 4 and March 9, 1940.
18   Anita Page, born 1947; Pamela Frances, born 1949; Amy Osborne, born 1953.
19   MC to Sarah McLaughlin, August 2, 1935.
20   Lawrence Dame, "Santayana's Last Interview," *Harvard Alumni Bulletin* 59 (November 10, 1956): 146–48. Beth Gates to MCSC, March 11, 1964.
21   Wendy Goodman, The World of Gloria Vanderbilt (New York: Abrams Books, 2010), 134.
22   JOC to MC, April 24, 1921. MC to Charles Perkins, July 25, 1935.

CHAPTER 9: MARY McLAUGHLIN'S
DEADWOOD, 1889–1913

1   William's brother Daniel, also a lawyer, later became a well-known press writer in San Francisco. *See* McLaughlin Brothers' Papers, Special Collections, Georgetown University Law Library, Washington, D.C.
2   Helen married Deadwood native and Pasadena lawyer George Martin and had two sons, William and George, Jr.
3   MC, "Early Family Memories," CFP.
4   *See* Estelline Bennett, *Old Deadwood Days* (Lincoln & London: University of Nebraska Press, 1982), originally published 1928. On the life of W. L. McLaughlin, *see* "A Tribute," by M. H. Barry, *Deadwood Pioneer Times*, July 30, 1911. George Martin, Jr., to Sarah McLaughlin Anderson, September 1, 1982. Martin was a writer, radio broadcaster, international newsman, and reporter for CBS in Los Angeles.
5   MC, "Gold in the Homestake, A Reminiscence," 1958, CFP. MC to Edward Manion, June 24, 1938.
6   Bennett, back cover. See page 240 for Ellen McLaughlin's story of the young Calamity Jane.
7   *See* Eleanore C. Sullivan, *Georgetown Visitation since 1799* (Washington, D.C.: Georgetown Visitation Monastery, 2004).
8   "Wm. L. McLaughlin Has Passed Away," *Weekly Pioneer Times*, August 3, 1911. "WM.L. M'Laughlin Burial Here Monday," *Deadwood Daily Pioneer Times*, July 30, 1911.
9   Snead to MMcL, January 8, 1912.
10 MC, "Gold in the Homestake."

CHAPTER 10: SANTA BARBARA:
THE ANACAPA ILLUSION

1   *Anacapa* was a word used by the Chumash people to describe "an illusion or a pleasing mirage." Kevin Starr, *Material Dreams: Southern California through the 1920s* (New York: Oxford University Press, 1990), xii, 300, 302.
2   Following the death of her husband Judge McLaughlin in 1903, Ellen lived with Mary and her family until her death in Pasadena in 1914.
3   Information concerning Southern Pacific was provided by Cara J. Randall, California State Railroad Museum, Sacramento.
4   Ted Paramore to MMcL, October 16, 1915. Brando in discussion with author, June 2, 2007.
5   Paramore's motion pictures include *The Virginian* (1929), *Three Comrades* (1938, in collaboration with F. Scott Fitzgerald) and *The Oklahoma Kid* (1939, in collaboration with James Cagney). James Cagney, *Cagney by Cagney* (New York: Doubleday, 1976), 84. Following his Hollywood career, Ted became a regular contributor to the *Detroit Athletic Club News*. In April 1956, on his way back from New York to Santa Barbara, Paramore, wishing to retrieve his car himself, ignored the warnings of a garage attendant and "mounted an employee-only elevator made up of small foot stands on a moving belt. When he reached the top, they said his clothing apparently caught and he was carried up and over the wheel on which the belt moved. He dropped ten feet and landed on his head on the concrete." He died the next day. "Film Writer Killed In Garage Accident," *Washington Post*, May 2, 1956.
6   Edmund Wilson, *The Twenties* (New York: Farrar, Straus and Giroux, 1975), 160–172, 479. "Mr. Ed," Wilson's tribute to Paramore, first appeared in the *New Republic* LV, no. 712 (July 25, 1928): 251–54.
7   Ibid, 162–3.
8   1914 Student Monthly Report, CFP.
9   "The Week: Parties, Receptions, Dinners, Weddings and the Like …," *Los Angeles Times*, September 12, 1915.
10 "The Merry-Go-Round of Society," *Morning Press*, October 13, November 12, 1916.

CHAPTER 11: JAMES OSBORNE CRAIG,
FROM SCOTLAND TO AMERICA, 1888–1916

1   Bernard Aspinwall, *Portable Utopia, Glasgow and the United States 1820–1920* (Aberdeen: Aberdeen University Press, 1984), xi, 12.
2   Built between 1860 and 1880, 43 Carlibar Road, Barrhead, remains a residence.
3   1891 census.
4   Through the efforts of Scottish researcher Alison Spring, the ninety-page journal titled *The Osborne Family Story* was found in 2007 to be in the possession of Mrs. George Hunter of Glasgow, granddaughter of the journal's author. Eileen Osborne Hunter, born in 1924, is the daughter of Herbert Osborne, Osborne Craig's first cousin. George Hunter transcribed the original document in 1997.
5   Unless otherwise noted, all quotes and information about the Osborne family come from the 1919 journal.
6   Faulds Farm, purchased in 1848, remained in the Osborne family until the early 1900s when it was turned over to Mr. Osborne's nephew John Whiteford. Rysland, now called Croyland, 202 Ayr Road, is listed with the East Renfrewshire Council's Heritage Collection of historic mansions.
7   A. B. Leggat, *Winning the Soldier, A Faith That Removed Mountains, A Brief Sketch of the Life and Work of Mrs. Todd Osborne* (Glasgow: Pickering & Inglis, 1932), 2, 7.
8   "Tile To Commemorate James Osborne Craig, Architect, at El Paseo," *Santa Barbara Daily News*, December 7, 1928.
9   Leggat, 7, 8, 10. See Alice Todd Osborne to William Mackinnon, April 21, 1891, Sir William Mackinnon Papers, Archives & Special Collections, School of Oriental

and African Studies, London. "Soldiers' Friend, Mrs. Todd Osborne Dies at Cairo," *Glasgow Herald*, April 20, 1926.

10 The 1901 Scottish census lists Osborne, age twelve, at 248 Kenmure Street, Glasgow, and a "scholar, 5th Parish Ward, Ecc. Parish of Govan, School Board District of Govan, Burgh/Ward of Pollokshields." The technical school was renamed the Royal Technical College in 1912. Known today as Strathclyde University, student archives confirm Craig's enrollment in 1904–05. Gavin Stamp, "An Architect of the Entente Cordiale: Eugéne Bourdon (1870–1916)—Glasgow and Versailles," *Architectural Heritage* 15, Edinburgh University Press (November 2004): 96, 97.

11 Ellis Island Records.

12 George A. Crofutt, *Crofutt's Grip-Sack Guide of Colorado, II* (Omaha, Nebraska: Overland Publishing Company, 1885), 120, 122.

13 Aspinwall, 186.

14 Joan Palmer and Ilene Bergsmann, *Architects of Colorado: Database of State Business Directory Listings 1875–1950* (Colorado Historical Society, 2006).

15 Crofutt, 82-83

16 Osgood's name would forever be associated with the 1914 Ludlow Massacre. "The Newest Figure in Finance, Remarkable Career of J. C. Osgood," *New York Times*, September 7, 1902. See Darrell Munsell, *From Redstone to Ludlow: John Cleveland Osgood's Struggle against the United Mine Workers of America* (Boulder: University Press of Colorado, 2009). Sylvia Ruland, *The Lion of Redstone* (Boulder, Colorado: Johnson Books, 1981). "Village of Redstone Design Guidelines, 2004," Redstone Historic Preservation Commission.

17 Colorado Springs, 1910 Census. See "George M. Bryson," *Western Architect* 27, no. 9 (September 1918): 82. "Noted Architect Dies Suddenly," *Architect and Engineer* LIV, no. 3 (September 1918): 114. "Burial Will Be in Evergreen Cemetery," *Colorado Springs Gazette*, August 13, 1918. "G.M. Bryson Dead," *Deseret News* (Salt Lake City), August 12, 1918. Bryson's life in Utah courtesy of Burtch W. Beall, Jr., FAIA.

18 Supporting needy causes in the Scottish homeland, the Caledonian Society was a men's charitable fraternity devoted to preserving Scottish heritage. Caledonian Society Collection Records, January 1910, page 236, Colorado Springs Pioneers Museum.

19 See The James M. MacLaren Society at http://www.jmmaclaren.org. See Alan Calder, "Thomas MacLaren: The European Years," *The James M. MacLaren Society Journal* 4 (Summer 2007): 1–25. Duncan McLachlan, "Master Draftsmen, XIX, Thomas MacLaren," *Pencil Points* 7, (December 1926): 711–26. D. MacDougall, Editor-In-Chief, *Scots and Scots' Descendants in America* (New York: Caledonian Publishing Company, 1917). Office of Archeology and Historical Preservation, Colorado Historical Society, Denver.

20. "Thomas MacLaren, Architect," interview with Edward L. Bunts by Vicki Overholser and Tom Walters, North End, Homeowners Association, Historic Restoration, Tape #1, Interview #1, May 19, 1978. Typed transcript courtesy of Special Collections, University of Colorado at Boulder Libraries.

21 McLachlan, *Pencil Points*, 726.

22 With the exception of his first trip to America in 1905, no ship manifests have been found documenting Craig leaving for or returning from Europe, making his itinerary virtually unknown. "Tile Honors James Craig," *Santa Barbara News Press*, December 8, 1928.

23 M. J. Riordan, *Foot Prints of the Spanish Padres in New Mexico and Arizona* (Los Angeles, California: The Tidings Company, 1900), 3.

24 See Kathleen M. Farretta, "Progressive Era Community-Builders: The Riordan Brothers of Flagstaff, Arizona Territory, 1884–1904" (master's thesis, Northern Arizona University, 2004); Platt Cline, *Mountain Town, Flagstaff's First Century* (Flagstaff: Northland Publishing, 1994); Richard and Sherry Magnum, *Flagstaff Past and Present*

(Flagstaff: Northland Publishing, 2003). David F. Myrick, *The Santa Fe Route, Railroads of Arizona* 4 (Berkeley: Signature Press, 1998). Riordan Family Collection, 1883–1931, AHS–ND, 4, Northern Arizona University, Cline Library, Flagstaff, Arizona.

25 Richard Magnum, e-mail to author, April 12, 2012. Craig's daughter was always told her father went to Flagstaff for his health. Mark Jackson, "Divine Stramonium: The Rise and Fall of Smoking for Asthma," *Medical History* 54 (2010): 171–94.

26 Stephen Fried, Appetite for America (New York: Bantam Books, 2010), 233–45.

27 Fernand Lungren, *Some Notes on His Life* (Santa Barbara: Santa Barbara School of the Arts, 1933), 129. John A. Berger, *Fernand Lungren: A Biography* (Santa Barbara: The Schauer Press, 1936), 74–5. The curriculum brochure for fall 1920 shows Craig teaching "History of Architecture and House Planning." Subject files, Santa Barbara School of the Arts file, Gledhill Library, Santa Barbara Historical Museum.

28 See Patricia Gardner Cleek, "Francis W. Wilson, Architect," *Noticias* XXXI, no. 3 (Fall 1985): 41–53. "Francis Wilson with Santa Fe, Well Known Architect is Appointed to a Position in Construction Department," *Morning Press*, September 23, 1905. Romy Wyllie, Bertram Goodhue, *His Life and Residential Architecture* (New York: W.W. Norton & Company, 2007), 113–117.

29 Mission preservation, a cause to which Craig rallied, was also of foremost concern to author and activist Charles Fletcher Lummis, whose outspoken views were well known in Santa Barbara circles in the 1920s In his earlier years in the Southwest (where he had met Fernand Lungren), Lummis and the Riordans were allies in their goal to protect and preserve the area's Native American culture. See Turbese Lummis Fiske and Keith Lummis, *Charles F. Lummis: The Man and His West* (Norman: University of Oklahoma Press, 1975), and Charles Fletcher Lummis Manuscript Collection, Braun Research Library, Autry Institute, Los Angeles.

30 "Noted Artist Here," *Coconino Sun*, October 8, 1915.

CHAPTER 12: SANTA BARBARA, 1917–1922

1 See Prynce Hopkins, *Both Hands Before the Fire* (Penobscot, Maine: Traversity Press, 1962). Dr. Ronald R. Koegler, M.D., "A Renaissance Prince: Prynce Hopkins," *Noticias* LII, no. 4 (2008): 139–81. "Boyland Has New Instructor," *Morning Press*, November 4, 1917.

2 "The Merry-Go-Round of Society," *Morning Press*, April 26, 1917.

3 *The Hill News* 19, no. 8, (November 12, 1920): p.4. "The Merry-Go-Round of Society," *Morning Press*, July 26, 28, 1918. *New York Times*, "Newcomers Among The Playwrights," *New York Times*, February 27, 1927.

4 JOC to MMcL, September 23, 29, October 5, 24, 1919. Craig's quote from English poet William Cowper is from the poem "Light Shining out of Darkness."

5 MMcL to JOC, October 20, 1919. "Miss McLaughlin to Wed Mr. Craig," *Santa Barbara Daily News*, November 15, 1919.

6 Jessie Mary Bryant, "The Daily Round of Society," *Morning Press*, February 8, March 18, March 20, March 24, 1920.

7 Jessie Mary Bryant, "The Daily Round of Society," *Morning Press*, April 10, 13; May 13; July 25, 1920. "Society," *Morning Press*, July 28, 1920.

8 JOC to MMcL, October 18, 1919.

9 MC to Sarah McLaughlin, [Winter]1920.

10 Geoffry Lawford to David Gebhard, October 4, 1971, copy from Hoffmann House Library. The English-born Lawford, a 1921 graduate of Santa Barbara High School, received his architectural degree from Cornell University in 1929. In 1946 he became a founding partner in the New York firm of Brown, Lawford and Forbes.

11 Hunt's master plan for Mrs. Burnes' Fernald Point prop-

erty was published in 1918. David Allison, "The Work of Mr. Myron Hunt," *Architect and Engineer* LIII, no.1 (April 1918): 39–68. "James N. Burnes Dead in California," *St. Joseph News Press*, August 22, 1913. "James Burnes Called by Death," *Pasadena Star*, August 23, 1913. Diane Fox Downs in discussion with author, April 23, 2007.

12 Harold Bryant Cody (1887–1924) received a Bachelor of Science in Architecture in 1908 from the University of Pennsylvania. First working for Myron Hunt, in 1915 Cody became a partner with Los Angeles architect Lester H. Hibbard. His drawings for the Citrus Experimental Station at the University of California, Riverside, and for the Northeast Branch Public Library, Los Angeles, won the praise of architect Elmer Grey who wrote: "Mr. Cody's inimitable renderings have been the admiration of Los Angeles architects for years." Elmer Grey, "Fifth Annual Architectural Exhibit at Los Angeles," *Architect and Engineer* XLIV, no. 3 (March 1916): 38. Never fully recovering from tuberculosis, Cody died at the age of thirty-seven.

13 JOC to MC, November 30, 1920.

14 JOC to MC, December 3, 1920.

15 The baby was delivered at St. John's Hospital in Oxnard by Dr. W. R. Livingston, famous for his use of the drug scopolamine (referred to as "twilight sleep") for a pain-free childbirth. Jeffrey Wayne Maulhardt, *Legendary Locals of Oxnard* (Charleston, South Carolina: Arcadia Publishing, 2013), 26–7. JOC to MC, March 7, 1921.

16 Elizabeth Pitman, in conversation with author, September 20, 2007. After Craig's death, Pitman worked for architect Carleton Winslow, managing Winslow's Santa Barbara office. "Richard Pitman," *Morning Press*, August 6, 1964. He assisted Winslow in building many significant structures in Southern California. His son, John Pitman, AIA, (1930–2007) was a highly regarded architect in Santa Barbara. Richard Pitman's papers are archived at the ADC.

17 John Taylor Boyd, "The Florida House," interview with Addison Mizner, *Arts and Decoration* 32 (January 1930): 40. *Thomas Hastings Architect. Collected Writings Together with a Memoir by David Gray* (New York: Houghton Mifflin, 1933), 11.

18 JOC to MC, January 31, 1921.

19 Carleton Winslow, "Rough Sketch," 1939, ADC.

20 Carleton Winslow, "Liberals," October 1939 and "Outline of Address, Santa Monica Arts Association," January 8, 1934, ADC.

21 Ann Seymour Sheehan, Winslow's niece, in discussion with author, January 19, 23, 2009. Mrs. Carleton Winslow, Jr., in discussion with author, January 19, 2009. Untitled ms., Winslow Papers, ADC.

22 Wagner to Chase, December 7, 1921. Lobero Theatre, Series I (Community Arts Association Ledgers), III, V, IX (Scrapbooks). See letters dated December 6, 1921 and January 5, 1922, Chase Papers.

23 Jim Paramore to Ted Paramore, January 17, 1922. Death certificate of James Osborne Craig, Ventura County Recorder, March 16, 1922. Estate Papers. JOC to MMcL, October 9, 1919.

24 "Craig Funeral to Be Held Saturday in Ojai Valley," *Santa Barbara Daily News*, March 17, 1922. The cross remained in place until 2008 when, badly deteriorated, it was removed. Through the generosity of many, notably Tanny and Kent Hodgetts and William Mahan, AIA, who drew plans to match the original design, a replica was created by artist/iron-smith David Shelton. The new cross was dedicated by family and friends on April 12, 2008. The original cross now stands at the Hoffmann House.

25 Margaret Craig to MC, June 8, 1924. Morrow to Hoffmann, May 23, 1922, CDCC, Plans/Planting/CAA/ Incoming, 1922–1925, Chase Papers. Wire, Chase to MC, March 18, 1922, CFP. Starr, 282. Bernhard Hoffmann to R. J. Munro, September 4, 1922, CAA, Plans and Planting, Outgoing, 1922–1925, Chase Papers.

26 C. Sumner Greene, "Architecture as a Fine Art," *Architect* XII, no. 4 (April 1917): 219. Rotogravure Special Section, *Santa Barbara Daily News*, May 20, 1922. "Tile Honors James Craig," *Santa Barbara Daily News*, December 7, 1928. Irving F. Morrow, "A Step in California's Architecture," *Architect and Engineer* LXX, no. 2 (August 1922): 56–8.

CHAPTER 13: MARY CRAIG, DESIGNER, 1922–1939

1 This area of Constance Street was later renamed Garden Street.

2. Armitage's State of California license #844 was issued February 11, 1915. Information on the life of Ralph Armitage comes from over one hundred pages of his military records from 1941 to 1946, on file at the National Personnel Records in St. Louis, MO, as well as from interviews with Mary Craig Skewes-Cox, and Jeanne Armitage Henderson, Ralph's granddaughter; and from the Archives and Records, The American Institute of Architects, Washington, D.C. Further biographical information on the life of Ralph Armitage is included with the Craig papers at the Architecture and Design Collection, University of California, Santa Barbara and at the Library of Congress.

3 MC to Joe Leiter, June 17, 1924, Levi Z. Leiter papers and Leiter estate papers, 1852–1969, Chicago History Museum. Joe Leiter to MC, July 15, 1924. MC to Joe Leiter, August 8, 1924.

4 In 2008 historian Ronald Nye submitted a report on the Campbell Ranch dovecote to the Marine Science Institute, University of California, Santa Barbara. See Anita Guerrini, "The Story of the Campbells, From Montecito to Goleta and Back," *Montecito Magazine* XXX, no. 1 (Spring/Summer 2010): 58–66. Researchers Anita Guerrini and Jennifer Dugan have made a major contribution to the ecological and historical significance of the Campbell property, now owned by the University of California, Santa Barbara.

5 Joe Leiter to MC, March 3, 1925.

6 From the diaries of Gertrude Wesselhoeft Hoffmann, courtesy of her granddaughter, Caroline Ghigo, and shared with the author in January, 2012.

7 Lummis to Hoffmann, July 29, 1925. See essay by Charles Lummis, "Two Years Later," Series I, CAA, Additional Records, 1920s–1930s, Chase Papers.

8 See Mary Louise Days, "Landmarks Committee Staff Report, Plaza Rubio Landmark Designation," May 6, 1992, 4–12. Michael Redmon, "Pioneering Partnership," *Santa Barbara Seasons*, XLIX, no. 1, (March 2003): 36–7.

9 "W. A. Slater Dies in Washington," *Norwich Bulletin*, February 26, 1919. *See* the Slater Memorial Museum, Norwich, Connecticut. Ellen Slater to MC, n.d., Mary Craig papers, Slater File, ADC.

10 Alisal Guestbook, August 29, 1937, courtesy of C. E. Perkins, IV.

11 In 1929 they travelled to England and Ireland and, in 1932, to Cuba. In 1934, leaving on the *S.S. Lurline*, they went on a four-month tour of the Pacific and Asia.

12 Minutes, Southern California State Board of Architectural Examiners, 1924–1936, Sacramento, California.

13 T. L. Lingham (1904–1978) was the son of Santa Barbara developer and realtor Francis H. Lingham (1872–1936). His friendship with Ralph Armitage made for an easy entry into the Craig office. Though unlicensed, the longevity of his employment throughout the 1920s and early 1930s indicates he was clearly valued. Biographical information on T.L. Lingham courtesy of his daughter, Carol Lingham. Barone returned to New York in 1927 and worked for Delano & Aldrich until 1933. He practiced in New York until his death. *The AIA Historical Directory of American Architects*, s.v. "Barone, Henry Mario," (ahd1002241), http://www.aia.org/about/history/aiab082017 (accessed December 10, 2013). Obninsky obtained a New York architect's license while working for Platt, but never attempted to get a California license. Victor Peter Obninsky (son) in discussion with author, May 8, 2012.

14 MCSC to author, December 12, 2013.

15 Donald Culross Peattie, "Teacher of the Troubled," Donald Culross Peattie and Louise Redfield Peattie Papers, Mss 94, Department of Special Collections, University Libraries, University of California, Santa Barbara.

16 See Alexander Alland, Jessie Tarbox Beals, First Woman Photographer (New York: Camera/Graphic Press, 1978). The Papers of Jessie Tarbox Beals, Schlesinger Library on the History of Women in America, Radcliffe Institute, Harvard University. Beal's Santa Barbara photographs, archived at Harvard's Loeb Library Special Collections, include the Craig and Slater houses, and the properties of Hoffmann, Jefferson, Gavit, du Pont, Thorne, Bryce, Fleischmann, Knapp, and Parshall.

17 Minutes, Southern California State Board of Architectural Examiners, 1924–1936. An August 20, 2007 e-mail to the author from Shaundra Lee Cashdollar, Public Information Technician, California Architects Board, confirmed that neither Osborne nor Mary Craig "followed through on the exams."

18 MC to Sarah McLaughlin, Summer, 1932.

19 Reginald Johnson to MC, March 17, 1933.

20 Lewis Walker Dies; Founded Zipper Industry," New York Times, January 25, 1938. See Judy Pearce, "Fernald Point," Montecito Magazine XVII, no. 1 (Spring 1997): 30–6.

21 MC to MOC, February 8, 1937. Mary's daughter attended the Foxcroft School from 1935 to 1938.

22 The Hodges friendship with the Roosevelt family came about when Wetmore was on the War Production Board and the Business Advisory Council to the President in 1934 and 1935. William Hodges in discussion with author, August 29, 2009.

23 MC to May Roberts, September 23, 1939.

24 William Hodges to author, January 23, 2008.

CHAPTER 14: WINDING DOWN, 1940–1964

1 William Craig to Mary Craig, December 9, 1946.

2 Mary's mother, Sarah McLaughlin, died in March after falling and breaking her hip.

3 Diary, MC, May 11, 27, 1950.

4 Adrian Halsey Malone (1915–2006) began his professional career in San Francisco. Later he settled in Big Horn, Wyoming. Working from his Sheridan, Wyoming, office, Malone's long and noteworthy career includes projects in California and Wyoming, and the Plains Indian Museum in Cody, Wyoming. Joan Skewes-Cox Malone in discussion with author, December 8, 2007.

5 River House was designed by architect Arthur W. Lord, Head of the School of Architecture at Columbia. Postponing changes to River House until 1956, Terhune hired architect Charles E. O'Hara to carry out substantial renovations. Mary referred to the house as "Dr. Hiden's house"; Hiden lived there earlier. MC to Terhune, January 28, 1957. MC to Terhune, March 18, 1957.

6 MC to Hayes, August 12, October 14, 1953.

7 MC to Armitage, April 5, 1955. MC to Hayes, November 28, 1955.

8 See societyofthecincinnati.org and Candace Shireman's To be Preserved for All Time: The Major And The President, White House Historical Association, 2009, 36–55. Percy Blair's autobiographical notes from vertical file, The Society of the Cincinnati, Washington, D.C. Douglas in discussion with author, November 16, 20, 2009.

9 Oswald Da Ros in discussion with author, May 2008.

10 Eugene Louie, e-mail message to author, October 8, 2009. William Louie (1908–2006), a solitary and intelligent man of great personal integrity, worked for Mary Craig from the mid-1930s to the early 1940s.

11 From William Shakespeare's Measure for Measure. MC to Homestake president Donald H. McLaughlin, October 5, 1959, Mary McLaughlin Craig Collection, Colorado School of Mines, Arthur Lakes Library, Golden, Colorado.

POSTSCRIPT

1 Joan Skewes-Cox Malone to author, March 14, 2008.

AFTERWORD

1 "Betty Sherrill, 91, Decorator for New York's White-Shoed," New York Times, May 25, 2014.

ACKNOWLEDGMENTS

For the greater part of her career as a designer, Mary McLaughlin Craig worked out of a small cottage on her property in Montecito. Just before the house sold in the late 1970s, my mother, Mary Osborne Craig Skewes-Cox, found tucked into a recess of a cupboard, several large rolls of drawings on tracing paper. Unknown to her, they were the documents representing her parents' careers. It would not be until 2004 that a handful of letters written by Osborne Craig to Mary was found. For the first time, two lives began to take on greater clarity. Following eight years of research, aided by the impeccable memory of my mother, now ninety-four, James Osborne Craig and Mary McLaughlin Craig have at long last been brought out of the deep historical slumber that has, until now, marked their lives.

I was unaware of my grandparents' architectural careers while growing up. Mary Craig died when I was thirteen; an age hardly receptive to asking questions about her profession or her husband who died in 1922. But I did know well the house on Buena Vista Road which my sisters and I visited at least once a year. I can remember every room, especially the small library, filled to the ceiling with my grandfather's architectural books and ones later collected by my grandmother. In the 1950s Montecito was magical for any child. My sisters and I had the freedom to roam in and about many of the fine houses my grandparents and their colleagues built, yet we were oblivious as to their importance.

Awareness and curiosity came later, in the years after I studied architecture in college. On the advice of architect Ted Dominick, who had known and worked with Mary Craig, the Craig drawings were given by my parents in 1981 to the Library of Congress and to the University of California, Santa Barbara. Beforehand, I was fortunate to receive a number of them, as well as many of the architectural books. Living with these drawings and books on a daily basis began to instill an appreciation of my grandparents' unique talents. I wanted to learn more.

I asked my mother if she knew anyone in Santa Barbara who might remember Osborne Craig. The only person she could recall her mother mentioning was Elizabeth de Forest, wife of landscape architect Lockwood de Forest. "She was very fond of your father," Mary Craig told my mother. With that I wrote a long letter to Elizabeth de Forest, a woman of great talent and intellect, hoping that she would reply and fill in all the blanks about a man whom I was just beginning to appreciate. But the reply never came; Elizabeth died shortly after, in 1984. The Craigs took a back burner while my priorities shifted to family and focus on my career as a ceramic artist and teacher.

Eventually Osborne's letters to Mary would be the catalyst for me to begin research for this book. As I proceeded to review the hundreds of archived drawings and track down the descendants of the Craigs' clients, I realized the need to work with an architectural historian. A friend suggested I contact Robert Sweeney, who was completing a book on Casa del Herrero. With my mother, whose instincts I trusted, we agreed to meet over lunch at El Paseo. Bob professed a longstanding interest in the Craigs and agreed to take the project on. His own research, insights, and professionalism have contributed greatly to the unfolding story of the Craigs' work. He has also been an extraordinary "teacher" in the best sense. Most of what I have learned about classical architecture, I have learned from him; the tour he gave me of the Boston Public Library and Trinity Church was memorable. These last eight years working with him have been a great privilege.

The author W. C. Heintz referred to writing as "building a stone wall without mortar. You place the words one at a time, fit them, take them apart and refit them until they're balanced and solid." And in our case, factual, I might add. Such has been the process of the Craig book, concluding in as balanced and solid with the facts testament to their lives and legacy as any two people (Robert Sweeney and I) could hope to achieve.

The story begins in Scotland. We are indebted to Alison Spring for her prodigious investigation of Osborne Craig's early life. Describing herself as a Glaswegian who enjoys the "hunt" by being "a bit of a bloodhound who loves to find her quarry," Alison proved her worth when she discovered the 1919 Osborne Family Journal in the hands of a family relative. Others who helped in Scotland are Kristeen Croll and Dr. Anne Cameron/Strathclyde University; Mrs. G. R. Dun, Mrs. Eileen Hunter, Neil Kilpatrick, Eric Osborne, Mike Whiteford, Jenny McGhie/ Giffnock Library, East Renfrewshire Council; Vicky Clark/Special Collections, Mitchell Library, Glasgow; and Barrhead and Neilston Historical Association and the Mearns History Group. Scottish historian, author and educator Bernard Aspinwall, provided keen insight into Scotland at the turn of the last century; his generosity of time and commentary by e-mail were invaluable.

Craig's trail led from Scotland to Colorado and Arizona. In Colorado we thank Leah Davis Witherow/Colorado Springs Pioneers Museum; Ruth Kahn; Suzannah Reid/Colorado College; Michelle Falke/University of Colorado, Boulder; Jenny Vega/History Colorado; Dennis Daily and Amy Ziegler/Special Collections, Pikes Peak Library District; and Zilla May Brown/Montrose Historical Society. The authors are indebted to Darrell Munsell, Jay Trask/Archivist, Bessemer Historical Society; and Cindy Hines/Frontier Historical Museum, Glenwood Springs; for their help in identifying Colorado locations in Craig family photos.

Except for a few photographs, Craig's years in Flagstaff were undocumented at the time we began this project. Bob's trips there on four occasions finally gave us answers. Peter Runge, Head, Special Collections and Archives at NAU's Cline Library, and his staff, gave repeated assistance in tracing Craig's local activities and his association with the Riordan and Babbitt families. Ramon Bazurto, Design Coordinator, Capital Assets, retrieved archival plans for the campus dormitories on which Craig worked. Joe Meehan, Park Manager, Riordan Mansion State Historic Park, was most helpful in establishing the original location of the stone entrance gate Craig designed for the Riordan compound. Others who gave important leads are Richard Mangum, Vincent Murray, Karen Malis-Clark, Kathy Farretta, Bill James/Arizona State Library, Pat Foley/Mohave Museum, Kingman, James Babbitt, Caroline Malmgren Davis, and Peter Malmgren.

Information about Mary McLaughlin's early years in Deadwood was fleshed out with the assistance of City Archivist Michael Runge, Adams Museum and House; Carol Hauck/Deadwood Public Library; Ken Stewart/South Dakota State Archives; and Carolyn Weber and Jessica Michak/Homestake Adams Research and Cultural Center.

The mother lode of information about Santa Barbara is the Gledhill Library at the Santa Barbara Historical Museum and its director, Michael Redmon. Michael and his staff have consistently been responsive to our numerous requests over the last eight years. His review of our finished manuscript was thoughtful and instructive. He is sincerely thanked, as are contributors Sondra Aggeler, Kathi Brewster, Martha Hassenplug and Roy Regester. We also wish to thank Jocelyn Gibbs, Curator, Architecture and Design Collection, University of California, Santa Barbara, and her predecessor Kurt Helfrich, who made their rich collections of material on the Craigs, Myron Hunt and Carlton Winslow available on numerous occasions. Their staff, notably Jennifer Whitlock, Melinda Gandara, Christina Marino, and Alexandra Adler, was a pleasure to work with. The vast Pearl Chase archive at UCSB's Davidson Library, Department of Special Collections, was another rich and largely untapped source of information on the Craigs. We thank Edward C. Fields, Jennifer Mundy Johnson, Amanda Demeter, and Daisy Muralles for their help.

Maria Herold, longtime keeper of the Montecito Association History Committee and one of the doyennes of Santa Barbara history opened numerous doors, both physically and intellectually; she is sorely missed. Others in Santa Barbara whose assistance was invaluable include Maria's replacement, Trish Davis; Laura Menahen/Montecito Water District; Kellam de Forrest; Patricia Gebhard; and Mary Louise Days. Edward Carty graciously arranged for access to early minutes of the University Club in Santa Barbara. We also called on Rose Thomas; Alex Cole; Dorothy Oksner; Neal Graffy; Hattie Beresford; Pamela Post; Joan Conway Cota; Jack Look; Dora Bradley; Daphne Ireland; Jo and Willard Thompson; Molly Outwater; Kimberlee Taylor/Santa Barbara County Court House; Jake Jacobus/Planning Archivist; Map and Imagery Laboratory staff/UCSB; librarians Erica Scranton, Lydia Emard, Susan Moon and Ellen Corrigan/UCSB Arts Library; Anne Petersen/Santa Barbara Trust for Historic Preservation; Joe Cantrell/Santa Barbara Public Library; Santa Barbara Museum of Natural History; Santa Barbara Botanic Garden; Anne Dewey/Ganna Walska Lotusland; and the Santa Barbara Museum of Art. All are acknowledged with appreciation.

Information on specific projects and the people who commissioned them came from many sources. There is a reciprocal relationship between prolific building activity and surviving documentation on Bernhard and Irene Hoffmann: most of their personal papers seem to have been destroyed. Still, the recollections of Elizabeth Longstreet, Caroline Williams, Janet Ghigo, Margaret B. Hoffmann, and Martin Hoffmann were critical. The ambitious story of Margaret Andrews' many bold enterprises was clarified by Robert Forsyth, her grandson, and his wife Jane, and Carol Lingham, granddaughter of Plaza Rubio site developer Frances H. Lingham.

Descendants of two other early clients—Mrs. Theodore Sheldon and Mrs. William Slater—were equally forthcoming. Sheldon family members Bruce Wirtz MacArthur, Mrs. Edward MacArthur, Mary MacArthur Schneider, Robert MacArthur Gardner, and author Loren Ruff, shared numerous anecdotes, documents and photographs. Though the stories are very different, Mr. and Mrs. William Slater, III, and Mrs. Barnaby Conrad were similarly generous with information about the Slater family. Further documentation came from the Otis Library and the Slater Museum, both in Norwich, Connecticut.

Information on Mrs. James Nelson Burnes and her extended Armstrong family was provided by Diane Fox Downes and Orien Armstrong. Similarly, Harry Peter Gantz shared information about his and his parents' lives in Santa Barbara in the 1920s and 1930s. Charles Elliott Perkins, IV; Mary Russell Perkins Willis; Forbes Perkins; Wendy Wilder Larsen; Pamela Wilder Barnes Heminway; Nancy Kennick and Eve Perkins were generous with stories and family albums. Access to the Alisal guest book was a rare treat.

Neville and Pat Cramer shared recollections of two houses Mary Craig designed: one for his mother and a later one for himself. The Cramers also injected bits of spice in describing Mary's activities over the many years they were friends. Betty Lasky, joined by Reggie Sully, held our attention over lunch at the Hotel Bel Air with stories of the house her parents built.

Stephanie Glatt, Carol Carrig, and archivist Anna Maria Prieto of La Casa de Maria and its Center for Spiritual Renewal provided crucial ongoing access to old records and blueprints, as well as room and board many years in a row during my research visits to Santa Barbara. Theirs and their staffs' hospitality are deeply appreciated.

Patrick Yochum and John Page deserve special mention. Pat, with indefatigable energy, had the patience and skill to not only navigate through but to copy and transcribe by hand hundreds of pages of deeds and early property records which answered many important questions. John Page, with a gift for finding the most elusive of the Craig clients, has been with us on this project for almost ten years, showing remarkable talent in tracking down people from all over the world so that we might get the facts. We owe them deep gratitude for efforts we could never have duplicated. You are both extraordinary sleuths!

Ron Johnson, introduced to us through Patricia Owen, redrew the plans of several of the most important buildings. The plans not only serve a didactic function in their clarity, they provide a more contemporary appearance in the book. Ron, we look forward to working with you again. Daniel McQuaid took charge of our digital art program, improving the appearance and organizing hundreds of drawings and photographs we were considering for the book. Dr. James R. Marston helped with questions about geography and, as always, was a good listener. Isrrael Fuentes was an erudite guide while exploring the wonders of Morelia and Pátzcuaro. Later he tracked down the obscure "Gallery in Patio" in Cuernavaca, the source of Osborne Craig's Street in Spain.

Discussions with many noted writers and educators were a great privilege. Thanks especially to Mary N. Woods, Romy Wyllie, Sam Watters, Kevin Starr, Richard Longstreth, Richard Guy Wilson, Thomas Hines, Arnold Berke, Char Miller, Lewis Dabney, Ernest D. Peixotto, Robert Winter, Jay Belloli, Stephen Fried, Peter de Bretteville, Stefanos Polyzoides, William Deverell, Phoebe Cutler, Christopher Long, Alison J. Clarke, Marc Appleton, Peter Wild, Kathryn Masson, Alan Calder, Neil Hooper, Walter Nelson-Rees, Nancy Kriplen, Dr. Ian Robert Dungavell, Dr. Thomas Yeomans, Judith Triem, Ken and Carol Pauley, and Julia Costello.

In the discovery phase of this project, several individuals expressed special appreciation for the Craigs' accomplishment. They were Tanny Keeler and Kent Hodgetts, Michael Towbes, Astrid and Lawrence Hammett, Alison de Frise, and Julie Folger. Tanny and Kent acquired the Hoffmann House under conditions few would consider. With extraordinary passion—and no small expense—they labored to restore it to its original condition. It stands today as a tribute to their efforts and to Osborne Craig's talent. They have supported this book since its inception.

Michael Towbes acquired the old Logan's Garage building in 1973. With an eye of appreciation for Mary Craig's work in the process of reconstruction, he replicated the arcade, the original building's distinguishing feature. William Cowles, Larry Hammett's grandfather, was a client of both the Craigs. The Hammetts became interested in our research early on, sharing family history and photographs. Larry gave me a tour of Eucalyptus Hill, recalling it as he knew it in his youth. Without his assistance, one of Osborne Craig's extant buildings would have been missed. Alison Campbell de Frise and Julie Campbell Folger, the Campbells' granddaughters, who shared stories, letters and photographs, made a significant contribution to the understanding of their grandparents' great American dream of making an honorable and unique life for themselves and others when they left England for California in 1919. Julie Folger was forthcoming with a great deal of material on the life and legend of her great-uncle Joseph Leiter and, similarly, Alison de Frise transcribed important and revealing letters by Nancy Campbell which even the Chicago History Museum found impossible to decipher.

Numerous homeowners opened their properties allowing not only new photography but an opportunity to study the buildings. For their patience and generosity we thank: Barbara Ann Baker, Britt Weleniger Beauvoix, Greta Breeden, Betsy Carlson, Marcy Carsey (by Jeanene Pierce), Amy Clark, Rolland Denny Cox, Betsy Dennison (by Margaret Matson), Robert and Jane Forsyth, Foxcroft School, Orman Gaspar, Bill and Danielle Hahn, Diane and John Handloser, Julie Hansen, Stephen Harby, Barbara Hilaire, Audrey Johnson, Wolfgang Kubetschek, La Casa de Maria and its Center for Spiritual Renewal, Nicole Maloney, Mrs. James T. McClintock, Dennis McGowan and Rudie J. Vanbrussel; Jane Keck Meade, Bill Morgan, Dudley Morris, Natalie Fleet Orfalea (by Arlene Bailey), Dr. Ted Polos, Jaquelin Reed, Robert Rickard, Cathy Ross, Jamie Ann Ruffing, Richard Sherman, Mr. and Mrs. Mark Shields, Ronn Sturgis, Leslie Tolan, UCSB/Campbell Ranch house (by Chuck Klein), Alice Willfong, Helen Williams, and Nicolas Zwick. The complicated trail to the du Pont house led from Albert Hinckley to Ann Copeland to Suzy Racobaldo, to Nathan and Marilyn Hayward, and finally to its current owners, Dr.and Mrs. Gary Lyons.

We owe to David Bisol the great honor of our association with the Santa Barbara Historical Museum. David had a vision for Santa Barbara, "a small city of international importance." He understood and was anxious to trumpet the Craigs' definitive role in its architectural development. His successors, Warren Miller and Lynn Brittner, have supported David's initiative and carried it through to reality. We also thank Loretta Reynolds for managing our budget.

John Woodward has worn several hats in this undertaking. He has helped with funding, he has helped with research, he has helped with legal technicalities, and he has been the critical bridge in our partnership with the Santa Barbara Historical Museum. John: Salut!

We are honored by Ford Peatross' introduction to this book. His generosity of time in giving us repeated access to the Craig Collection at the Library of Congress was critical to our understanding of the progression of the Craigs' work. He and his staff, especially Elizabeth Terry Rose, accommodated us on numerous visits.

During our protracted negotiations, David Morton of Rizzoli asked, "We are going to have a beautiful book, aren't we?" His colleagues Douglas Curran, Abigail Sturges and Ron Broadhurst made it so. All were a pleasure to work with.

Of course, for many, the beauty of the book will lie in Matt Walla's photographs. Matt faced numerous challenges: not all the buildings were ready to be photographed. But he has an eye and instinctively overcame obstacles. The results do the Craigs proud.

Countless individuals in their official capacity as researchers, librarians, archivists and heads of special collections assisted us in our research. Though this list is by no means complete I would like to especially thank Gillian Holroyd, Harrison Memorial Library/Carmel; Dan McLaughlin/Pasadena Public Library; Charles Johnson/Museum of Ventura County; Janet Parks/Avery Architectural & Fine Arts Library, Columbia University; Dennis Copeland/Monterey Public Library; Waverly Lowell/Environmental Design Archives, UC Berkeley; Rebecca Bogart/Goodnow Library, Sudbury, MA.; Desiree Goodwin and Mary Daniels, Loeb Library, Harvard University; Nancy Hadley/Archivist and Records Manager for the American Institute of Architects; St. Joseph Public Library; St. Joseph Historical Society; Hannah Parris/Special Collections, Newberry Library, Chicago; Chicago History Museum; Jeri Vogelsang and Sally McManus/Palm Springs Historical Society; Kristine Krueger/Margaret Herrick Library/Academy of Motion Pictures Arts and Sciences; Louis Jeffries/Hill School Library; Beinecke Rare Book and Manuscript Library/Yale University; Manuscripts and Archives/Yale University Library; Huntington Library, San Marino; Andrew Wenburg/Fulmer Library, Sheridan, Wyoming; Sheila Benedict/Santa Inez Mission Archives; Lynn Bremer and Brian Burd/Santa Barbara Mission Archives; Ellen Clark/The Society of the Cincinnati; Georgetown University Law Center; Laura Verlaque/Pasadena Museum of History; and Tim Gregory/The Building Biographer.

Information about the Craigs' clients, colleagues and friends was graciously provided by the following: Amy Adams Boyington; Marie Biel, Brian Andrews; Lawrence Charles Ford, Jr.; Cynthia Criley Williams; Mr. and Mrs. Kinton Stevens, Jr.; Mrs. Arden Stevens; Barbara Tallant Mann Bauer; Barbara Stevens Bauer Yelverton; Louis Bauer; Paula Trotter; Neal Hotelling; Anita Guerrini; Jenifer Dugan; Phyllis Olsen; Janis Johnson; Joan Churchill; Allen Snow; Dennis Whelan; Jean-Guy Dube'; Joanna Bard Newton; Mary Canby Slater; Joan Canby; James B. Canby, IV; Harold Whiting; Judy Whiting; Vee Obern; Martha Clyde; Elaine Chesebrough; Mary Ann Hobart Gibbons; Andrea Currier; J. Michael Frease; Dr. Benjamin Hammett; Victoria Hines; David Tucker; Nancy Lloyd Kittle; Jill Cramer Bryson; Carl Cramer; Ginger Frere; Elizabeth Marino; Stephanie Merchant; Bob Merchant; Mr. and Mrs. Norris Wood; Michael McDonald; Karl Ward, Walter Davis; James Jones; Anne Fleming Sighicelli; Samuel Sighicelli; Walter Lewis; David Sullins; Alan Renga; Eleanor Park Beronius; Fran Calene; Patricia Murphy; Mrs. William Gring; Eric Swaine; Ginger Williams/Cate School; Katherin Chase; Helen Harvey Mills; Joy Harvey; Kay Harvey; Mrs. Alfred Bruce; Ted Bruce; Elliot Hayne; Alston Hayne; Heather Porter/Silver Hill Hospital; Robert Hiden, Jr.; William Hodges; Henry and Mary Hodges; Joel Morris; Susan Johnson; Carol Storke; Dr. Carole Owens; Rev. Charles H. Clark; Mrs. Donald K. Auxier; Moya Henderson; Jane Hoff; Mrs. Edmund Harrison; Samuel Pitts Edwards; Virginia Sharkey; Hillary Dabney; Thomas Dabney; Mrs. Samuel Dabney; Harry Laws; Helen Laws Elliot; Holly Baer; Mark Penn; Ron Sickafoose; George Collins; Sidney Whelan; Elizabeth Dominick; Julie Howard/School District of Santa Barbara; Bill Ellzey; Stacy Pulice; Ken Voyles/Detroit Athletic Club; James Main; Mike Gracie; Robert Youngman; Cecelia Pruter; Georgia Lee Bakewell and Ted Funsten; Laurel B. Barrack; John Curran; Hugh Curran, Jr.; Madelyn Foster; Dee Pascal Cox; Victor Peter Obninsky; Ruth Redington; Lanny Eberstein; Norma Riedell; Dona Senning; Gail Fanaro; Brother Timothy Arthur, O.F.M./Provincial Archivist/Santa Barbara Mission; Mrs. Robert Jamplis; Margaret Leighton/Pebble Beach Co.; Mr. and Mrs. Chris Weiser; Oswald da Ros; Harwood White, Jr.; Richard Allison; Sally Stokes; Christina Allison; Margaret Carpenter; Ed Carpenter; Dudley S. Carpenter; Sharon Soboil; Shelby Gray; Mrs. Robert Cenedella; Jennifer Hopkins; Resa Hull Rivers; Eleanor Hunt Tucker; Paul Myron Tucker; Jim Norris; Martina Lee Albright; Billy Little; Robert Livermore, III; John Douglas; George and Kerry Martin; Dr. Sarah Martin; Marvin Martin; Jim Schiffer; John Pitman, AIA; Peter Edwards, AIA; Leonard Bucklin; Thomas Shiels; Marie Birdsall; Julius Lotterhos; Rachel Lotterhos Wills; Michael Bekins; Lexi MacLane; Stowe C. Phelps and Charlton Yarnell Phelps; Gloria Vanderbilt; Dr. Michael Kelly; Mrs. Carleton Winslow, Jr.; Dr. Constance Monroe Winslow; Jane Winslow; Ann Seymour Sheehan; Natalie House/Damariscotta Historical Society; Jerry Boyer; Blake and Melanie Haverberg; Taffy Tucker; Father Michael Johnson; Sister Mada-Anne Gell, VHN; Sister Mary Berchmans Hannan; Frederica Sterling Bacher; Betsy Rea; Robin Cederlof; Cynthia Carvery; Terry Hill; Dave Mason; Tony Thacher; Anson Thacher; Nick Thacher; Ruth Thomas; Michael Hermes; Patricia Fry; Susan Clark Ogden; Kam Jacoby; Curt Cragg; Mary Christina Wood and Mardi Wood.

For wisdom and moral support I thank my mother Mary Osborne Craig Skewes-Cox whose special place in my grandparents' story gave me unique personal insight. I also thank my aunt and uncle, Adrian and Joan Skewes-Cox Malone whose understanding of Mary Craig the designer offered another important personal perspective. My daughters Sarah Anderson Thompson and Mary Brooke Anderson; my sister Anita Skewes-Cox McCann; Anna Paramore Brando, and my friends Elsie Hull and Renée deYoe, were unflagging in their support.

Finally, we thank Mary Braga, Nancy de L'Abre, Lee and Julie Folger, Mr. and Mrs. Kent Hodgetts, Elsie Y. Hull and Dr. James Sprague, Robert Maxim, David Myrick, Alexandra Campbell Totten, Michael Towbes, and Eleanor Van Cott. Theirs has been an extraordinary display of support.

Pamela Skewes-Cox
Sudbury, Massachusetts

with

Robert Sweeney
Pacific Palisades, California

April 26, 2015

INDEX

PHOTOGRAPHY AND ILLUSTRATION CREDITS

Unless otherwise indicated here or throughout book, color photography is by Matt Walla.

New floor plans and site plans by Ron Johnson. (Hodges House, Tucson, drawn by Diana Kelly.)

American Country Houses of Today (New York: Architectural Book Publishing Company, 1927, p. 36), 101 (right)

Courtesy of Marc Appleton, 252 (Bryce Beach Cabana)

Architecture and Design Collections, University of California, Santa Barbara, 135 (bottom), 242, 244–245, 248 (Hoffmann House, Casa Santa Cruz)

Courtesy of Eleanor Park Beronious and Fran Park Calene, 252 (Gates House)

Pearl Chase Collection, Department of Special Collections, Davidson Library, University of California, Santa Barbara, 36–37 (Alexander), 39, 66–67, 134 (bottom), 135 (bottom, photo by Jessie Tarbox Beals), 146 (top), 150, 154 (top), 163 (photo by Jessie Tarbox Beals), 249 (Babcock)

Courtesy of the Chicago History Museum, The Levi Leiter Photo Collection, 104

Courtesy of Joan Churchill, 108 (bottom), 110, 111

Cline Library, Special Collections and Archives, Northern Arizona University, 18, 19, 20

Courtesy of the Craig Family, 7 (portrait of Mary Craig and her daughter by Clarence Mattei), 13, 17, 26–27, 30–31, 32, 38, 52 (bottom), 53, 67, 93 (bottom), 97 (bottom), 108 (top), 110–111, 148 (top), 149 (bottom), 153 (top), 192, 195 (bottom), 203, 204, 205, 207, 208, 209, 211, 214, 215, 216, 217, 219 (top right), 220–221, 223, 226, 229, 241, 248 (Parshall)

Courtesy of Mary Louise Days, 52 (top)

Jenifer Dugan, 230, 250 (Campbell Barn)

Courtesy of the Foxcroft School, 252 (House for Academic Head)

Courtesy Alison de Frise, 219 (bottom)

Diane Downs Collection, 46 (bottom)

Courtesy of Mrs. G. R. Dun, Heriot, Midlothian, Scotland, 213 (bottom)

Isobel Field Collection, Department of Special Collections, Davidson Library, University of California, Santa Barbara, 108–109

Isrrael Fuentes, 89

Courtesy of the late Patricia Gebhard, 74–75 (*Santa Barbara Daily News*)

Gledhill Library, Santa Barbara Historical Museum, 42 (Gift of Jo and Willard Thompson), 72 (top), 147, 247

Courtesy of the Frances Loeb Library, Harvard Graduate School of Design (photographs by Jessie Tarbox Beals), 149, 151 (top), 152, 161, 162, 232, 233

Courtesy Hagley Museum and Library, 181

Lawrence Hammett Collection, 93 (top), 248 (Cowles Reservoir)

Goodwin Harding, 178–179

Nathan Hayward, 183

Maria Herold, Montecito Association History Committee, 253 (Adams House)

Courtesy Henry and Mary Hodges, 184–185

Courtesy of the Hoffmann House Library, 62–63, 243

Elsie Hull, 182, 250 (Miley Guest House and fountain)

Courtesy of Mrs. George (Eileen Osborne) Hunter, Glasgow, 213 (top)

Courtesy of Immaculate Heart Center for Spiritual Renewal, 126 (bottom)

Frances Benjamin Johnson, 87

Louis La Beaume and Wm. Booth Papin, *The Picturesque Architecture of Mexico* (New York: Architectural Book Publishing Company, 1915, pl. 14), 86 (top)

Library of Congress, 21, 24–25, 34–35, 36, 43, 46 (top), 47 (top), 49, 70, 96, 106–107, 133, 163 (top), 227 (Paramore Scheme 1), 249 (Paramore, Scheme 2), 250 (Crow), 252 (du Pont Garage)

George Martin III Collection, 195 (top), 219 (top left), 237

Wayne McCall, 164, 189, 253 (Hayes House)

Mike McCreery, 212

Courtesy Palm Springs Historical Society, 248 (Kocher)

Courtesy of Charles E Perkins IV, 231

Picturesque Pasadena, 97 (top)

Courtesy of Santa Barbara Magazine, 179

Santa Barbara Morning Press, 82–83 (top)

Courtesy of the Santa Barbara Trust for Historic Preservation, 74

Schlesinger Library, Radcliffe Institute, Harvard University (photo by Jessie Tarbox Beals), 79 (bottom, left)

Courtesy of Thomas Schmidt, 40–41

Randy Seaver, 252 (Keck Mausoleum)

Courtesy of Kent Seavey, 33

Courtesy of Silver Hill Hospital, 253 (Terhune House)

Courtesy of Amy Skewes-Cox, 248 (Cowles Gardener's Cottage)

Pamela Skewes-Cox, 253 (Nevill Cramer House)

Jay Steffy/Architectural Digest/ © Conde Nast, 250 (Mary Craig House)

Courtesy of Marc Wanamaker/Bison Archives, 184

Harold White Collection, 47 (bottom)

Courtesy of John Woodward, 23, 72–73, 78, 79 (bottom right), 83 (bottom), 85, 86 (bottom), 101 (left), 132 (top), 230, 251 (Dieterich)